I0810868

Humble Aspiration

Constructing an Early Christian Ideal

Bernadette McNary-Zak

LITURGICAL PRESS
Collegeville, Minnesota

www.litpress.org

Cover design by Tara Wiese. Photo courtesy of Wikimedia Commons.

1 2 3 4 5 6 7 8 9

Library of Congress Cataloging-in-Publication Data

Names: McNary-Zak, Bernadette, author.
Title: Humble aspiration : constructing an early Christian ideal / Bernadette McNary-Zak.
Description: Collegeville, Minnesota : Liturgical Press, 2020. | Includes bibliographical references. | Summary: "Explores various concepts of Christian humility in late antiquity, looking closely at some of the ways humility has operated as a relational value in specific contexts involving ascetic women"— Provided by publisher.
Identifiers: LCCN 2019044348 (print) | LCCN 2019044349 (ebook) | ISBN 9780814684061 (paperback) | ISBN 9780814684313 (epub) | ISBN 9780814684313 (mobi) | ISBN 9780814684313 (pdf)
Subjects: LCSH: Humility—Religious aspects—Christianity—History of doctrines—Early church, ca. 30-600. | Women in Christianity—History—Early church, ca. 30-600. | Christian women—Religious life—History—To 1500.
Classification: LCC BV4647.H8 M36 2020 (print) | LCC BV4647.H8 (ebook) | DDC 241/.4—dc23
LC record available at https://lccn.loc.gov/2019044348
LC ebook record available at https://lccn.loc.gov/2019044349

"*Humble Aspiration* is a welcome addition to a growing body of scholarship on the meaning and practice of humility. In this thoroughly researched book Bernadette McNary-Zak illuminates the construction of Christian humility in the lives of fourth- to seventh-century female ascetics, demonstrating clearly its 'multivalent' nature and its centrality to their commitment to the way of Christ. While twentieth-century feminists were right to critique the much later construction of humility as a feminine virtue, ensuring women's submission to patriarchal power, McNary-Zak brings to life an assembly of early Christian women who stand strongly as equals, alongside their more celebrated male counterparts, in their imitation of the humble Christ. Christian humility was indeed a 'countercultural' force in the world of late antiquity, as McNary-Zak richly demonstrates."

—Jane Foulcher
Associate Head of School, School of Theology
Charles Sturt University

"Bernadette McNary-Zak offers a convincing portrayal of the polyvalent values attendant upon humility. *Humble Aspirations* represents McNary-Zak's comprehensive examination of humility in late antiquity, from Syriac and Coptic texts to texts penned by familiar representatives of the Latin church such as Augustine. Furthermore, McNary-Zak's facility in drawing out the very best from these primary sources is exemplary. She shows with remarkably fine detail how 'humble aspirations,' though shared by late antique Christian women and men as imitation of Christ, were more subversively realized in the late antique female ascetic than the male ascetic. And, women's 'humble aspirations' were authoritative for the Christian communities who witnessed them. Perhaps most importantly, McNary-Zak's models for understanding late antique expressions of humility, such as theological, social, intellectual, and moral, avoid the trap of re-inscribing ideologies of women's socio-cultural inferiority in her valorization of humility; instead, McNary-Zak's attention to how humility expressed wise understanding of oneself in relation to God and others through practices of solidarity and through internalization of such values as vulnerability and dispossession, continue to have relevance for readers, both women and men, today."

—Rachel Wheeler, PhD
Assistant Professor of Theology
University of Portland

"In a world where humility is often misunderstood, especially as applied to women, this book offers a deep and wide exploration of the concept. McNary-Zak gathers views of humility from ancient and modern sources into a resource unlike any other currently available."

—Judith Sutera, OSB
Mount St. Scholastica, Atchison, Kansas

In memory of Mariya

Contents

Acknowledgments

This book began with a question about the role of humility in the lives of early Christian women. I am grateful to those students, colleagues, family, and friends who served as conversation partners at various stages in its composition. I am appreciative, as well, of the institutional and departmental support of my colleagues at Rhodes College, and of Savannah Webb for her research assistance in the early stages of this project. Finally, I give tremendous thanks to the work of two anonymous referees, and to the publication team at Liturgical Press: Hans Christoffersen, Stephanie Lancour, Angela Steffens, Colleen Stiller, and Tara Durheim.

Chapter One

Introduction

"Picture in your mind His humility."[1]

Leander of Seville's late sixth-century imperative invites his sister, Florentina, and her fellow nuns to focus on the centerpiece of Christian humility. By imagining divine humility, with Christ as their exemplar, Leander asks the nuns to direct their attention beyond themselves, diminishing their self-concern and emphasizing their dependence. In doing so, the nuns may encounter humility as a relational act of theological, social, and intellectual consequence with the potential to form their monastic community. Given such outcomes, what did it mean for these nuns to be humble like Christ? This book indicates that the response is neither simple nor self-evident.

Humility was an especially prevalent topic for discussion and debate in Christian monastic circles like those of Leander and Florentina during the period of late antiquity (3c.–7c.). The centrality of humility as a distinctly Christian value would come to be defined in the contexts of evolving theological interpretation and ecclesiological development. An examination of select sources from this period retrieves areas of contestation and concern in emergent formulations of Christian humility. We see several types of humility operative in this period. These types, defined by the relationships they express, illumine how humility is conceptualized, represented, and inscribed as a value in late antique ascetic contexts. Specifically, these types reflect the ways ascetic women—real

[1] Claude W. Barlow, trans., *Iberian Fathers*, vol. 1, *Martin of Braga, Paschasius of Dumium, Leander of Seville* (Washington, DC: Catholic University of America Press, 1969), 206. Leander of Seville (534–600 CE) drew on a number of earlier monastic sources in his short book *The Training of Nuns*, directed to Florentina and her fellow nuns.

and ideal—are deployed for evaluative purpose, namely, to explore the capacity for humility to focus a Christian worldview.

Humility as a Christian Value

Monastic scholar Andre Louf reminds us that all forms of Christian humility are bound firmly "in the context of Jesus Christ."[2] This context forms the broader "background of significance" as "a wider picture of the goals of human life, or the best way of living" against which Christian humility is defined and measured in our sources.[3] This "background" is the call to follow the example of Christ. If we turn to Christ's teachings about humility in the synoptic gospels and "Q" source, we see frequent use of the word ταπεινόω[4] where, as Eben Scheffler observes, it "suggests not a mere state, but a disposition that the followers of Jesus must constantly fulfill."[5] The mandate of disposition emphasizes distinction as Scheffler explains that Jesus "prophetically preached humility in a Graeco-Roman context that was contravening it in thought and behaviour."[6] Indeed, Kari Konkola succinctly claims that neither the Greek nor the Jewish tradition "reached the conclusion that, if pride or hubris is evil, humility must be good. Only Christianity took this step."[7] Jane Foulcher writes that, in its Greco-Roman context, "humility . . . was primarily a condition of the socially inferior, whose servile status and dependence on physical labor precluded them from all that was considered in public life";[8] in its Jewish context, "care for the lowly or humili-

[2] Andre Louf, *The Way of Humility*, trans. Lawrence S. Cunningham, Monastic Wisdom Series (Kalamazoo, MI: Cistercian Publications, 2007), 9. See also Sheryl Overmyer, "Exalting the Meek Virtue of Humility in Aquinas," *Heythrop Journal* 56, no. 4 (2015): 660.

[3] John Cottingham, "What Difference Does It Make? The Nature and Significance of Theistic Belief," *Ratio* (*new series*) 19, no. 4 (December 2006): 408.

[4] Eben Scheffler, "Reflecting on Jesus' Teaching on Humility from a Positive Psychological Perspective," *Neotestamentica* 51, no. 1 (2017): 101. In Latin, *humus* or *humilis* is tied to earth.

[5] Ibid., 102.

[6] Ibid., 108.

[7] Kari Konkola, "Have We Lost Humility?," *Humanitas* 18, nos. 1–2 (2005): 183.

[8] Jane Foulcher, *Reclaiming Humility: Four Studies in the Monastic Tradition* (Collegeville, MN: Liturgical Press, 2015), 17.

ated emerged as a core value in the Hebrew Scriptures . . . with God taking the side of the oppressed and downtrodden."[9] According to Foulcher, both contexts directly inform humility in early Christianity. Vestiges of its Greco-Roman connotation lingered in those "readings of humility that begin to serve the interests of those in authority."[10] Vestiges from Jewish thought persisted by "affirm[ing] God's solidarity with the humiliated, but also . . . nam[ing] humility a central value."[11] The call to follow the example of Christ, then, meant following the humility of Christ as a nonnormative, primary religious value.

The formulation of Christian guidelines for this mandate took time. The centrality of humility emerged during an intense period of Christian self-definition. Under Constantinian and post-Constaninian rule, late antique Christians across the empire grappled with core questions about religious identity. They sought to determine those defining characteristics that would imprint indelibly what was "Christian." Questions about interpretation are present in debates regarding canon formation and ritual practice; doctrinal and liturgical developments framed heretical and orthodox ways of being Christian. Historian Peter Brown captures a sense of significance when he observes that "during the late antique period there was a slow shift from one form of public community to another—from the ancient city to the Christian church. The life of the individual, the life of the family, even matters as intimate as the perception of the body itself came to be seen in relation to changing social contexts, associated with the rise of new forms of community."[12] As these Christians constituted their values, humility would contribute unequivocally to define a Christian identity. The emergent centrality of humility would continue to set them, and their religious worldview, apart by linking their efforts, through lineage, to Christ. Such a lineage was constructed formally by the doctrinal decisions made by a series of ecclesiastical councils that stressed the anthropology and theology of Christ. Donald F. Winslow explains, "As the Trinitarian controversies reached a tentative resolution at the councils of Nicea (325) and Constantinople (381), where the preexistent Son was declared to be 'of the same substance with the

[9] Ibid.

[10] Ibid., 24.

[11] Ibid., 19.

[12] Peter Brown, *Late Antiquity* (Cambridge, MA: Harvard University Press, 1998), 23.

Father,' humility began to take on specifically theological connotations. The humility of Christ, that is, came to be perceived as the humilty of God. . . . It was divine humility, then, that was embodied and articulated by Jesus Christ."[13] In the contexts of stabilizing ecclesiologies and evolving christological formulations, this androcentric position would decisively inform the background of significance for the question of what it meant to be humble like Christ.[14]

The ideological implications of these decisions became embedded in prevailing constructions of the female Christian body.[15] Androcentric bias remained in the definition of female asceticism. Whereas ascetic renunciation offered women "an alternative to conventions of marriage and motherhood, and thus a kind of control over their sexuality,"[16] constructions of "liberation" were necessarily constrained and regulated by prevailing social and religious ideologies, according to Elizabeth Castelli.[17] In her groundbreaking 1986 article, "Virginity and Its Meaning for Women's Sexuality in Early Christianity," Castelli argues that in the period of late antiquity a woman's body—in marriage and in virginity—measured her value. She writes, "The religious system adopted the reigning idea of women's sexuality as token of exchange and reinforced it by investing it with theological significance" tied to her *redemptive* value.[18] In this way, virginity reinscribed prevailing restrictions on a woman's body and amplified its controlled status, thereby exacerbating competing perspectives regarding its religious value. As Castelli explains, "For women, their sexuality is synonymous with their identity in this cultural order; to demand its negation is to make a far more profound demand for alienation and renunciation of self than any demand for

[13] Donald F. Winslow, "Humility," in *Encyclopedia of Early Christianity*, 2nd ed., ed. Everett Ferguson (New York: Garland, 1998), 547–48.

[14] See Willi Braun, "Body, Character, and the Problem of Femaleness in Early Christian Discourse," *Religion and Theology* 9, nos. 1–2 (2002): 108–17.

[15] There is a strong body of scholarship on issues related to gender and sex in the contexts of early Christian asceticism and monasticism.

[16] Elizabeth Castelli, "Virginity and Its Meaning for Women's Sexuality in Early Christianity," *Journal of Feminist Studies in Religion* 2, no. 1 (1986): 85.

[17] Ibid., 88. See also Joelle Beaucamp, "Women," in *Late Antiquity: A Guide to the Postclassical World*, ed. G. W. Bowersock, Peter Brown, and Oleg Grabar (Cambridge, MA: Harvard University Press, 1999), 749.

[18] Castelli, "Virginity and Its Meaning," 86.

continence on the part of men."[19] These tensions were not dismissed as female ascetic practice "was moving from a self-generated alternative to family life toward an institutionalised alternative whose conditions were legislated by men, though women determined their application,"[20] according to Jo Ann McNamara. Such institutionalization would further marginalize the already "disadvantaged" female body that was "physically weaker than males . . . unlikely to be the intellectual equals of males, and had a more difficult time controlling bodily desires and the onslaughts of emotion."[21]

Virginia Burrus oberves the specific connection between heightened attention to the sexual bodies of women and doctrinal development in the fourth century in her 1994 article, "Word and Flesh: The Bodies and Sexuality of Ascetic Women in Christian Antiquity," where she writes that "female sexuality first comes to occupy a central and clearly articulated place in Christian thought."[22] Such attention would reinforce a binary interpretation of the female body as fraught with vice or capable of virtue. Burrus continues, "Significantly, the earliest treatments of female virginity and heretical harlotry are found in the writings of Alexander of Alexandria and coincide precisely with the onset of the Arian controversy and the accession of Constantine in the east,"[23] initiating the dissension that would culminate with the Council of Nicea. The "dramatic reconfiguration of Christianity" under Constantine introduced efforts to define Christian identity—self, communal, and organizational.[24] With these efforts, "the men who struggled to construct an imperial, catholic orthodoxy were drawn again and again to the problems of boundaries and social order—above all the order of the relations between men and women. Within this context the well-bounded and constrained virginal body came to carry much of the weight of ecclesiology, and female sexuality became almost unbearably heavy with symbolic meaning."[25] Male control of the narrative

[19] Ibid.

[20] Jo Ann McNamara, *The Ordeal of Community*, 2nd ed. (Toronto, ON: Peregrina, 1993), 7.

[21] Gillian Clark, *Women in Late Antiquity: Pagan and Christian Lifestyles* (Oxford: Clarendon Press, 1994), 119.

[22] Virginia Burrus, "Word and Flesh: The Bodies and Sexuality of Ascetic Women in Christian Antiquity," *Journal of Feminist Studies in Religion* 10, no. 1 (Spring 1994): 31.

[23] Ibid., 34.

[24] Ibid., 44.

[25] Ibid., 45.

construction of female sexuality influenced the definition of female values, including humility, as Elizabeth Clark demonstrated in her 1985 article, "Authority and Humility: A Conflict of Values in Fourth-Century Female Monasticism." Here, Clark examines how some of the early church fathers wrote about female monastic leadership. Their focus on the ways these women redistributed their considerable personal finances signals their humility for these ecclesiastical figures. Clark contends that "by their emphasis on the women's humility and abject lowliness, the Fathers were in effect highlighting, by way of contrast, the true source of authority the women possessed: status, family background, wealth."[26]

Ecclesiastical formulations about the identity of Mary further impacted the identification of the ascetic woman. Drawing on Louf's assessment, Foulcher explains that Origen "identified the humility of the Virgin Mary in the *Magnificat* as the classical virtue of *metriotes* (measure), which in turn became the Latin *mediocritas* (moderation)."[27] Such a view informed later thinkers, including Aquinas, at notable cost.[28] Fifth-century conciliar decisions about the status of Mary as Theotokos (God-bearer) at the Council of Ephesus (431 CE) were reinforced in subsequent ecclesiastical statements, including those at the Council of Chalcedon (451 CE), in which it was affirmed that Jesus Christ "was begotten by the Father before all ages according to his divinity and, in these latter days, he was born for us and for our salvation of Mary the Virgin, the Mother of God (*Theotokos*), according to his humanity."[29] In her study of Mary, Sally Cunneen observes that, "As God-bearer, Mary began to take over some of her son's functions; she was invoked for healing and protection."[30] Conciliar statements responded to broadening and deepening popular

[26] Elizabeth A. Clark, "Authority and Humility: A Conflict of Values in Fourth-Century Female Monasticism," *Byzantinische Forschungen* 9 (1985): 22. See also Elizabeth A. Clark, *Ascetic Piety and Women's Faith: Essays on Late Ancient Christianity* (Lewiston, NY: Edwin Mellen Press, 1986), 209–28.

[27] Foulcher, *Reclaiming Humility*, 29.

[28] Ibid., 30.

[29] "Definition and Canons of Chalcedon," in Bart Ehrman and Andrew S. Jacobs, eds., *Christianity in Late Antiquity, 300–450 CE: A Reader* (Oxford: Oxford University Press, 2004), 262.

[30] Sally Cunneen, *In Search of Mary: The Woman and the Symbol* (New York: Ballantine Books, 1996), 138.

and monastic access to Mary, as Patricia Ranft asserts: "After Ephesus devotion to Mary increased. It became a permanent, public, and official aspect of orthodox Christianity."[31] Serving as the only complete human witness to the humility of Christ in incarnation, birth, and death, Mary would come to hold a distinctive role in late sixth- and early seventh-century monastic sources for women.[32] In word and in image, Mary's example offers a fruitful site for interpreting monastic guidance in this post-Chalcedonian context. Jaroslav Pelikan writes, "The area of worship in which Mary performed as leader most effectively was in the adornment of icons."[33] Pelikan further explains, "As Theotokos, Mary—and that included the Mary of the icons—was the legitimate object of orthodox worship [*proskynēsis*]."[34] One of the implications of these decisions, as Kate Cooper maintains, was "to honor the spiritual achievement of virgins among the Christian faithful."[35] Many thinkers, like Leander of Seville, attest to the example of Mary for Florentina and her fellow nuns, especially with regard to the cultivation of humility. Due to Mary's increasingly exalted status as co-redeemer through her humility, she could do for them what she had done for Christ; she could serve them as she served Christ. Through their imitation of her humility they, in turn, could become daughters of Mary as their spiritual guide.

Humility as a Religious Value

Typically, constructions of humility contrast with constructions of pride.[36] The ideological implications and existential limitations of this binary opposition persist to this day. As Valerie Saiving observed nearly sixty

[31] Patricia Ranft, *Women and Spiritual Equality in Christian Tradition* (New York: St. Martin's Press, 1998), 90.

[32] See the discussions in Ranft, *Women and Spiritual Equality*. See also Miri Rubin, *Mother of God: A History of the Virgin Mary* (New Haven, CT: Yale University Press, 2010).

[33] Jaroslav Pelikan, *Mary through the Centuries: Her Place in the History of Culture* (New Haven, CT: Yale University Press, 1996), 99.

[34] Ibid., 102.

[35] Kate Cooper, "Virginity," in *Late Antiquity: A Guide to the Postclassical World*, ed. G. W. Bowersock, Peter Brown, and Oleg Grabar (Cambridge, MA: Harvard University Press, 1999), 744.

[36] See John Cottingham, "What Difference Does It Make?," 407.

years ago, in a patriarchal context women's sin is more accurately understood in terms of "underdevelopment or negation of the self" rather than "pride."[37] Applying Saiving's insight to the contemporary role of humility as a feminist value, Elizabeth Hinson-Hasty contends further that "pride could not be women's sin when women have been forced to stand at intersections created for them by men and have been deprived of the power and freedom to shape their own destinies, projects, and identities . . . humility known only in acts of self-sacrificial love cannot be the means to redeem women's circumstances if women's freedoms have been taken from them."[38] Given these conditions, Hinson-Hasty maintains that "genuine humility" is "a choice made through one's own moral agency"[39] reliant on a relational sense of self.[40]

A similar intellectual move is made by the philosopher James Kellenberger. Kellenberger offers a particularly useful qualification when he acknowledges that there are many forms of humility, and proposes that "the more profound expression of humility is one that spontaneously and naturally excludes pride as a self-concerned reaction (and as well other self-concerned reactions, in particular that of shame). The person who is humble and has the moral virtue of humility in this way is not one who struggles to be humble in order to meet a pride ideal."[41] In a later work, Kellenberger explains that religious humility has a "cognitive aspect" that is "a recognition of oneself as one is, a recognition of God, and a recognition of one's relation to God."[42] Furthermore, "in light of that recognition, the expression of humility required for

[37] Valerie Saiving, "The Human Situation: A Feminine View," *Journal of Religion* 40 (1960): 109. See also James Kellenberger, *Relationship Morality* (University Park: Pennsylvania State University Press, 1995), 337.

[38] Elizabeth Hinson-Hasty, "Revisiting Feminist Discussions of Sin and Genuine Humility," *Journal of Feminist Studies in Religion* 28, no. 1 (2012): 109.

[39] Hinson-Hasty, "Revisiting Feminist Discussions," 110.

[40] Ibid., 112. See Andre Louf, *The Way of Humility*; Louf encourages consideration of the state of humility rather than the virtue of humility on 9–10. See also Stephen Pardue, "Kenosis and its Discontents: Towards an Augustinian Account of Divine Humility," *Scottish Journal of Theology* 65, no. 3 (2012): 271–88; Stephen Pardue, *The Mind of Christ: Humility and the Intellect in Early Christian Theology* (London: Bloomsbury, 2013).

[41] James Kellenberger, "Humility," *American Philosophical Quarterly* 47, no. 4 (2010): 330. See also Joseph Kupfer, "The Moral Perspective of Humility," *Pacific Philosophical Quarterly* 84 (2003): 249–69.

[42] James Kellenberger, *Dying to Self and Detachment* (New York: Routledge, 2016), 28.

religious humility is a turning away from self and self-concern."[43] This cognitive aspect indicates self-knowledge, what Vance Morgan refers to as an "awareness."[44] Joseph Kupfer prefers the term "orientation," as humility "directs our attention, thought and action in a sustained way."[45] As an orientation, humility informs knowledge of others and of the world. This is founded, according to Kupfer, on "radical dependence" that recognizes "just how much of our success depends on people, institutions, and circumstances outside of our control."[46]

These scholars further emphasize that humility assumes agency. Put succinctly, in the words of Jay Newman, "humility is a quality involving self-determination based on self-evaluation."[47] As a relational value, humility necessarily impacts not only the self but others. Humility consistently assumes a broader community, and it can operate as a common or collective end. This is due to the fact that, as George Schlesinger explains, humility is often interpreted in a nexus of other values: "the virtue of other-directedness, the core of humility, is the ultimate source for all other characteristics that involve an impartial concern for worthy ideals and causes, and that require sympathy for the well-being of others."[48] Humility is thereby typically recognized in relation to, and in relation with, other values, including obedience and charity.

An emphasis on the relational features and orientation of religious humility offers an expansive approach to the subject that hearkens to humility as a "disposition,"[49] suggested earlier in the teachings of Christ. Such resonances suggest that Christian humility intends an orientation beyond the self that "excludes pride as a self-concerned reaction."[50] In order to think about the tension between the real and the ideal in humility as it is found in our sources, I adopt the operative definition provided by

[43] Ibid., 26; see also Kellenberger, "Humility," 333.

[44] Vance G. Morgan, "Humility and the Transcendent," *Faith and Philosophy* 18, no. 3 (July 2001): 314.

[45] Kupfer, "The Moral Perspective of Humility," 251.

[46] Ibid., 252.

[47] Jay Newman, "Humility and Self-Realization," *Journal of Value Inquiry* 16 (1982): 282.

[48] George N. Schlesinger, "Truth, Humility, and Philosophies," in *God and the Philosophers: The Reconciliation of Faith and Reason*, ed. Thomas V. Morris (Oxford: Oxford University Press, 1994), 254.

[49] Scheffler, "Reflecting on Jesus' Teaching on Humility," 102.

[50] Kellenberger, "Humility," 330.

Lisa Fullam, who writes, "Humility is the virtue of true self-understanding in context, cultivated through the practice of other-centeredness."[51] Fullam's definition attends to the aspects of cognition, agency, affect, and relation in humility. Furthermore, her definition indicates that humility is a *practice*, a key defining feature in our sources; as a practice, humility not only shifts one's orientation beyond the self but does so with the potential for excluding a reaction of self-concern, thereby leaving open divine humility as exemplar, the very issue that is being confronted in our sources. Moreover, her definition recognizes the role of context in defining humility. In our sources, Christian humility has a recognizeable background of significance formed by Christian scriptures that orients the self toward a divine presence in a way that acknowledges the social implications of radical dependence. Dependence signals hierachy as Sheryl Overmyer explains, humility "is primarily found in our reverence for God. . . . Humility secondarily concerns others through primary subjection for God."[52]

Humility as an Ascetic Value

When we turn to our sources, we must be mindful of what they can and cannot tell us, of their potential and their limitations. Many of our sources function as "orthodox attempts to frame and order experience and doctrine into a single, monolithic image of Christian existence."[53] As well, we need to read with awareness that our sources were written by and attributed to individuals, primarily men. In many cases, our authors were directly connected to their subjects and to their audiences. In all cases, writing served as a relevant means of interrogating and asserting identity; these authors named and reified their own ideologies and ideals in their works.[54]

[51] Lisa Fullam, "Humility and Magnanimity in Spiritual Guidance," *Reflective Practice: Formation and Supervision in Ministry* 32 (2012): 38.

[52] Overmyer, "Exalting the Meek Virtue of Humility in Aquinas," 655.

[53] Castelli, "Virginity and Its Meaning," 65.

[54] Ibid., 63–64. See also Claudia Rapp, "Storytelling as Spiritual Communication in Early Greek Hagiography: The Use of Diegesis," *Journal of Early Christian Studies* 6, no. 3 (1998): 431–48; Claudia Rapp, "Figures of Female Sanctity: Byzantine Edifying Manuscripts and Their Audience," *Dumbarton Oaks Papers* 50 (1996): 313–44; Derek Krueger, *Writing and Holiness: The Practice of Authorship in the Early Christian East* (Philadelphia: University of Pennsylvania Press, 2004); David Brakke, "The Lady Ap-

Our sources attest to the ways in which humility is framed by "its literary expression in the narratives," to borrow a phrase from Virginia Lieson Brereton.[55] We are fortunate that this "literary expression" enables us to witness humility as an operational value in lived experience. If we are attentive to linguistic and relational cues,[56] we can identify situations in which humility functions for early Christian individuals and communities.[57]

As our authors grappled with how to identify humility as a *Christian* value with "specifically theological connotations,"[58] they chose the ascetic woman—real and ideal—to imagine and to think about their subject. The ascetic woman became a site for evaluating how theological humility, social humility, intellectual humility, and mutual humility were performed. The ascetic woman figured the inevitable murkiness in efforts to define and legitimate a "Christian" humility in this period. Efforts to stabilize and to routinize humility as they weigh the Greco-Roman emphasis on submission and obedience to authority with the Jewish emphasis on humility as solidarity with the socially outcast alongside an emergent Christian orientation of humility as a social value. Such efforts belie concerns about the structure of humility in pedagogy, expressions, rituals, and texts; they make connections to authority, servanthood, solidarity, and charity. They also posit the potential of humility

---

pears: Materializations of 'Woman' in Early Monastic Literature," *Journal of Medieval and Early Modern Studies* 33, no. 3 (Fall 2003): 387–402; Gillian Clark, *Women in Late Antiquity*; Ranft, *Women and Spiritual Equality*, 53–93; Gillian Cloke, *This Female Man of God: Women and Spiritual Power in the Patristic Age, AD 350–450* (New York: Routledge, 1995); Elizabeth A. Clark, "Ideology, History, and the Construction of 'Woman' in Late Ancient Christianity," *Journal of Early Christian Studies* 2, no. 2 (1994): 155–84.

[55] Virginia Lieson Brereton, *From Sin to Salvation: Stories of Women's Conversion, 1800 to the Present* (Bloomington: Indiana University Press, 1991), xiii. See also Sebastian Brock and Susan Ashbrook Harvey, *Holy Women of the Syrian Orient* (Berkeley: University of California Press, 1987), 3.

[56] Mary Gerhart, *Genre Choices, Gender Questions* (Norman: University of Oklahoma Press, 1992), 4. See also Stuart Hall, ed., *Representation: Cultural Representations and Signifying Practices* (Thousand Oaks, CA: Sage Publications, 1997), 23.

[57] I am indebted to the foundational work on Christian monastic humility by many scholars including Jane Foulcher, Andre Louf, Douglas Burton-Christie, and Stephen Pardue. My approach shares an emphasis on humility as a situational value and focuses distinctly on female representations of monastic humility.

[58] Winslow, "Humility," 547.

to function as a value "that spontaneously and naturally excludes pride as a self-concerned reaction"[59] by reinforcing the dispositional concept of "radical dependence."[60] Put simply, our sources provide an operating framework for the ways some late antique Christians imagined Christian humility as a relational value.

Why explore humility in this way? By examining how humility operates in narrative sources that focus on ascetic women in late antiquity, I intend to complement the considerable body of existing studies on early Christian humility. While a focus on male ascetics may present similar results, I think that the second-class status of women in ecclesiastical and social contexts in this period suggests a particular suitability to discussion of Christian humility as a value. The tension between possibility and restraint for ascetic women, in particular, affords a distinct opportunity to imagine the potential in humility as a Christian value that included attention to the "lowliness" of Christ. Furthermore, a focus on ascetic women maps several types of humility and attends to concomitant values that continued to inform a distinctively Christian interpretation of humility. Finally, examination of ascetic women reveals Christian humility as a value—both real and ideal—that contributes to an eschatological imagination.

In order to consider humility as a relational value in the period of late antiquity, the next four chapters examine closely some of the ways humility operated in specific contexts involving ascetic women. Each chapter explores a particular type of humility. We begin with theological humility as radical dependence on a divine power through a process of submission and obedience. Theological humility is the foundation for a construction of Christian humility; from theological humility necessarily emerges social humility, those expressions of humility between individual persons. Both theological and social humility are informed by intellectual humility as they require a willingness to engage in ongoing interpretation and application of Scripture. Theological, social, and intellectual humility come together in a distinctly monastic form in constructions of mutual humility found in monastic rules composed to guide communal expressions of submission, obedience, and prayer. These chapters examine particular types of humility not to suggest compartmentalization but, rather, to consider distinct features. Each

[59] Kellenberger, "Humility," 330.

[60] Kupfer, "The Moral Perspective of Humility," 252.

type of humility functions to define the ascetic woman through external behaviors that illumine and uphold internal values. These external behaviors and internal values inform a broader construction of Christian humility in the context of an eschatological imagination.

We begin by examining how select fourth- and fifth-century hagiographies and sayings (apophthegms) craft a pedagogy of theological humility. Our specific consideration of how humility is learned in the formation of female spiritual guides in the *Life of Syncletica* and the *Life of Thais* attends to the inclusion of biblical and religious figures as role models and instructors for these ammas; consideration of how theological humility is taught in those sayings attributed to the female spiritual guides Theodora, Sarah, and Syncletica interprets their ascetic authority as vulnerable. Collectively, these female hermits demonstrate a process of becoming humble through learning and of being humble through teaching. Their humility attests to a process of submission and obedience that shifts their orientation toward a divine power.

Theological humility extends in relationship to others. In chapter 3 we examine how expressions of social humility in several fourth- and fifth-century monastic sources are represented in the intimacy of encounter and exchange between ammas and their visitors in the particular context of hospitality. Our sources demonstrate some of the ways people interpreted humility as qualitatively Christian by providing an awareness, born in the vulnerability implicit in the encounter, of the ongoing presence of Christ. We consider first how humility is heard in two exchanges between monks and their monastic visitors. We then turn to how humility is visualized in the feigned madness of the unnamed nun, the weeping posture of Domnina, and the prayerful orientation of Shirin.

Theological and social humility apply the examples and teachings contained in Christian scripture. In chapter 4 we explore practices of intellectual humility, with a focus on prayer, in the late fourth-century travel narrative of the Christian woman Egeria. Egeria's experiences of receiving hospitality inform our reading of the ways vulnerability and anonymity factored into her pilgrimage. The decentering perspective she adopts through the repetition of patterns of prayer with others before a divine presence over the course of her travels indicates a type of intellectual humility, a capacity for learning through the ongoing interpretation of Scripture. Egeria's intellectual humility offers a worldview featuring solidarity and fellowship with others in a broadly defined Christian community.

Theological, social, and intellectual humility are all present in the construction of mutual humility embedded in monastic rules for ascetic women in the period of late antiquity. In chapter 5 we weigh teachings about mutual humility in monastic rules composed by episcopal leaders for their biological sisters. We begin with the fourth-century thinker Augustine of Hippo and then turn to the ways his interpretation of mutual humility informed the subject for the late antique reformers Caesarius of Arles and Donatus of Besançon. Mutual humility in these monastic contexts seeks to embody the Christocentric focus of Christian humility. This embodiment is stabilized in those rules that stress dispossession. Here, we see how mutual humility strives to create and structure a community spirituality centered on submission, obedience, and charity before a divine power and following the example of Christ.

The final chapter shifts our focus to assess how the four types of humility supply a broader operating framework for defining Christian humility in this period. What are the implications for using ascetic women to represent Christian humility? Our sources indicate a rich, robust response by inviting us into narrative spaces in which humility disrupts and unsettles operating norms and prevailing views. These humble ascetic women are exemplars for authors and audiences.[61] Stuart Hall draws attention to the dual meanings of representation as both to "stand in the place of, and at the same time, stand for."[62] He contends that "representation is the production of meaning through language,"[63] referencing the real and the ideal. Preserving societal, ecclesiastical, and patriarchal norms that bound their access and agency, these humble ascetic women—real and ideal—stood for and in the place of Christ.

[61] Richard Valantasis, *The Making of the Self: Ancient and Modern Asceticism* (Eugene, OR: Cascade Books, 2008), 162–63. See also Patricia Cox Miller, "Visceral Seeing: The Holy Body in Late Ancient Christianity," *Journal of Early Christian Studies* 12, no. 4 (Winter 2004): 391–411.

[62] Hall, *Representation*, 16.

[63] Ibid., 28.

Chapter Two

Pedagogies of Theological Humility

A sizable portion of the *Sayings of the Desert Fathers* addresses humility, including these words attributed to the fourth-century female hermit Amma Syncletica: “Just as one cannot build a ship unless one has some nails, so it is impossible to be saved without humility.”[1] Juxtaposing a ship with salvation and nails with humility, this saying creates a figurative space deeply contextualized by a specific geographic environment. Its referent, the Egyptian seaport of Alexandria, was a vibrant metropolitan city serving as a significant site of cultural diversity and exchange in the later Roman Empire. This urban center and its surrounding desert regions would have been recognizable to its immediate audience. Although Syncletica’s words may locate her initiative and resolve, we are encouraged to read them as an evaluative statement about humility as a Christian value.[2]

[1] This saying is attributed to Amma Syncletica in both the apophthegmata as well as in the life story that bears her name. For the translation used here, see *Sayings* 26 in Benedicta Ward, trans., *The Sayings of the Desert Fathers: The Alphabetical Collection* (Kalamazoo, MI: Cistercian Publications, 1995), 235. On the use of sailing imagery in the teachings of Syncletica, see Mary Forman, “Amma Syncletica: A Spirituality of Experience,” *Vox Benedictina* 10, no. 2 (1993): 216. See also Bernadette McNary-Zak, “The Soul is Like a Ship: Sailing Imagery in Early Egyptian Monastic Literature,” *Coptica* 8 (2009): 41–51.

[2] On the authorship of the *Life of Syncletica* see Pseudo-Athanasius, *The Life and Regimen of the Blessed and Holy Syncletica*, trans. Elizabeth Bryson Bongie (Toronto, ON: Peregrina, 1999), 5. Subsequent references to the *Life of Syncletica* in this chapter are from this translation and include section and page numbers. For context, see the discussion in Susanna Elm, *“Virgins of God”: The Making of Asceticism in Late Antiquity* (Oxford: Oxford University Press, 1994), 227–34.

The analogy expressed in the saying is more fully contextualized by appeal to the description in the *Life of Syncletica*. According to this hagiographic depiction, Syncletica removed herself from the Alexandrian environment to a more secluded location, adopting ascetic practices of fasting and prayer and striving for purity of heart through a single-minded focus on, and awareness of, a divine power. Like many other contemporary Christian hermits, Syncletica's example summoned the attention of those who learned of her efforts, and groups of women in particular are said to have sought her wisdom, counsel, and guidance. Hagiographic preservation and transmission of the words and deeds of holy persons like Syncletica (in vitae and in sayings) signal a prominent role for memory construction in an early Christian worldview.

This chapter appeals to the evidence of several ascetic women—Syncletica, Thais, Theodora, and Sarah—as instruction about theological humility. Theological humility stresses a "radical dependence" on a divine power; for our purposes, theological humility is possible "from a recognition of and attunement to a reality that is other and greater than oneself."[3] The hagiographies of Syncletica and Thais disclose a process of learning about theological humility structured by stages of submission and obedience to a divine power; over time, this orientation is embodied and culminates in the acquisition of an authority characterized by theological humility. Our sources are clear that this process has ancient religious roots by appealing to the examples of key figures in the Hebrew Bible and that it has currency in the present by appealing to martyrs and prominent ascetic figures in early Christian tradition. This authority is evident in the wisdom teachings, or sayings, of Syncletica, Theodora, and Sarah. When these ascetic women exercise their authority they, in turn, teach others about theological humility.

Theological humility operates as a learned value for women in the *Life of Syncletica* and the *Life of Thais*. The *Life of Syncletica*, composed by an anonymous author in the fifth century in Egypt, presents its subject as having an extraordinary capacity for theological humility. Syncletica's ascetic discipline, practiced as a desert hermit, produces a state of holiness that leads to her apotheosis; in the ultimate expression of theological humility, Syncletica bears extreme bodily suffering as a form of prayer,

[3] Morgan, "Humility and the Transcendent," 312. I have added the qualifier, theological, here in order to emphasize the role of radical dependence on a divine power.

in conjugal union with a divine presence. Syncletica's theological humility is acquired through a common hagiographic process of hearing, transgressing, and transforming; this process is reflected, as well, in the sixth-century *Life of Thais*, also composed by an anonymous author in Egypt. Thais repents her harlotry by obeying the conditions of extreme confinement and ascetic discipline imposed on her. Gradually, Thais grows in holiness; her theological humility is signified by the state of her soul, as confirmed through divine prophecy. In addition to a common process for obtaining holiness, the hagiographies of these women demonstrate a concerted emphasis on the part of their male hagiographers to depict their subjects' theological humility as culminating in an act of complete dependence on a divine power; in each hagiography, the female subject undergoes a period of trials close to the end of her life which she chooses to embrace as a turning of self over to a divine power for strength. Each hagiography contains a highly descriptive, communally and relationally oriented account of this final period of trials as others are aware of the subjects' struggles. In order to think about how theological humility operates as a female Christian value in these hagiographies, we focus our discussion on two distinguishing features of these hagiographies: the explicit roles of spiritual guides to facilitate learning theological humility and of detailed bodily practices to teach humble suffering.

The hagiographers' attempts to grapple with Christian humility in the stories of Syncletica and Thais are not isolated ones in late antiquity, nor are the conceptions of theological humility depicted in their works. The *Sayings of the Desert Fathers* are another relevant source for spiritual formation and guidance in this period, as evident in the insight attributed to Amma Syncletica at the opening of this chapter. Describing ascetic discipline and practices, as well as values and principles, the *Sayings* provides a snapshot of a significant period of ascetic experimentation centered in the deserts of Egypt. This seedbed would prove foundational to operative constructions of theological humility in later Christian tradition. In the second part of this chapter, we will build on differences in form and content between individual sayings in order to examine how theological humility grounded the authority of these ammas. In all of these sayings, theological humility operates against misguided assumptions and false conceptions; the teachings of these ammas invite application and testing so that audiences might imagine various ways of thinking about theological humility. Collective analysis of these sayings about theological humility reveals efforts to destabilize or disavow a monolithic interpretation. By situating theological humility in the authority of the amma, these sayings depict their subjects as embodied sites of knowledge and insight rooted in radical dependence on a divine power and directed beyond self-concern.

The Humility of Learning

Hagiography is a hybrid literary form in the ancient world; it adopts a variety of structural and narrative features from existing genres connected to memorializing individuals. These genres, including the encomium and the martyrology, signify that hagiographic origins lie in narrative representation. Hagiography serves its contemporary audience by identifying a particular type of Christian holiness.[4] Since the formulaic structure of the hagiographic subject's life constructs resemblance with the life of Christ, hagiography operates as a testament to the power of God. Allison Goddard Elliot observes that "while names, places, and dates may differ in hagiographic accounts, many stories employ a common narrative grammar and framework . . . for audience and author alike shared a common horizon of expectation concerning narrative deep structure of saintly behavior."[5] Hagiographies are social, public texts intended to expose the presence and activity of a divine power in the life of a holy person (ἅγιος), a Christian saint.[6] The quest for a strictly historical reconstruction about a hagiographic subject will remain unfulfilled. Rather, we must begin by acknowledging that hagiography bears a different didactic purpose. Given its use in monastic and liturgical settings, hagiography aims to explain a process of becoming a type of Christian. Very often, the words, actions, and behaviors of the hagiographic subject

[4] Daniel J. Sahas, "Hagiography," in *Encyclopedia of Early Christianity*, ed. Everett Ferguson, Michael P. McHugh, Frederick W. Norris, and David M. Scholar (New York: Garland, 1990), 409.

[5] Allison Goddard Elliott, *Roads to Paradise: Reading the Lives of the Early Saints* (Hanover, NH: University Press of New England, 1987), 8.

[6] See Andrew H. Merrills, "Monks, Monsters, and Barbarians: Re-defining the African Periphery in Late Antiquity," *Journal of Early Christian Studies* 12, no. 2 (2004): 217–44.

exemplify for the hagiographer and the audience the stages by which a Christian subject chooses to accept and live a more strictly ascetic or monastic way of life. Hagiography deals partially with partial subjects. As Alexander Kazhdan explains, "Hagiographical works present, usually in a sequence of episodes, the system of Christian values, among which chastity naturally holds a place of honor."[7] Adopting a more solitary existence, confronting trials and testing, the hagiographic subject appears to develop a dependence on a divine power. This dependence is a mark of their holiness recognized by other Christians.

And so, interpreting early Christian hagiography requires an attentive approach. As Susan Ashbrook Harvey and Sebastian Brock observe, the "variation in historicity does not detract from the worth of these texts as social documents for their period of composition, offering us insight and information on the world from which they come."[8] As social documents, early Christian hagiographies offer narrative sites for experimenting with ideas and behaviors, as hagiographers and their audiences imagined ways of being Christian in the context of empire. Gender identity is necessarily constrained by the broader social parameters of an androcentric, patriarchal world. These parameters contribute to the construction of holiness advanced in these texts, as Andrew Merrills contends that "the literary paradigm of the biblical wild *man* proved to be a fundamental one in late antique hagiography."[9] This paradigm presents an added challenge for interpreters of hagiographies with female subjects. To what extent are these female subjects depicted as women? We must remember that male authorship informs the vast majority of the representations of women and of womanhood, as well as the ways in which gender operates in these texts. Here, purity and personal relationships feature prominently and interactions are localized and circumscribed within a limited social environment. Although humility is a distinguishing mark of the holiness depicted in hagiography, it requires further qualification for female subjects. As hagiographers grapple with constructions of female sanctity, they must attend to the ways in which the humility of their subjects exemplifies that of their male savior.

[7] Alexander Kazhdan, "Byzantine Hagiography and Sex in the Fifth to Twelfth Centuries," *Dumbarton Oaks Papers* 44 (1990): 131.

[8] See Brock and Harvey, *Holy Women of the Syrian Orient*, 3.

[9] Merrills, "Monks, Monsters, and Barbarians," 221. Italics added.

The early sections of the *Life of Syncletica* illustrate well those familiar narrative features foreshadowing the inevitable conversion of a Christian subject to a more ascetic form of discipleship. At the start of the text, the hagiographer introduces Syncletica's family. They are staunchly Christian immigrants from Macedonia who migrated to Alexandria, where, full of joy and surprise, they are pleased with their fellow Christians.[10] Syncletica's siblings are "esteemed for their religious way of life,"[11] and Syncletica is eager, early on, "to train her soul in the love of God."[12] From here forward in the text, the hagiographer describes Syncletica's progress in the spiritual life: by strengthening her resolve and commitment to bodily discipline and prayer, she will develop an acute awareness of her created state that marks her growth in theological humility.

Syncletica learns about theological humility from the examples of two predecessors, the early Christian saint Thecla and the biblical figure Job.[13] Syncletica is a model student, as she will come to surpass the example of both teachers. Historian Stephen J. Davis writes, "The biographer of Syncletica presents her as a disciple moulded in Thecla's image and urges

[10] Pseudo-Athanasius, *Life of Syncletica* 4, p. 10.

[11] Ibid. 5, p. 11.

[12] Ibid. 6, p. 11.

[13] Several scholars have assessed literary connections between the *Life of Syncletica* and other texts, as well as between Syncletica and these figures. See Virginia Burrus, *Saving Shame: Martyrs, Saints, and Other Abject Subjects* (Philadelphia: University of Pennsylvania Press, 2008), especially 100–109; Kevin Corrigan, "Syncletica and Macrina: Two Early Lives of Women Saints," *Vox Benedictina* 6, no. 3 (July 1989): 241–57; Stephen J. Davis, *The Cult of Saint Thecla: A Tradition of Women's Piety in Late Antiquity* (Oxford: Oxford University Press, 2001); Susan Dreyer, "Syncletica: Urban Ascetic and Desert Mother," Graduate Papers/Theses, paper 14, 2006, College of Saint Benedict/ Saint John's University School of Theology and Seminary; Forman, "Amma Syncletica"; Annabelle Parker, "The Vita Syncleticae in the Synagoge: The Citations of Synkletike of Alexandria Used by Paul of Evergetis," in *Work and Worship at the Theotokos Evergetis: 1050–1200*, ed. Margaret Mullett and Anthony Kirby, 143–51, Belfast Byzantine Texts and Translations 6.2 (Belfast: Belfast Byzantine Enterprises, 1997); Rachel Wheeler, "Growing Wings Like Eagles: Women's Bodies and Women's Work in *The Life of Syncletica*," *Magistra* (Summer 2014): 76–96; David Brakke, *Demons and the Making of the Monk: Spiritual Combat in Early Christianity* (Cambridge, MA: Harvard University Press, 2006); Elizabeth A. Castelli, "Mortifying the Body, Curing the Soul: Beyond Ascetic Dualism in *The Life of Saint Syncletica*," *differences: A Journal of Feminist Cultural Studies* 4, no. 2 (1992): 134.

his monastic readers to envision both Thecla and Syncletica as models for their own piety."[14] Regardless of whether "this identification of Syncletica as a disciple of Thecla might be interpreted merely as a rhetorical gesture on the part of the hagiographer,"[15] Davis's observation that the connections between Thecla and Syncletica build on existing practice and belief stands. It is clear that the hagiographer envisions Thecla as a model of theological humility for Syncletica.

In the *Life of Syncletica*, explicit connections between Thecla and Syncletica exist alongside more indirect inferences in order to depict education in theological humility as a continuous process. Thecla's story is recounted in the earlier apocryphal text *Acts of Paul and Thecla*. Here, the author deploys the highly sensory, experiential site of the window as a space of encounter for his female subject. The window is a prominent physical space that marks the stages of Thecla's emerging holiness: hearing, transgressing, and transforming. Early in the *Acts*, we find Thecla at the window as she sits and listens to Paul's preaching and teaching; she is converted by a hearing that is possible only through the open window.[16] Furthering her desire to appear before Paul, she observes, again from the window, others going to him.[17] Her reluctance to remove herself from the window to visit with her fiancé, Thamyris, alerts the reader to her changing state as the window develops from a space of possibility into one of transgression. Despite reprimand and rebuke, Thecla maintains a composed posture at the window as confrontation between Thamyris, herself, and her mother escalates. While Thamyris and Theocleia are concerned with the seeming seduction and apparent loss of Thecla who is, in the words of her mother, "clinging to the window like a spider,"[18] Thecla is transfixed, consumed by the discourses of

[14] Davis, *The Cult of Saint Thecla*, 192.

[15] Ibid., 108.

[16] For the version of the *Acts of Paul and Thecla* used in this chapter, see Patricia Cox Miller, ed., *Women in Early Christianity: Translations from Greek Texts* (Washington, DC: Catholic University of America Press, 2005), 155–56. Subsequent references in this chapter are from this translation and include section and page numbers. Miller, *Acts of Paul and Thecla* 7, 157. See also the discussion of the *Acts of Paul and Thecla* in Lynn H. Cohick and Amy Brown Hughes, *Christian Women in the Patristic World* (Grand Rapids, MI: Baker Academic, 2017), 1–25.

[17] Miller, *Acts of Paul and Thecla* 7, in *Women in Early Christianity*, p. 157.

[18] Ibid. 9, p. 158.

Paul and their impact on others. Here, again, the window marks a changed state from a site of transgression into a venue for discipleship. Unveiling a new way of being, for Thecla, the window thus serves as a symbol for the tensions created and confronted by her decisions to contest boundaries between marriage and chastity, and for her resolve to be "led on by faith, rejoicing exceedingly."[19]

The *Life of Syncletica* employs the compelling symbol of the window for similar ends. Thecla's act of consumptive hearing by giving herself over to Paul's preaching is reflected and yet simultaneously transposed in the *Life of Syncletica*. Here, the hagiographer describes Syncletica's desire to attain a similar quality of hearing: "by closing her senses as if they were windows, she continued to converse in solitude with her bridegroom, referring to the following passage: *I belong to my beloved and my beloved belongs to me*."[20] Unlike Thecla, Syncletica's claim redirects this intellectual conversion toward a single-minded focus on her divine beloved. Syncletica reorients her attention more directly on contemplation; "by closing her senses as if they were windows," Syncletica chooses her partner and decides to give herself over to the word as shared with her bridegroom, Jesus Christ.[21]

In subsequent sections of the *Life of Syncletica*, Thecla's example of courage and fortitude, through transgression and transformation, functions as a benchmark for Syncletica's formation to again exceed.[22] Instructed in Scripture, Syncletica's practice turns inward as she strives to ready her soul through application of the word. Through a single-minded focus, in conjunction with ascetic disciplines, especially fasting, Syncletica perseveres.[23] Syncletica's interior state is reflected in a series of actions undertaken shortly after the death of her parents; seeking to intensify her commitment, Syncletica transgresses societal expectations. She leaves home for a tomb outside the city, sells her remaining posses-

[19] Ibid. 7, p. 157.

[20] Pseudo-Athanasius, *Life of Syncletica* 9, p. 13; italics in the text.

[21] As Elizabeth A. Castelli observes about the role of sight in the *Life of Syncletica*, "The senses, like the windows of a house, control what enters the space inside" ("Mortifying the Body," 147). See also Elizabeth A. Clark, "The Celibate Bridegroom and His Virginal Brides: Metaphor and the Marriage of Jesus in Early Christian Ascetic Exegesis," *Church History* 77, no. 1 (March 2008): 1–25.

[22] See Brakke, *Demons and the Making of the Monk*, 189–91.

[23] Pseudo-Athanasius, *Life of Syncletica* 10, p. 13.

sions and distributes the proceeds to the poor, and requests that her hair be cut, an act recognized by the author as "a sign that her soul had become unadorned and pure."[24] The hagiographer further identifies this act as a significant mark of Syncletica's humility when he concludes that, through it, she "laid aside all 'worldly glory.'"[25] Whereas this transformation mirrors that of her teacher, Thecla, it serves Syncletica as a foundation for a more radical embodiment of theological humility.

Educated by Thecla, Syncletica would eventually receive a "more piercing brand of evil"[26] from Satan, who confronted her "from within through her own contrary and destructive thoughts."[27] As the *Life of Syncletica* unfolds, the hagiographer's description of Syncletica's practices of fasting and food consumption demonstrate a remarkable strength and resolve. In the final sections of the *Life of Syncletica*, the slow and steady disintegration of Syncletica's body, ravaged from within, presents in vivid descriptive detail as the author writes that the devil attacks Syncletica with a series of debilitating illnesses.[28] The devil's attacks are most intense during Syncletica's eightieth year of life, when she is given the "trials of Job."[29] In this case, the devil "assailed her with torments from wounds on the inside; for by afflicting her inner organs, he allotted her to more severe and arduous suffering."[30] The hagiographer's reference to the opening chapters of the biblical book of Job frames the interpretive context for Syncletica's suffering. These chapters constitute part of an early folktale questioning the source of Job's virtue by posing the question "Does Job fear God for nothing?"[31] Job is a "blameless and upright" person,[32] a man of great material wealth who "feared God and turned away from evil"[33]

[24] Ibid. 11, p. 14.

[25] See Davis, *The Cult of Saint Thecla*, 110. See also Castelli, "Mortifying the Body," 148.

[26] Pseudo-Athanasius, *Life of Syncletica* 8, p. 12.

[27] Ibid. 8, p. 12. See Brakke, *Demons and the Making of the Monk*, 189ff.; Wheeler, "Growing Wings Like Eagles," 85–86; Burrus, *Saving Shame*, 105; Corrigan, "Syncletica and Macrina"; Forman, "Amma Syncletica."

[28] Pseudo-Athanasius, *Life of Syncletica* 104, p. 65.

[29] Ibid. 106, p. 66.

[30] Ibid.

[31] Job 1:9.

[32] Job 1:1.

[33] Ibid.

and who is rightly reckoned simply as "the greatest of all the people of the east,"[34] protected with "a fence around him and his house and all that he has, on every side."[35] Unlike those around him, Job is singled out for temptation by the divine and the adversary. The attack of the Sabeans against Job's oxen and servants, the fire of God that burned up Job's camels and servants, the raids of the Chaldeans on Job's sheep and servants, and the onslaught of the desert wind that collapsed Job's house, causing the deaths of his sons and daughters—all recounted in the first chapter of the book of Job—strike Job without mercy. Yet, in the face of these tragedies, Job appears neither debilitated nor paralyzed. He seeks neither blame nor retribution. Rather, Job hears the challenge posed to him by the haunting prophecy of the messengers responsible for informing him of these tragedies. Their common cry, "I alone have escaped to tell you,"[36] halts briefly the description of the devastation brought with each tragedy in order to name clearly Job's own vulnerability. Because Job values these prophetic voices and the content of their message, he is empowered to act rather than to react, as he does in the face of these tragedies for, acknowledging his own accountability, Job "tore his robe"[37] and "shaved his head."[38] While such acts were associated with mourning, shame, and repentance in the ancient world, their meaning here is unambiguous, as Job then "fell on the ground and worshipped."[39] Job's first vocalization in the text is a public recognition of theological humility: "Naked I came from my mother's womb, and naked I shall return there; the Lord gave, and the Lord has taken away; blessed be the name of the Lord."[40] Job's resulting resolve lingers for "In all this Job did not sin or charge God with wrongdoing,"[41] thereby maintaining his theological humility. Thus, in his sustained response to these tragedies, Job continued to choose to be blameless and accountable; he continued to act righteously and justly before a divine power and before his fellow human beings. In

[34] Job 1:3.
[35] Job 1:10.
[36] Job 1:17.
[37] Job 1:20.
[38] Ibid.
[39] Ibid.
[40] Job 1:21.
[41] Job 1:22.

his response Job articulates his theological humility as radical dependence, as a complete submission before God, lacking self-concern.

In the *Life of Syncletica*, the hagiographer's analogy to the suffering of Job has the effect of heightening the intensity and emphasizing the depth of Syncletica's suffering. Syncletica, like Job, is given over to the adversary for the purpose of testing;[42] however, as in the previous comparison with Thecla, Syncletica's sufferings and their impact again exceed. Whereas Syncletica's response to her suffering is similar to Job's,[43] her efforts appear to have a broader healing influence on others than those of her male predecessor.[44] Like Job, Syncletica's knowledge of her "nothingness" appears as an intentional, willful act of recognizing herself as created and as creature that is directed not toward the self but toward a divine power. Yet here, too, there is an extended dimension to Syncletica's response; whereas Job's "nothingness" is an awareness of his presence before a divine power, Syncletica's "nothingness" is cast as a merging with that power.[45]

The stories of Thecla and Job present relevant narrative frameworks for demonstrating the theological humility of Syncletica to the audience. Thecla's example supplies a process for learning about theological humility that becomes embodied when Syncletica confronts trials akin to those of Job. In this way, Syncletica's education in humility will move beyond resemblance to surpass that of Thecla as she is challenged to become like Job. And yet, again, Syncletica's exceptional capacity for theological humility will exceed as the hagiographer introduces a most extreme, unreplicable expression of theological humility in the form of self-destruction.[46] The hagiographer's emphasis in both comparisons suggests a desire not merely to equate his subject with these figures but to set Syncletica apart from these figures through her particular experience of theological humility. Thecla and Job are figures known for their theological humility; through her instruction in their example, Syncletica becomes a figure of theological humility as well. Serving to guide and

[42] Pseudo-Athanasius, *Life of Syncletica* 105, p. 65.

[43] Ibid., 106, p. 66.

[44] Ibid., 107, p. 67.

[45] Wheeler, "Growing Wings Like Eagles," 86.

[46] Burrus, *Saving Shame*, 103. My intent is to explore how Job functions as a model of humility for Syncletica.

instruct both Syncletica and, by extension, the audience of her vita, the hagiographer's inclusion of the example of Thecla lays the groundwork for theological humility as a christological concept that is then given a soteriological interpretation through appeal to the example of Job. Specifically, theological humility is cast as a Christian eremitic value grounded in—and extending beyond—its foundational scriptural context. Job's theological humility, rewarded by recompense for his suffering while he is still alive, becomes the basis from which Syncletica's theological humility attains new eschatological significance. By framing Syncletica's humility as an experience of union with her divine bridegroom, the hagiographer offers his audience a reconstituted category grounded in familiar theological features and incorporating contemporary christological elements.

Theological humility, as self-aware and intentional dependence on a divine power, is the central teaching in the later hagiography, the *Life of Thais*. This vita presents a similar process for obtaining holiness grounded in hearing, transgressing societal expectations, and transforming identity through conversion to a monastic life.[47] Thais was a prostitute who was visited by a monk in disguise, Paphnutius, for the purpose of her redemption; when Paphnutius speaks with Thais in the bedroom, the site of her fornications, she openly admits to knowing of the constant presence of the Christian God. Paphnutius chastises Thais for choosing to lead others and herself away from the path of righteousness. Listening deeply and desiring forgiveness and conversion, Thais then sets ablaze all of the possessions and distributes all of the money given to her by her former lovers. She allows herself to be led by Paphnutius to a convent of women, where she is cloistered in a cell containing a small window through which food and other necessities might be passed. When she asks Paphnutius about her excrement, she is told that she should sit in her filth; when she asks Paphnutius what she should do in the cell, she is told to pray the words, "You who made me, have mercy on me,"[48] thereby appealing to a divine

[47] For the version of the *Life of St. Thais the Harlot* used in this chapter, see Benedicta Ward, *Harlots of the Desert: A Study of Repentance in Early Monastic Sources* (Kalamazoo, MI: Cistercian Publications, 1987), 83–84. Subsequent references to the *Life of Thais* in this chapter are from this translation and include section and page numbers.

[48] Ward, *Life of Thais*, cap. 2, p. 84.

power without the explicit use of the divine name. Thais is thus left alone to pray, repent, and worship in the confines of her monastic cell.

Like the author of the *Life of Syncletica*, the author of the *Life of Thais* employs a rhetoric of renunciation of material goods. Again, the symbol of the window heightens the female subject's changing status. Whereas Thais's focus "in the world" was on others seeing and thus recognizing her physical beauty, Thais's focus "in the cell" is on her seeing her own filth and sinfulness. As Thais knowingly admits, the divine "sees" the activities of both the bedroom and the cell.[49] This juxtaposition signifies Thais's changing status: she confronts her exterior, perverted beauty in the cell as inner moral sanctity becomes the mark of her Christian, eremitic beauty; the cell is a constructed site that signifies confrontation and personal transformation, bondage and liberation, sin and redemption. In the space of the cell, Thais is instructed to perform a series of acts intended to force her to confront her sinfulness in order to be open to a different form of sight and awareness of a divine power. Through continuous prayer, Thais exercises a form of recollection and remembrance with the potential for personal transformation.[50]

After three years of continuous appeal to a divine power through obedience in the cell, Thais's theological humility, like Syncletica's, has become embodied. No longer interested in "the world," Thais resides before and with a divine power. When Thais emerges from her cell, she articulates this understanding of theological humility as she states, "I call God to witness that since I came in here my sins have always been before my eyes as a burden; they have never been out of my sight and I have always wept to see them."[51] Thais's profession of theological humility names and defines her personal transformation.

The story of Thais is framed by the story of Paphnutius; the actions of Paphnutius drive the movement in Thais's story. Paphnutius first appeals to Thais, which leads to a series of decisions that culminate in her enclosure; when Paphnutius then appeals to Abba Antony of Egypt while she is in the cell, a round of prayers are issued that culminate in a vision

[49] Ibid., cap. 1, p. 83.

[50] See the discussion of the features of the cell as constructed monastic space in Darlene L. Brooks Hedstrom, "The Geography of the Monastic Cell in Early Egyptian Monastic Literature," *Church History* 78, no. 4 (December 2009): 756–91.

[51] Ward, *Life of Thais*, cap. 3, p. 84.

of acceptance; finally, Paphnutius appeals again to Thais, and she is removed from the cell. The story of Thais intentionally masks its subject behind the actions of the publicly recognized, religiously validated figure of the monk, Paphnutius. Such framing accounts for the series of events occurring outside of Thais's cell. While Thais is still in isolation, a group of monks debates her outcome. Her period of isolation concludes only when it is revealed in a vision that she has been forgiven. Just as Paphnutius initiated the sequence of events that led to Thais's entombment, he initiates the sequence of events that leads to her removal from the cell. When Paphnutius is uncertain about the outcome of Thais's isolation, he seeks the advice of Abba Antony to determine whether Thais has repented for a sufficient time. Paphnutius's uncertainty moves the narrative forward, and his indecisiveness is ironically juxtaposed with his prior assertiveness about the need for Thais to be removed from a society of males to a community of females. Like Thais's appeal to Paphnutius, Paphnutius's appeal to Abba Antony is an opportunity for further instruction in theological humility; like Thais, Paphnutius recognizes not only his own limitations but also the wisdom and insight of another person in his request for counsel. Rather than answering Paphnutius's question directly, Abba Antony instructs his followers to hold a vigil and wait for a sign to indicate a divine response. Abba Antony's instruction to his followers, like Paphnutius's instruction to Thais, is a sign of theological humility; when Abba Antony redirects the group of monks to issue their request to a divine power, he affirms that power as the only legitimate authority in this situation. Antony's admission of his own insufficiency to offer a response thereby reinforces how theological humility is acquired, as it parallels what Paphnutius had instructed Thais to do, namely, to redirect her focus and attention from the world to a divine power. Indeed, when Abba Antony tells his disciples to pray, he directs them to do what Thais has done by orienting their focus to accept God's revelation about the state of Thais's repentance.

For this reason, it is fitting that Thais's story concludes with a public confirmation of her profession of theological humility in the mouth of Paphnutius. After Abba Antony's instruction to his disciples to persist in prayer in order to receive a response to Paphnutius's query, another monk, Paul, receives a vision of three virgins. When Paul queries the three virgins about whether the glory they project is for Abba Antony, they explain that such glory is for Thais. When Paul then comes forward to share his vision before the group of monks, it is Paphnutius who "recognised the will of God"[52] in the vision and who then expressed it when he goes to Thais's cell to report this news. Thais's reluctance to depart the cell and her profession of theological humility are met with Paphnutius's pronouncement that she has been forgiven "not because of your penances but because you have always had the remembrance of your sins in your soul."[53] Paphnutius thus reinforces the claim that Thais's theological humility attains rightfully through the continuous reminder, the "remembrance," of her place and orientation before a divine power.

Audiences familiar with the *Life of Syncletica* or the *Life of Antony* would recognize that, like the holiness of the subjects of these hagiographies, Thais's theological humility must be learned. In their respective vitae, Syncletica, Antony, and Thais are divinely directed to ascetic discipline in response to hearing the word of God; all three subjects transgress societal expectations by renouncing their material wealth and spending a period of time sealed in a confined area, whether a tomb or a cell, where they undergo trial, testing, and a "death" to the self; and all three subjects are said to exit their isolated confinement transformed in body. Like Antony, Syncletica and Thais initiate ascetic discipline under the direction of male authorities and spiritual guides. Unlike Antony, by submitting to the spiritual guidance of recognized male figures, the obedience of Syncletica and Thais necessarily reinscribes their submissive social status. Although "women were not valued as women," their worth was acknowledged "as true followers of Christ" by early Christian hagiographers.[54]

Obedience also highlights a preexisting state of "illness" as the context for theological humility: whereas Syncletica's theological humility is demonstrated as emerging from her attitudes around the treatment of her disease, thought to be inflicted on her by demons, Thais's theological humility is demonstrated as emerging from her attitudes around the treatment of her sin, thought to orient her toward vice. In the tomb and in the cell, Syncletica and Thais assume a solitary pursuit of ascetic discipline and prayer. The physical containment of each woman represents her entrapment: Syncletica is trapped in her decay, the context for her insistent dependence on a divine power; Thais is trapped in her sin, the context

[52] Ward, *Life of Thais*, cap. 3, p. 84.

[53] Ibid.

[54] Brock and Harvey, *Holy Women of the Syrian Orient*, 26.

for her insistent dependence on a divine power. In both cases, other human beings are visible and present. Acting as witnesses and audience, their watchfulness serves to validate the events presented. The hagiographers' closing description of the bodily transformation of each woman includes a verification by her peers; her obedience and containment are thereby recognizable public markers of a new, humble status.

While the historical veracity of such entrapment remains unverifiable for Syncletica and Thais, the implicit relationship between containment and disease does not. In the world of late antiquity physical illness, of body or of mind, could merit sequester from others. Claustration from the ecclesia was commonplace for menstruating women, and Jennifer Schultz has shown that medical and biological theories informed such practices.[55] In Egypt, this intentional compartmentalization of women occurs in conjunction with "a highly developed interest in illness, health, and healing"[56] by which holy men "used the panoply of prayer together with their medical skills, folk wisdom, and herbal lore to cure the ills of others" as a key component of their holiness.[57]

The quest for a divine power to heal thus bears cultural and religious significance. By decrying human assistance and seeking a divine power, both women operate in contexts familiar to their audiences. By redirecting their pain as an offering, their exercise of humility requires the ability to know that one is being humble. This is possible by modeling the example of Christ: Syncletica's connection to Christ's persecution, suffering, and death frames her body's demise; Thais's connection to Christ's wilderness experience shapes her body's purification. Like Christ, Syncletica and Thais choose to respond to their respective forms of disease

[55] Jennifer Schultz, "Doctors, Philosophers, and Christian Fathers on Menstrual Blood," in *Wholly Woman, Holy Blood: A Feminist Critique of Purity and Impurity*, ed. Kristin De Troyer et. al. (Harrisburg, PA: Trinity Press, 2003), 97–116.

[56] See R. J. S. Barrett-Lennard, "The Canons of Hippolytus and Christian Concern with Illness, Health, and Healing," *Journal of Early Christian Studies* 13, no. 2 (Summer 2005): 137–64.

[57] Stanley Harakas, "The Eastern Orthodox Tradition," in *Caring and Curing: Health and Medicine in the Western Religious Tradition*, ed. Ronald L. Numbers and Darrel Amundson (Baltimore, MD: Johns Hopkins University Press, 1986), 151, as cited in Amanda Porterfield, *Healing in the History of Christianity* (Oxford: Oxford University Press, 2005), 48.

in continuous prayer. Healing aligns the female body with Christ, the "great physician." For this reason, humility occurs through a displacement of self that retains rather than refutes the female sex; the quest of Syncletica and Thais, according to their hagiographers, is not to become male but to become one with the divine presence by following the example of Christ. Syncletica's self-resignation before her impending death and Thais's self-identification upon the reopening of her cell are demonstrations of a divine power.

Syncletica and Thais learn theological humility through instruction that draws on other human beings as exemplars. These exemplars initiate the female subjects' consideration of theological humility as a value; over time, each female subject progresses in understanding through further education as theological humility becomes embodied and lived under the direct guidance of a divine power. As we consider the primary examples of theological humility offered to Syncletica and to others, we witness the hagiographers' attempts to identify the theological humility of their respective subject. In the *Life of Syncletica*, when the hagiographer appeals to the demonstrated theological humility of two predecessors, Thecla and Job, he describes Syncletica as a student of their example; she learns to such an extent that she not only extends but surpasses the theological humility of her guides. Instruction in theological humility appears again in the later story of the harlot saint, Thais. Here the hagiographer incorporates the example of theological humility in the monk, Paphnutius, in order to educate Thais in theological humility. Obedient to the instruction given, Thais learns to adopt an alternative way of being Christian. In both hagiographies, the subject learns about theological humility in the immediate context of material attachment. Syncletica's theological humility entails renunciation of worldly glory; by adopting material poverty, Syncletica learns theological humility through a poverty of self as the physical health of her physical body steadily declines. Her hagiography highlights the transformation that results from this ultimate sacrifice of bodily attachment. Misguided use of the body opens the hagiography of Thais. Thais's theological humility requires renunciation of worldly profit; by accepting physical confinement, Thais learns theological humility through repentance as her physical body aligns with a divine power. As a result of their respective decisions, Syncletica and Thais become, in turn, teachers of others like those ascetic women whose teachings are preserved in the *Apophthegmata Patrum*.

The Humility of Teaching

Akin to proverbs and other types of gnomic literature, the *Sayings of the Desert Fathers* is practically oriented and centers on ethical matters.[58] The spiritual direction in the *Sayings* reflects attempts to interpret Scripture in a specifically monastic setting.[59] Here, spiritual direction occurs in the teachings of ammas (desert mothers) and abbas (desert fathers). These figures are recalled for the caliber of their lived ascetic experience as *monachoi*, monks and hermits; thus, the content of the *Sayings* imparts guidance and teaching from those endowed with a type of authority and knowledge familiar and valuable in the ancient world.[60] As a type of *paraenesis*, namely, "moral exhortation to follow a given course of action or to abstain from a contrary behavior,"[61] the *Sayings* are gendered in form. They "are told from the point of view of a male celibate"[62] and intended for a predominantly male audience. Like hagiographic representation, accurate attribution of a saying is most often unverifiable.[63]

Direct in tone and didactic in delivery, many of the *Sayings* elicit pungent and searing commentaries on contemporary norms and thought patterns. This may be most apparent in those sayings that address or include women. William Harmless observes, "Women are often cast in a negative

[58] For evidence evincing relationships between proverbs and the *Apophthegmata Patrum*, see Lillian I. Larsen, "Excavating the Excavations," in *Monastic Education in Late Antiquity: The Transformation of Classical Paideia*, ed. Lillian I. Larsen and Samuel Rubenson (Cambridge: Cambridge University Press, 2018), 101–24.

[59] See William Harmless, *Desert Christians: An Introduction to the Literature of Early Monasticism* (Oxford: Oxford University Press, 2004), 245–51; Douglas Burton-Christie, *The Word in the Desert: Scripture and the Quest for Holiness in Early Christian Monasticism* (Oxford: Oxford University Press, 1993), 236–60. See also Per Rönnegård, *Threads and Images: The Use of Scripture in* Apophthegmata Patrum (Winona Lake, IN: Eisenbrauns, 2010).

[60] See Lillian I. Larsen, "The Apophthegmata Patrum and the Classical Rhetorical Tradition," *Studia Patristica* 39 (2006): 409–16. See also Ward, foreword to *The Sayings of the Desert Fathers*.

[61] Everett Ferguson, *Backgrounds of Early Christianity*, 2nd ed. (Grand Rapids, MI: William B. Eerdmans, 1993), 302. See also Larsen, "The Apophthegmata Patrum and the Classical Rhetorical Tradition."

[62] Harmless, *Desert Christians*, 440. See also Margot H. King, *The Desert Mothers: A Survey of the Feminine Anchoretic Tradition in Western Europe* (Toronto, ON: Peregrina, 1984).

[63] See Rönnegård, *Threads and Images*, 7. See also Samuel Rubenson, *The Letters of Antony: Monasticism and the Making of a Saint* (Minneapolis: Fortress Press, 1995), 152.

light—as temptresses, sometimes human, sometimes demonic, who come at night to taunt monks, rousing their lust or luring them to abandon their monastic commitments and return to the settled land for the amenities of family life. But here and there, one finds scattered reports of women who took up residence in the desert."[64] Laden with deceptive and duplicitous characterization and a gendered construction privileging males, how are we to read and interpret theological humility in the sayings of those ammas who are said to have chosen such a "residence in the desert?"

Like other types of gnomic literature, the *Sayings* were used in an instructional context. Recent scholarly focus on this context by Lillian I. Larsen and others yields fresh insights into early monastic educational practices. These insights advance a response to long-standing questions about the development and diversity of the sayings by gauging what Larsen refers to as their "malleability." Larsen explains that, "in an ancient frame, the merit of a saying was not measured in terms of its 'authenticity', but rather its 'aptness'. Sayings were understood to be infinitely malleable. A saying's attribution to a particular individual, its prompting circumstance or setting, and the structure of the statement itself were each widely recognized as eminently variable."[65] The malleability of the sayings enabled a hermeneutic fluidity that, in turn, facilitated their learning, as core structural characteristics and repeated phrasing across the sayings eased recitation and content could be truncated or expanded as circumstances required.[66]

In order to attend to its familiar and distinct features, the *Sayings* has been studied from a variety of approaches. Such approaches highlight the spiritual, religious, and educational value of the sayings for past and present audiences. The approach taken in this chapter recognizes how the sayings demonstrate variability in teachings about theological humility attributed to those women identified explicitly as professed ammas in the *Sayings*. Christian humility is a central feature of the *Sayings*, as Douglas

[64] Harmless, *Desert Christians*, 440. See also Caroline T. Schroeder, "Women in Anchoritic and Semi-Anchoritic Monasticism in Egypt: Rethinking the Landscape," *Church History* 83, no. 1 (March 2014): 1–17. See also Kate Cooper, *Band of Angels: The Forgotten World of Early Christian Women* (New York: Overlook Press, 2013), 237–46.

[65] Lillian I. Larsen, "The Apophthegmata Patrum: Rustic Rumination or Rhetorical Recitation," *Patristica Nordica Annuaria* 23 (2008): 24.

[66] See the examples provided by Larsen, "The Apophthegmata Patrum: Rustic Rumination or Rhetorical Recitation," 24–29.

Burton-Christie explains: "The *Sayings* is filled with questions about the meaning of humility and about how to acquire and cultivate it: its importance was equaled only by its elusiveness. The monks' questions about humility focused on and drew upon various words of Scripture and in particular the witness of Christ."[67] Despite the paucity of female representation in the *Sayings*, those ammas identified by name, including Theodora, Sarah, and Syncletica, attest to an impact on teaching about theological humility rivaling that of their male counterparts. Because these women are inscribed in thought and in action as masculine, they perform the feminine identity their acquired wisdom claims to transcend.

Our approach draws on Carole Fontaine's study of biblical proverbs in the ancient world. Fontaine's attention to the relationship between the structure and reception of a proverb applies to the sayings attributed to these ammas. Fontaine maintains that "if the proverb is an oppositional one, ancient women hearers/users must decide between two options, neither of which may concern itself with the real alternatives allowed women. If the saying works, on the other hand, by an extended comment on a topic, there is not much likelihood that either the topic or the comment is reflective of a female 'point of view.'"[68] By recognizing the way structural differences in form meet distinct didactic aims, such an approach to the proverbs bears similar purchase in the *Sayings*. Larsen's argument about the malleability of the sayings shows how the reformulation of a simple saying might offer "alternate" or "increasingly complex narratives,"[69] thereby suggesting possible parallels with the ways in which a proverb functioned for its female audiences in Fontaine's terms. Here, I treat those teachings about theological humility attributed to Theodora, Sarah, and Syncletica as a collective work with specific attention to their immediate context of spiritual guidance as personal encounter. I'll look first at how the religious authority of these ammas appears in sayings that are "oppositional," Fontaine's first classification, and then at those that serve as "extended comment on a topic," Fontaine's second classification, in order to note how differences in form supply

[67] Burton-Christie, *The Word in the Desert*, 236–60. See also Pardue, *The Mind of Christ*, 72.

[68] Carole Fontaine, *Smooth Words: Women, Proverbs and Performance in Biblical Wisdom* (London: Sheffield Academic Press, 2002), 13.

[69] Larsen, "The Apophthegmata Patrum," 28.

alternative sites for interrogating the authority of these ammas. In those sayings containing juxtaposition, we'll see how authority is tied to obedience to, and discernment of, a divine power; in those sayings that serve as extended commentary, we'll note how this construction of authority is founded in theological humility. The latter sayings, in particular, expose tensions over visitors' expectations about the amma's role as religious authority. These tensions meet a clear pedagogical aim by offering the reader an opportunity to confront alterity in the amma's response about the operation of theological humility.

Like that of their male counterparts in the *Sayings*, the religious authority of Theodora, Sarah, and Syncletica is born in a purity of heart. A saying attributed to Amma Sarah reads, "If I prayed God that all men should approve of my conduct, I should find myself a penitent at the door of each one, but I shall rather pray that my heart may be pure towards all."[70] This saying professes purity of heart as the foundation and condition for right relations between the self and others in a simple and systematic manner. In this context, purity of heart commences with prayer, rightly directed and rightly oriented outward, beyond the self, toward a divine power; this orientation, in turn, substantively affects how the individual amma engages in human affairs and relationships. There is a teasing tension in the saying intended to test operating assumptions, as the conditional language used in Sarah's statement is heavy with possibility, exhorting her visitors—and so the audience of the *Sayings*—to engage her words in a framework of concern beyond their immediate personal encounter. In this way, the use of the personal pronoun in her saying names and then deflects self-concern. Sarah's teaching is a statement about self-responsibility; it is framed as a choice that she identifies, weighs, and then decides. As a statement of agency, her choice affects not only herself but also her audience.

In the *Sayings*, purity of heart grows a wisdom that is often cultivated as discernment, the ability to differentiate between truth and falsehood. Male predecessors and biblical figures are exemplars meriting imitation, as is evident in this saying attributed to Amma Syncletica: "We must direct our souls with discernment. As long as we are in the monastery, we must

[70] Amma Sarah, *Sayings* 5, in Benedicta Ward, trans. *The Sayings of the Desert Fathers: The Alphabetical Collection* (Kalamazoo, MI: Cistercian Publications, 1975; rev. ed., 1984), 230.

not seek our own will, nor follow our personal opinion, but obey our fathers in the faith."[71] Here, the collective "we" hearkens to a common experience presented in relational terms; by immediately orienting her audience in an interpersonal manner, Syncletica's opening call for self-discipline and oversight bears a firm tone and elicits a clear directive. The saying builds on this foundation. Syncletica guides as a fellow ascetic also striving to practice an obedience aligned with the examples of "fathers in the faith," those notable male predecessors whose lives serve as consummate models. Thus, Syncletica and her teaching are positioned alongside current and prior practitioners. Such conflation of past and present time is a common feature of the *Sayings*; in this case, it assures that Syncletica is interpreted in the context of a monastic lineage extending back to foundational narratives and figures and forward to the decisions of the receiving audience. Such contextualization facilitates the proper reception and application of her instruction about obedience in two ways: for the individual, obedience implies a self-imposed submission of self in relation to others; this, in turn, folds into the community, as obedience governs those living "in the monastery." By attesting to individual and communal dimensions, Syncletica represents an embodiment of her teaching. This supplies additional reason for her audience to accept her invitation to exercise discernment obtained through monastic obedience.

The effects of exercising discernment in this way are modeled again in a second saying attributed to Syncletica. Here, we see a relationship between obedience, discernment, and theological humility. The subjects' discernment elicits a type of power defined by theological humility. The saying reads, "Imitate the publican, and you will not be condemned with the Pharisee. Choose the meekness of Moses and you will find your heart which is a rock changed into a spring of water."[72] This saying relates two very different scriptural frameworks for correct discernment, and Syncletica's religious authority is located in her insight about their symmetry. The first statement in this saying refers to the parable of the tax collector and the Pharisee who are at the temple to pray.[73] In their study of Christian scriptures, Norman Perrin and Dennis C. Duling maintain that, by definition, a parable is "an imaginary story from normal, every-

[71] Amma Syncletica, *Sayings* 17, in Ward, *The Sayings of the Desert Fathers*, 234.

[72] Amma Syncletica, *Sayings* 11, in Ward, *The Sayings of the Desert Fathers*, 233.

[73] Luke 18:9.

day human life which can be localized in time and place, a story which challenges established and conventional perceptions of reality."[74] In the parable of the tax collector and the Pharisee, Jesus juxtaposes the comportment of each figure in order to demonstrate righteous behavior. Jesus describes the Pharisee, known for his close observance of the law, who judges the inadequacies of others against his own standards, and deems himself superior in his consistent prayer, tithing, and fasting practices. The Pharisee prays, "God, I thank you that I am not like other people: thieves, rogues, adulterers, or even like this tax collector."[75] In contrast, as Jesus explains, the tax collector who was a bit removed, with eyes downcast, readily acknowledges his sinfulness and prays for mercy.[76] Through this juxtaposition, Jesus names the false righteousness of the Pharisee: "I tell you, this man [i.e., the tax collector] went down to his home justified rather than the other; for all who exalt themselves will be humbled, but all who humble themselves will be exalted."[77] The parable begs interpretation because it overturns a presumably right way of thinking. Specifically, the parable confronts belief in a bifurcation between action and intent; in its place, the parable teaches that right action requires right intent. The placement of this parable, referring directly to the teachings of Jesus, as the first statement in Syncletica's saying provides an interpretive context that extends, furthermore, to the Exodus reference in the second statement in the saying.

The second statement in Syncletica's saying refers to events during the Israelites' journey from Egypt to Sinai, as recounted in Exodus 17. The Israelites consistently complain to their leaders, Moses and Aaron, of their abandonment by Yahweh. Seeking signs of Yahweh's protection and care, they question Moses' authority and beg him to intercede before Yahweh on their behalf. Camping at Rephidim and lacking water, the Israelites hurl insults at Moses. Turning to Yahweh, Moses pleads for assistance. In reply, Yahweh instructs Moses, "Go on ahead of the people, and take some of the elders of Israel with you; take in your hand the staff with which you struck the Nile, and go. I will be standing there in front

[74] Norman Perrin and Dennis C. Duling, *The New Testament: An Introduction*, 2nd ed. (New York: Harcourt Brace Jovanovich, 1982), 415.

[75] Luke 18:11.

[76] Luke 18:13.

[77] Luke 18:14.

of you on the rock at Horeb. Strike the rock, and water will come out of it, so that the people may drink."[78] Moses obeys, and the people are restored for a time.

When these two scriptural statements, one from the canonical gospels and one from the book of Exodus, are paired in Syncletica's saying, they invite the audience to consider an association between submission, obedience, discernment, theological humility, and redemption. Jesus' assertion about theological humility in the first statement creates a scenario built on cause and effect: to choose the example of the tax collector is to choose a righteous way of being rooted in theological humility as defined by radical dependence. In his statement, Jesus defines the theological humility of the tax collector by appeal to the tax collector's understanding of his place in relation to others and before the divine. Jesus' teaching about a right recognition of one's place then carries over into the second statement in the saying, as the meekness of Moses is upheld over the aggression and doubt of the Israelites. Here, again, the decision to choose theological humility is said to have a redemptive effect and theological humility is relational: Moses' meekness strengthens his bond to Yahweh. In Syncletica's saying, the implications for the receiving audience promise the same: "You will find your heart which is a rock changed into a spring of water." Like the tax collector, Moses presents a model of theological humility, and the words of Jesus mirror those of Yahweh. By observing the connection and identifying the symmetry, Syncletica's insight reveals discernment and extends options similar to those presented to the tax collector and to Moses to her audience.

Another saying attributed to Amma Theodora employs oppositional language more directly to harness theological humility as a component of right thinking and practice. Here, again, theological humility is interpreted primarily as it operates with others and before the divine as an expression of reliance on a divine power. In this particular saying, Theodora reflects on the constitution of monastic authority. Such placement informs interpretation, as Susanna Elm observes: "Those who compiled the *Apophthegmata Patrum* regarded Theodora as the perfect representative of the qualities an ideal teacher ought to possess."[79] Theodora's instruction issues an opportunity for her audience to assess the accuracy and presence of

[78] Exodus 17:5-6.

[79] Elm, *"Virgins of God,"* 265.

these qualities. "The same amma [Theodora] said that a teacher ought to be a stranger to the desire for domination, vain-glory, and pride; one should not be able to fool him by flattery, nor blind him by gifts, nor conquer him by the stomach, nor dominate him by anger; but he should be patient, gentle and humble as far as possible; he must be tested and without partisanship, full of concern, and a lover of souls."[80] Theodora's saying applies the teasing power of suggestion to propose a set of relations between the stated categories. Of particular note is the order of presentation. The saying opens with a positive, potential claim indicating aspiration, expectation, and evaluation: the teacher *ought* to bear these characteristics. There is a proposed juxtaposition between characteristics presented intentionally in two antithetical clusters: domination, vainglory, and pride are positioned in contrast to patience, gentleness, humility. Serving not only to situate and define each cluster against its opposite, this juxtaposition denounces what is unworthy and highlights what is valued. The first cluster is undergirded by degrees of self-absorption, self-promotion, and self-advancement, as explained in the brief series of qualifying statements that follow. Conversely, the second cluster is indicative of self-restraint and self-discipline. Here, the subsequent qualifying statements emphasize, again, a certain understanding of one's place; if domination, vainglory, and pride are primarily self-directed, theological humility is directed toward the divine power. Theological humility is decided. The amma, as teacher, has chosen to exercise theological humility in engagement with others; as a "lover of souls," the amma and her teaching model an awareness of place before the divine and her audience.

In the sayings examined, we can see how the amma's monastic authority is qualified by her submission, obedience, discernment, and theological humility. Theological humility signals the amma's orientation beyond self-concern; it is a choice expressly defined. The amma's authority, exercised as a form of theological humility, originates in the ability of others to identify her choice to be humble. Such choice is qualified further, as Kate Cooper writes: "The point of humility was not to think ill of oneself but to protect oneself from this craving for status."[81]

[80] Amma Theodora, *Sayings* 5, in Ward, *The Sayings of the Desert Fathers*, 83. Ward's translation is from J. P. Migne, Patrologia Graeca, vol. 65, col. 71-440.

[81] Cooper, *Band of Angels*, 240.

When we turn to the sayings of Theodora, Sarah, and Syncletica structured as an "extended comment" on theological humility, there is a notable hermeneutic shift; unlike those sayings that teach through an oppositional statement, these sayings teach through story. The stories contained in sayings about theological humility exhibit a pattern wherein the stability of the amma's religious authority is first contested and then championed. These sayings are structured like a parable and often bear similar purchase. Like parables, the story in these sayings suspends the element of choice in order to increase the imagination, and so the engagement, of the audience. Moments of uncertainty disclose a perceived ambiguity about the wisdom of the amma as the operating assumptions of her visitors' false thinking are judged, overturned, and replaced with right thinking.

In one saying attributed to Theodora, the amma frames her teaching in a story about an encounter between an anchorite and the demons. Theodora demonstrates discernment as she again advances her belief in the soteriological significance of theological humility.

> She [Theodora] also said that neither asceticism, nor vigils nor any kind of suffering are able to save, only true humility can do that. There was an anchorite who was able to banish the demons; and he asked them, "What makes you go away? Is it fasting?" They replied, "We do not eat or drink." "Is it vigils?" They replied, "We do not sleep." "Is it separation from the world?" "We live in the deserts." "What power sends you away then?" They said, "Nothing can overcome us, but only humility." "Do you see how humility is victorious over the demons?"[82]

The story of the anchorite and the demons frames and illumines Theodora's teaching by providing both an evidentiary foundation and experiential support in a distinctly eremitic context. The structure of the saying bears attention for its contribution to this end: by bookending the story of the anchorite with Theodora's opening claim and concluding question, the presentation of this saying preserves its pedagogical purpose to instruct and to challenge its audience.

Theodora's opening claim introduces the story through the lived experience of a fellow ascetic and proposes that theological humility be evaluated comparatively in a common list of items related to the lived

[82] Amma Theodora, *Sayings* 6, in Ward, *The Sayings of the Desert Fathers*, 84.

practice of an ascetic; her claim thereby invites her audience to consider theological humility within a familiar cognitive framework. Her words propose a hierarchy that positions the value of theological humility over the practices of asceticism, suffering, and vigils. In relation to these practices, theological humility is distinct; theological humility serves as the appropriate orientation for these pursuits, and while these pursuits may contribute to the cultivation of theological humility, they are presented as neither sources of nor requirements for theological humility.

In the story, the anchorite's interrogation of the demons illustrates how one might arrive at the validity of the opening claim. The questions posed by the anchorite encourage the demons to clarify the source of their rejection. Fasting, vigils, and physical withdrawal from the world are proposed and denounced; against these practices, theological humility is touted as the anchorite's defense. Over the course of the story, the anchorite and the audience are educated by the demons about their habits; both the anchorite and the audience witness the demons' assessment of ascetic practices in order to learn about the privileged role and specific value of theological humility.

Theodora's concluding question adopts the querying voice of the anchorite and moves the audience's attention beyond the story by encouraging her audience to apply the line of reasoning demonstrated to their own thinking about theological humility. Her question is a summons to evaluate the extent to which her opening claim has been illustrated by the story. Theodora beckons her audience to weigh the relevance of her teaching in the context of their own experience. The final response to Theodora's question is left unanswered, as it is to be determined; the succinct, confrontational tone of the question "Do you see?" suspends what is familiar and known. Working together, then, the opening claim, the story, and the closing question form a tightly constructed teaching intended to invite the audience to consider the role and value of theological humility.

Amma Theodora's insights about theological humility in relation to the other characteristics, including pride, are shared by her eremitic contemporary, Amma Sarah. In this case, the saying includes a story of two men who want to provoke Sarah and test her ascetic authority. Cultivating the characteristics of a teacher presented in the previous saying attributed to Theodora, Sarah confronts their binary reasoning in a way that has the potential to expand their thinking about theological humility. "Another time, two old men, great anchorites, came to the district of

Pelusium to visit her [i.e., Sarah]. When they arrived one said to the other, 'Let us humiliate this old woman.' So they said to her, 'Be careful not to become conceited thinking to yourself: "Look how anchorites are coming to see me, a mere woman."' But Amma Sarah said to them, 'According to nature I am a woman, but not according to my thoughts.'"[83] This saying demonstrates how theological humility is learned in the immediate context of familiar cultural constructions and practices of hospitality.[84] Here, a female host invites her male visitors, as guests, into a space of hospitality. Tracy McNulty explains that in Latin and in Greek the terms for hospitality apply to both host and guest so that "the foundation of the institution of hospitality as a social practice is thus the compensatory relation, the reciprocal bond of obligation linking members of an extended society."[85] Hospitality, in this sense, constructs a social network built on a core set of values. As Thomas Reynolds observes in his study of hospitality, "Especially in a nomadic context all would experience being a stranger in one circumstance or another. This ethic of exchange indicates that human beings share a base-line vulnerability that is worthy of protection; it fosters a dependence on the generosity of others."[86] Vulnerability and generosity—in guest and in host—were practical goods. Jibrail S. Jabbur explains, "The traveling stranger was not able to carry enough to sustain him on his wanderings, hence it became necessary for him to stop as the guest of others."[87]

In the *Sayings*, the vulnerability and generosity embedded in acts of hospitality bear added signification. As a desert Christian practice, hospitality is a means of welcoming the stranger as Christ.[88] McNulty explains that, in a Christian context, "the stranger or guest as 'pretext' is an anticipation or prefiguration of another text or logos, the Word that

[83] Amma Sarah, *Sayings* 4, in Ward, *The Sayings of the Desert Fathers*, 230.

[84] See Irina Aristarkhova, "Hospitality and the Maternal," *Hypatia* 27, no. 1 (Winter 2012): 163–81.

[85] Tracy McNulty, *The Hostess: Hospitality, Femininity, and the Expropriation of Identity* (Minneapolis: University of Minnesota Press, 2007), x.

[86] Thomas E. Reynolds, "Toward a Wider Hospitality: Rethinking Love of Neighbour in Religions of the Book," *Irish Theological Quarterly* 75, no. 2 (2010): 175–87.

[87] Jibrail S. Jabbur, *The Bedouins and the Desert: Aspects of Nomadic Life in the Arab East* (Albany, NY: SUNY Press, 1995), 311.

[88] Kyriaki Karidoyanes FitzGerald, "Hospitality: Keeping a Place for the 'Other,'" *Greek Orthodox Theological Review* 56, nos. 1–4 (2011): 161–77; see discussion on 165.

must both enter into the exchange and be reproduced by it if the hospitality relation is to have any symbolic significance or value."[89] The hospitality exercised in Sarah's saying thereby becomes a spiritual practice. Lines of vulnerability and generosity expose sites for the operation of power. The shifting power dynamics in this saying attest to shifts in vulnerable subjects. The two male anchorites who visit Sarah do so with the intent of imposing a form of dominance on her. Their intent to humiliate her co-opts and inverts the positive expectations affiliated with their roles as guests. Their intent seeks to define Sarah in the framework of a socially determined, traditionally gendered construction of womanhood whereby she is identified and known in subjection to them; this subjection is both culturally and religiously conditioned, as their intent is to diminish her status as both female *and* amma.[90] Sarah's response reverses and subverts their expression of dominance against her; by recasting the categories of womanhood and of power, Sarah's reply dismantles their operating assumptions about religious authority (to which they present no reply) while not diminishing, in any way, her stature of theological humility before them.

In this saying, the wordplay on humility as humiliation heightens the narrative tension as the audience anticipates the amma's response. The challenge of pride is upheld as the site for potential humiliation; the test of Sarah's ability to remain humble rests on her response to the presence and attention of her male visitors. As the saying concludes, Sarah's response to the visitors overturns their operating assumption that humility is strictly understood as the antithesis of pride and indicates a depth of interpretation as she states, "According to nature I am a woman, but not according to my thoughts." Noting the significance of Sarah's statement of gender identification in this saying, Harmless observes that this, and similar statements attributed to ammas in the *Sayings*, indicates "the way asceticism can transfigure gender."[91] Indeed, as Elm contends, "For the perfect ascetic the question of male or female no longer exists, because he or she has risen above the limits determined by the body; asceticism

[89] McNulty, *The Hostess*, 12.

[90] See David Brakke, "The Lady Appears," 390. See also Elizabeth A. Clark, "The Lady Vanishes: Dilemmas of a Feminist Historian after the 'Linguistic Turn,'" *Church History* 67, no. 1 (March 1998): 1–31.

[91] Harmless, *Desert Christians*, 441.

means annihilation of sexual distinction. The desert 'mothers' present the opportunity to introduce yet another nuance into the development of this concept."[92] In these terms, Sarah's statement articulates the capacity for alternative thinking about restrictions imposed by gender boundaries. Sarah's theological humility "strengthens rather than diminishes [her] sense of self-worth" as a *human* being, to borrow a phrase from the Benedictine author Laura Swan.[93] Swan contends that "Sarah knew who she was and did not waver—this is genuine humility. She both challenges the arrogance of presuming one is better than another due to gender, education, position in society, or anything else, and challenges her hearer to pursue spiritual maturity."[94] The saying thereby depicts theological humility as a type of self-knowledge voluntarily obtained and exercised through right understanding and right relations with others.

Vulnerable Humility

How does theological humility as learned and taught by these ascetic women inform the broader construction of Christian humility in this period? The ammas depicted in the *Sayings* are representative; as with female hagiographic subjects, we know that there were more women than are identified who chose to abide as desert ascetics, and that the inclusion of these ammas in the *Sayings* was an intentional decision. Whereas the *Sayings* retain the gendered hierarchy in place throughout the ancient world, they do appear simultaneously to offer a space in which the audience might imagine the capacity for an alternative type of ascetic relationship between fellow Christians. In some sense this space provided a shifting emphasis from male–female relations defined predominantly by societal roles to male–female relations defined by a shared pursuit and acquisition of knowledge. This shift, in turn, may be a recognizable product of a shared condition, as both ammas and abbas claimed a Christocentric origin for their ascetic authority, as evident in a saying attributed to Amma Theodora about the resurrected body. In response to an old man's query, "How shall we rise?," Theodora states, "As pledge,

[92] Elm, *"Virgins of God,"* 267. See also Brakke, "The Lady Appears," 390.

[93] Laura Swan, *The Forgotten Desert Mothers: Sayings, Lives, and Stories of Early Christian Women* (Mahwah, NJ: Paulist Press, 2001), 68.

[94] Ibid., 41.

example, and as prototype we have him who died for us and is risen, Christ our God."[95] When Theodora explains that "we" have Christ "as pledge, example, and as prototype," this shared condition has clearly moved beyond its immediate context to a broader referent. The "we" is inclusive of her male visitor and marks a clear sense of their radical dependence on a divine power. It is Christ's humility as submission, obedience, and discernment that serves as the consummate example and guide.

The acknowledgment of this shared condition allows us to account for these ammas' appeals to the experiences and narratives of male ascetics and visitors in their sayings. As we have seen, Amma Syncletica recalls the "meekness of Moses" as an example for imitation; Amma Theodora and Amma Sarah present stories of male anchorites to illustrate their teachings. Whereas the content of the sayings of these ammas may mark, in the terms of Harmless and Elm, "the way asceticism can transfigure gender," the function, form, and content of their sayings reinforce and reinscribe traditional gender hierarchy. Given the male authors and audiences of the sayings, this is not surprising. However, there need not have been female spokespersons for this content (and yet there were) in the figures of Theodora, Sarah, and Syncletica. Thus, the sayings of these ammas demonstrate the reality and the potential; the sayings needed to appeal to the examples and narratives of males because that is how legitimacy and credibility was defined in this cultural context. References to these ammas, therefore, are not readily dismissed as tokenism but are indicative of a type of ascetic authority not constrained to gender. This is evident, again, in the way in which Syncletica is shown to speak as a stable ascetic authority tied to male predecessors and biblical figures; her words are framed and appear to audiences as a credible interpretation of Scripture and invite application in the ascetic life.

This construction of ascetic authority in the *Sayings* is situated in the particular religious context of the fourth and fifth centuries. It is telling that, as Gillian Clark explains, in this period deaconess "was the highest official status which the Church offered women, since it accepted the cultural assumption that women were not suited to positions of authority."[96] This was a context of contestation and codification over christological formulas. Christopher A. Beeley explains that "disagreements about the

[95] Amma Theodora, *Sayings* 10, in Ward, *The Sayings of the Desert Fathers*, 84.

[96] Gillian Clark, *Women in Late Antiquity*, 54.

identity of Christ—and thus about the Christian faith—including especially those about his unity and duality, are not uniquely fifth-century concerns, as they are often imagined. In formal terms they date to the fourth century, with deep roots in the work of Origen and faint precedents in even earlier theologians—all fueled by the ongoing interpretation of Scripture in the church's liturgical, ascetical, and theological life."[97] The fifth-century councils thus continued the work of defining orthodox doctrine; in particular, these councils sought to address the implications and ongoing controversies from the decisions and creedal formula adopted at what is often characterized as the first ecumenical council, the Council of Nicea, convened in 325 CE. Among the series of statements affirmed at the Council of Chalcedon, convened by Emperor Marcian in 451 CE, was that Christ was "perfect God and perfect man, consubstantial with the Father in his Godhead, and with us in his manhood."[98] The council reinforced prior teaching about the incarnation, stating that Christ was "like us in all things apart from sin" and that Christ was born "for us and for our salvation from Mary the Virgin, the Theotokos, as regards his humanity."[99]

The preservation of the *Sayings* was influenced by the changing contours of this context. Even though the monks may not have been interested in Chalcedon, they were connected to its bishops.[100] Nicholas Marinides's observation that the desert fathers "held to a certain orthodoxy and sought to share that orthodoxy with others"[101] may serve as support for the apparent tensions we have seen in the sayings about theological humility examined in this chapter. Scholars continue to debate details of transmission and the extent to which the sayings circulated orally first and were then written down in a time and place distinct from their origins. Whereas specific questions about transmission remain subjects of scholarly debate, the *Sayings'* narrative setting in fourth-

[97] Christopher A. Beeley, *The Unity of Christ: Continuity and Conflict in Patristic Tradition* (New Haven, CT: Yale University Press, 2012), 277. See also Frances M. Young with Andrew Teal, *From Nicaea to Chalcedon: A Guide to the Literature and Its Background*, 2nd ed. (Grand Rapids, MI: Baker Academic, 2010), 241–44.

[98] Henry Chadwick, *The Early Church* (London: Penguin Books, 1984), 204.

[99] Beeley, *The Unity of Christ*, 281–82.

[100] See the discussion in Harmless, *Desert Christians*.

[101] Nicholas Marinides, "Religious Toleration in the *Apophthegmata Patrum*," *Journal of Early Christian Studies* 20, no. 2 (2012): 237.

century Egyptian desert figures and practices incorporates later fifth-century Palestinian concerns related to an emerging Christian orthodoxy.[102] For this reason, the sayings, like their proverbial predecessors, are a product of attempts to solidify teachings in writing. Codification of proverbs occurred under the circumstances of exile as a means of preserving a collective identity. Joseph Jensen explains that "Proverbs is not a unified composition but rather an anthology of wisdom literature. The collected sayings which form the bulk of it are mainly from monarchic times, though the completed book is postexilic."[103] In this way, proverbs sustained teachings across generations.

In the post-Chalcedonian context of the written preservation of the sayings, Christians grappled with claims about Christ's identity, weighing how Christ was both human and divine and ousting those "Christians" deemed heterodox. As a result, the *Sayings* illustrate, to some extent, the "working out" of an ascetic authority in accordance with the emerging, officially approved depiction of Christ and interpretation of Scripture. Their structure, as a teaching in the mouth of a credible spiritual guide, implies that this interpretation originates in an institutionally recognized source. The value of the *Sayings*, like hagiography, resides in the ability of the figure speaking, and on the content of a saying to be interpreted, in a broader Christocentric context. If the humility of Christ was a site of interpretation, then it is not surprising that there are alternative ways of envisioning theological humility in the *Sayings*.

According to Burton-Christie, "It is Christ's own example of humility—his kenosis or self-emptying (Phil 2)—whose shadow falls most dramatically across the *Sayings*."[104] This example, as indicative in the sayings about theological humility, refused a monolithic interpretation. Clearly, the inclusion of the amma and the identification of her teachings in the *Sayings* present theological humility as situational; the sayings of these ammas emphasize the distinctly relational quality of theological humility.[105] Most clearly, they reflect theological humility as radical

[102] Harmless, *Desert Christians*, 170–71.

[103] Joseph Jensen, *God's Word to Israel* (Wilmington, DE: Michael Glazier, 1988), 236.

[104] Burton-Christie, *The Word in the Desert*, 240.

[105] See Robert Louis Wilken, *The Spirit of Early Christian Thought: Seeking the Face of God* (New Haven, CT: Yale University Press, 2003).

dependence on a divine power that strives for a lack of self-concern. Here theological humility facilitates attainment of the Christian telos for the human person, female and male, and contains a universal aim that is modeled in the amma's example. Theological humility, located centrally in the eremitic life, is interpreted as a widely recognized venue for encounter with Scripture; the eremitic life, with its emphasis on solitary pursuit, is offered as ideal space for learning about theological humility through interaction with the amma, her understanding of Scripture, and her imitation of the example of Christ. Imitation can occur across the entire lifespan, given the distinct focus of theological humility in each of our sources: the hagiography of theological humility recalls Christ's self-abnegation in suffering and death, and the *Sayings* evince a theological humility of incarnation. Like the holy women represented in the hagiography of the period, the ammas of the *Sayings* serve as models of theological humility for their visitors and for the audiences who receive their teachings. Both sources attest to the countercultural dimensions of theological humility, to the ways in which theological humility overturns operating assumptions, norms, and hierarchies about the self and others in order to emphasize theological humility as a Christian value with distinct symbolic and soteriological purchase.

In the evidence for Syncletica, Thais, Theodora, and Sarah, theological humility as radical dependence on a divine power serves as a foundation for Christian discipleship, for following the example of Jesus Christ. In our sources, the rhetorical construction of theological humility is a clear, chosen self-awareness of place before a divine presence that rests on an intellectual reorientation rooted in a reconception of the self that emphasizes a Christocentric focus moving its female subject beyond self-concern. Here, to imitate Christ as the epitome of Christian humility calls for renunciation and reconciliation, for self-discipline and prayer. The pedagogy of theological humility, the process of learning and teaching, creates relational ties to the past through the example of key predecessors, and to the present through service to those seeking instruction.

Learning and teaching require vulnerability, depicted as a willingness to trust in a divine power by suspending self-concern. Although vulnerability is a characteristic of humble predecessors, the vulnerability of Christ serves as the consummate example. Consistently vulnerable by trusting completely, Christ embodies theological humility; imitation of his vulnerability distinguishes theological humility in its Christian context by stressing the full humanity of Christ. In this state, as attested by early Christian writings including the canonical gospels, Christ exemplified "being humbled in the existential sense" by "be[ing] made aware of the limitations of the human condition."[106] Such experience of the human condition bears the vulnerability capable of orienting the self as radically dependent on a divine power.

As we have seen, theological humility, the primary orientation of the Christian who follows the example of the humility of Christ, is necessarily relational; it is cultivated with other Christians and shapes Christian community. Given its foundational status, theological humility informs the types of social humility, intellectual humility, and mutual humility to be explored in subsequent chapters. Here, we'll explore further social humility in the encounter of hospitality and, more specifically, in the exchange between ascetic women and their male visitors in several fourth- and fifth-century sources, including monastic histories.[107] Our sources demonstrate some of the ways in which social humility was a means of upholding the concomitant value of anonymity.

[106] Nancy E. Snow, "Humility," *Journal of Value Inquiry* 29, no. 2 (1995): 208. Here, I apply Snow's qualification.

[107] As Foulcher explains, "Understandings of humility are always embedded in contexts (traditions) and surrounded by practices" (*Reclaiming Humility*, 33).

Chapter Three

Expressions of Social Humility

". . . but emptied Himself, taking the form of a servant, being made in human likeness." (Phil 2:7)[1]

The sources examined in the previous chapter demonstrate some of the ways early Christians imagined a pedagogy of theological humility as a process of learning and teaching about radical dependence on a divine power through imitation of the example of Jesus Christ. This chapter builds on that foundation by turning our focus to the ways in which early Christians sought to imitate the social humility of Christ. Social humility concerns the type of humility expressed in relations between individual persons; it presents in behaviors consisting of words and gestures.[2] Social humility originates in theological humility. Furthermore, it betrays what James Spiegel, writing about humility in a different context, observes: "The humble person places others before herself and maintains a proper estimate of her own moral worth."[3] For early Christians, social humility provided a way to imitate Christ's consistent foregrounding of the needs of the other before the self. In a Christian context, social

[1] For the present purpose, I take this passage to indicate both a theological or doctrinal statement as well as an ethical orientation; see Pardue, *The Mind of Christ*, 56–57. See also the discussion in Klaus Wengst, *Humility: Solidarity of the Humiliated* (Philadelphia: Fortress Press, 1987), 43–53.

[2] On the performance of humility see Nancy E. Snow, "Humility," 203–16.

[3] James S. Spiegel, "The Moral Irony of Humility," *Logos: A Journal of Catholic Thought and Culture* 6, no. 1 (2003): 142.

humility was therefore a disposition dependent on the foundation of theological humility. Through theological humility, the Christian embraces radical dependence on a divine power that necessarily informs an awareness of the created state of others; this awareness elicits recognition of a shared vulnerability capable, when interpreted in imitation of Christ, of embodying a form of servanthood. Social humility is, in the end, an expression of Christian servanthood.

In lived experience, social humility is performed; that is to say, it is accomplished or enacted in specific situational contexts through recognized behaviors. The sources we examine in this chapter present evidence for the performance of social humility in the explicit contexts of ascetic hospitality. Our sources capture those moments when the social humility of a holy woman (amma) shows her willingness to be vulnerable in some way before her male guest. The amma's vulnerability has the potential to strengthen or damage the guest–host relationship, as unmet expectations are possible. However, expectations are not only met but exceeded in our sources. Here, the amma's vulnerability is connected to her desire for anonymity; the amma's anonymity enables her to exercise ascetic hospitality as a way of imitating the servanthood of Christ.[4] For this reason, our sources locate social humility as a positive value for audiences. As servant to others, these holy women represent social humility as a Christocentric bond of spiritual friendship.

In our sources social humility is recalled and constructed through memory. If "interpretation is the hinge between language and lived experience,"[5] then our sources narrate expressions of social humility as distinctly Christian. They confirm Paul Ricoeur's contention that "lived experience is expressed through language then transcribed into a text and interpreted" by others.[6] As guests, our authors begin their recollections with the lived experience of an encounter with a holy woman known for her social humility; as visitors and as seekers, they maintain a willingness for their lived experiences to influence their thinking. Their quests are informed by their own identities and locations; their maleness and

[4] Spiegel, "The Moral Irony of Humility," 139–41. See also Pardue, *The Mind of Christ*, 37–38.

[5] Rene Geanellos, "Exploring Ricoeur's Hermeneutic Theory of Interpretation as a Method of Analysing Research Texts," *Nursing Inquiry* 7, no. 2 (2000): 113.

[6] Ibid.

status as relatives, neighbors, travelers, fellow monks and, in some cases, bishops, facilitates their ability to write about their experiences. As authors, these men are simultaneously disciples of their female subjects: personally influenced by their hosts, they construct memory in the contexts of Scripture and the Christian life. They strive to reify and publicize a type of Christian holiness rooted in ascetic practice and discipline; they provide testimonials shaped by their own professed claims of experiencing personal insight and transformation.

In the first part of the chapter we consider expressions of social humility performed in speech acts; in each source a speech act provides an opportunity for the listener to adopt a humble way of being. We see this specifically in two exchanges, that between Pachomius and Mary in the hagiographic *Life of Pachomius*, and that between Eucharistus, Mary, and their monastic visitors in the *Sayings of the Desert Fathers.* We'll then turn to three situations in monastic histories in which social humility is performed visually; in each source, observing the behavior of the holy woman supplies a model for the viewer's own consideration of the effects of social humility. We examine the feigned madness of the unnamed nun as recounted in Palladius's fifth-century work, *The Lausiac History*, the weeping posture of Domnina in Theodoret of Cyrrhus's fifth-century collection *A History of the Monks of Syria*, and the prayer of Shirin in Sahdona's seventh-century volume, *The Book of Perfection.*[7]

Together, our sources provide an opportunity to explore efforts to define qualitatively Christian features of social humility. By highlighting the role of vulnerability implicit in the encounter of ascetic hospitality

[7] This chapter is informed by the scholarly work of many others who have contributed to an understanding of asceticism and the family. See Brock and Ashbrook, *Holy Women of the Syrian Orient*; Susan Ashbrook Harvey, "Sacred Bonding: Mothers and Daughters in Early Syriac Hagiography," *Journal of Early Christian Studies* 4, no. 1 (1996): 27–56; McNamara, *The Ordeal of Community*; Rebecca Krawiec, "'From the Womb of the Church': Monastic Families," *Journal of Early Christian Studies* 11, no. 3 (2003): 283–307; Georgia Frank, "Macrina's Scar: Homeric Allusion and Heroic Identity in Gregory of Nyssa's Life of Macrina," *Journal of Early Christian Studies* 8, no. 4 (2000): 511–30; Andrew S. Jacobs, "'Let Him Guard Pietas': Early Christian Exegesis and the Ascetic Family," *Journal of Early Christian Studies* 11, no. 3 (2003): 265–81; Alice-Mary Talbot, "The Byzantine Family and the Monastery," *Dumbarton Oaks Papers* 44 (1990): 119–29; Derek Krueger, "Writing and the Liturgy of Memory in Gregory of Nyssa's Life of Macrina," *Journal of Early Christian Studies* 8, no. 4 (2000): 483–510.

exercised by these holy women, we see a consistent desire for anonymity. This desire for anonymity draws our attention to what Spiegel refers to as "the moral irony of humility," namely, the fact that whereas "the humble person . . . increases in actual moral worth and is therefore deserving of greater moral credit" because of her humility, "she manages to avoid the natural tendency to dwell on her own accomplishments, be they moral or otherwise."[8] The desired anonymity of the holy women in our sources signals for author and audience a way of imitating the servanthood of Christ that is ever cognizant of the human condition and its radical dependence on a divine power.

The Humility of Hearing

Mary and Pachomius

Hagiography supplies considerable evidence for ascetic hospitality between biological siblings in late antiquity. Jane Schulenburg observes that "the Lives of saints are a unique source in the portrayal of familial relationships and sentiments—and particularly the cultural valuation of sibling bonds across the centuries. They provide us with examples of sisters sharing in, or publicly reflected in, their brothers' political or religious prestige. In eulogizing their brothers, for example, the vitae shed light on the glory or *fama sanctitatis* of the sisters."[9] This is certainly the case in the *Life of Pachomius*, which upholds the role of Mary, and of the biological monastic sibling relationship, in the monastic leader's teachings about social humility. The vita's depiction of the emotional vulnerability between Pachomius and Mary serves, as Fiona Griffiths observes in other hagiographies of male monastic leaders, to "celebrate men's attention to the spiritual lives of their sisters, implicitly condoning, or even advancing, the legitimacy of the sibling bond."[10] The depiction of emotional vulnerability marks a notable place for Mary. Mary's presence demonstrates a significant impact on Pachomius's monastic growth and development. Rather than serving as anecdote to further heighten

[8] Spiegel, "The Moral Irony of Humility," 142.

[9] Jane Tibbetts Schulenburg, *Forgetful of Their Sex: Female Sanctity and Society, ca. 500–1100* (Chicago: University of Chicago Press, 1998), 272.

[10] Fiona J. Griffiths, "Siblings and the Sexes within the Medieval Religious Life," *Church History* 77, no. 1 (March 2008): 31.

the memorialization of Pachomius, attention to Mary serves a dual purpose: to attest to the virtuous life of a Christian woman ascetic who would not be recalled in her own vita, and to uphold her social humility as example for others.

The *Life of Pachomius* is a testament to Egyptian monastic expansion and stability in the fourth century. Recognizing the organizational prowess of its subject, the hagiography incorporates information about foundations for women.[11] As Peter Brown explains, "The great Pachomian monasteries at Tabennisi, Phbow, and their dependencies rapidly emerged as alternative villages in miniature."[12] The monastery for women, one of several in the Pachomian federation, was regulated by later precepts that included teachings about humility. It is telling, then, that the vita suggests that Pachomius instructed Mary in social humility and that she learned to express social humility to such an extent during her ascetic life that she later educates her brother in death.

According to the vita, while Pachomius was settled in his monastery at Tabennesi, he receives word that his sister, Mary, would like to visit him. Rather than meeting with her, Pachomius sends word of his well-being and instructions that she consider following his example by founding a monastery for women. When she agrees to do so, the monks build a monastery nearby that attracts the attention of many women who "practiced *ascesis* eagerly with her, and she was their mother and their worthy elder until her death."[13] Pachomius then establishes a formal relationship between the monasteries and records "the rules of the brothers" for them.[14] In his work on the Pachomian federation, Philip Rousseau attends to the formation and application of these monastic rules. Rather than imposing a strict set of regulations from the start, Pachomius's monastic rules evolved from the demands and rigors of ascetic life. Rousseau explains that Pachomius encouraged Mary "to join him in his experiment

[11] See the extensive discussion of the foundation of the female monastery in Elm, *"Virgins of God,"* 283–310.

[12] Peter Brown, *The Body and Society: Men, Women, and Sexual Renunciation in Early Christianity* (New York: Columbia University Press, 1988), 247.

[13] *Pachomian Koinonia*, vol. 1, *The Life of Pachomius and His Disciples*, trans. Armand Veilleux (Kalamazoo, MI: Cistercian Publications, 1980), SBo 27, p. 50.

[14] Ibid. See Jo Ann McNamara, *Sisters in Arms: Catholic Nuns through Two Millennia* (Cambridge, MA: Harvard University Press, 1996), 70.

so that she might find mercy, self-knowledge, the reflection born of quietness, and (though last of all) an opportunity to live with others called to join her by the Lord. Like mutual support and the fear of God, those would be recurrent emphases in Pachomian doctrine. They reinforce the impression that Pachomius's early disciples attached themselves much more to an attitude of mind, a spirituality, than to a mere system or regime."[15] This "attitude of mind" would leave room for teachings about the role of humility in the ascetic life.

Rousseau has also shown that Pachomius's actions with his sister align with those taken in the foundation of other monasteries that became part of the Pachomian federation.[16] Given that "relatives were closely involved in the process of adhesion to the monastic life,"[17] the hagiographer's presentation suggests that Pachomius avoided the visit with his sister for practical reasons. It is also possible, though, that the hagiographer includes Pachomius's dismissal as an expression of social humility. We know that, as Susanna Elm has shown, by locating a way to incorporate his sister into the monastic life, Pachomius "created an ideal way in which two seemingly contradictory demands of an ascetic's life could be combined: the ascetic, like Pachomius himself, could completely sever all ties with his family without having to relinquish all responsibilities towards it."[18] Integration appears consistent with the result.[19] Pachomius's reply to his sister may also reflect part of a monastic formation process that intentionally sought to minimize his position of authority. It is significant that, when Pachomius is informed of her arrival, he asks his fellow monk to respond on his behalf with the following words:

> I see you have learned that I am alive. Do not be distressed, however, because you have not seen me. But if you wish to share in this holy life so that you may find mercy before God, examine yourself on every point. The brothers will build a place for you to retire to. And doubtless, for your sake the Lord will call others to you, and they will be saved because of you. Man has no other hope in this world but to do good before he departs

[15] Philip Rousseau, *Pachomius: The Making of a Community in Fourth-Century Egypt* (Berkeley: University of California Press, 1999), 73.

[16] Ibid., 69.

[17] Ibid.

[18] Elm, *Virgins of God*, 291.

[19] McNamara, *Sisters in Arms*, 70.

> from the body and is led to the place where he shall be judged and rewarded according to his works.[20]

Two items in Pachomius's instruction direct our attention to social humility. First, Pachomius prioritizes an orientation of theological humility. By emphasizing the role of a divine power as a source of mercy, direction, and judgment, Pachomius situates Mary's request in a broader christological context. When Pachomius then offers her "a place," he issues an invitation to become more permanently disposed in this orientation. The hagiographer's description attends to the placement and words of Pachomius. In his reply, Pachomius positions his words at the center of the encounter between his sister and his fellow monk, thereby indicating that the monastic foundation and her consideration of participation are based not on him or his intentions but, rather, on a decision for life in community with others. Pachomius's absence thereby enforces his advice to his sister in the dissemination of his words and request that she undertake thoughtful reflection on her involvement in monastic life. If Pachomius acts as he does to model and to instruct his sister, then his introduction presents his specific construction of community life, including structural differences from traditional family life; to adopt his counsel is to espouse distinctly monastic ideas about lineage since, like her brother, she would renounce the capacity for bearing children and perpetuating the family line.

There is support for a reading of Pachomius's reply as an expression of social humility in the *Precepts* of Pachomius. The *Precepts* provide guidelines for interaction between the Pachomian monasteries and the monastery of virgins that is eventually built for Pachomius's sister and other women. Regulations governing visits are explicitly defined in the *Precepts*. Visits may be made only to relatives and are overseen by "the elders appointed to the virgins' ministry."[21] Finally, visits are conducted "*with all discipline and fear of God.*"[22] Rousseau has argued for a development of this phrase reflecting the maturing of Pachomius: "From what may have been a naïve generosity and a crude fear of hell, he

[20] *Pachomian Koinonia*, vol. 1 (SBo 27, p. 49).

[21] *Pachomian Koinonia*, vol. 2, *Pachomian Chronicles and Rules*, trans. Armand Veilleux (Kalamazoo, MI: Cistercian Publications, 1981). The quoted passage comes from the *Precepts of Saint Pachomius* (Precept 143, p. 167).

[22] Ibid. Italics added.

progressed to a careful balance between many acknowledged social obligations and a self-effacing but ardent desire for union with God."[23] Given the connection to discipline, the use of the phrase in regulations regarding visitation are best read in this context, as a reference to the monastic principle of being always in the presence of a divine power. If the appeal to discipline is the appeal to self-restraint and behavior, activity and comportment, then the appeal to fear of God is the appeal to the framework for that behavior, which would imply reference to the presence of a divine power in the context of all communications and forms of hospitality between visiting monks and nuns. In this context, then, the appeal to the fear of God is an appeal to theological humility, to an awareness of one's place of radical dependence in a theocentric context; the interactions between visitors should be conducted as expressions of social humilty with theological humility at their core.[24]

If Pachomius's absence from Mary in her initial visit described in the vita serves this purpose, then the remainder of the account of the founding of her monastery and her involvement in the oversight and development of monastic life and practice among the nuns is evidence that she incorporated and followed his example. According to the vita, when Mary received Pachomius's words from his fellow monk, "she wept, and she accepted the advice."[25] Hearing of her reply, Pachomius acknowledges "that her heart inclined to the good and right life"[26] and encourages the community to invest in his promise "to do good"[27] in this world by supporting her monastic intent. Mary's tears are evidence, then, of the veracity of her brother's counsel, an expression of submission, willing obedience, and trust in his assurances for her future.

Pachomius functions as brother and as monastic leader. Clearly, Mary's visit and response recognize Pachomius's institutional authority and his responsibility for the monastic community. Mary's commitment to accept her brother's teachings initiates her into the community and serves as an etiology for the construction and ongoing support of the women's founda-

[23] Rousseau, *Pachomius*, 133.

[24] See Rousseau, *Pachomius*, 130–34.

[25] *Pachomian Koinonia*, vol. 1 (SBo 27, p. 49).

[26] Ibid.

[27] Ibid.

tions in the vita. The inclusion of Mary's visit thereby designates and explains a role for her, as a family member of Pachomius and as a fellow monastic practitioner under the direction of his monastic rule, in the stabilization of Christian monasticism in the region. In the framework of this sibling relationship, the public, social, and structural authority of monastic leadership places a divine power at the center; correspondingly, the teachings about social humility thus interpret the sibling relationship as a Christian relationship focused around a divine presence.

According to Pachomius's vita, Mary's initial response as a gesture of social humility continues to influence her brother and the members of her female monastic community. We see this especially when we read that under the guidance of Pachomius's monastic rules, Mary served those who joined her in the monastery as "their mother and their worthy elder until her death."[28] Mary's oversight of all matters related to the death of members in the community enabled an important expression of social humility. Echoing Pachomius's initial instruction upon her visit that "Man has no other hope in this world but to do good before he departs from the body and is led to the place where he shall be judged and rewarded according to his works," it is telling that Mary would have assumed responsibility for assuring proper burial arrangements at the women's monastery. Pachomius's vita contains a description of this process in basic outline form: the death of a nun is followed by bringing the body to the oratory, where the amma is responsible for covering the corpse with a white cloth and notifying Apa Peter (from the men's monastery), who then comes with a select group of monks to "stand in the entryway"[29] and pray the psalms as the body is being preparared for burial. Then the body "was placed on a bier and carried to the mountain"[30] in an ordered procession led by the amma. According to the *Life of Pachomius*, "When the deceased was buried they prayed for her and returned with great sorrow to their dwelling."[31] As the original amma of the female monastery, Mary would have been the first to implement such teachings and to direct care for the preparation of her sisters.

[28] Ibid., 50.

[29] Ibid.

[30] Ibid.

[31] Ibid., 51.

Christian monastic death rituals mark transition.[32] As Duncan Sayer has argued, the construction of death rituals is "the result of an interpretation dependent on both the identities of the participants . . . and their relationships to the deceased."[33] The relevant and authoritative presence of Mary at death rituals belies the ultimate significance of social humility. Expressions of social humility in the context of death as related in hagiographies emphasize two areas of emotional vulnerability. The first area pertains to bodily decay, and the second area addresses the question of an afterlife.[34] Such a view is contained in Pachomius's message to Mary upon her initial visit. Mary's role in the burial preparations and procedures for the members of her female monastic community betrays explicit concern with treatment of the physical body and with resurrection, a concern attested in Egyptian burial practices among Christians in late antiquity, as Françoise Dunand writes: "But it is probable that in Coptic Egypt, as in other Christian societies, most people thought that it was essential to put dead bodies in good, secure tombs to grant them resurrection. Earth was assimilated to the motherly womb, inside which the dead would be born again."[35] The deliberative attention to the preparation as well as to the placement of the buried body apart from the monastery indicates a shift in Christian burial against its pagan counterpart in which, as Sofia Torallas Tovar has shown, "mummies were often carried and preserved at home, for family worship."[36] In a Christian context, spatial distance, from the monastery to the mountain, marks physical separation; burial on the mountain indicates a recognition of finality in life and a

[32] For a discussion of death as transition see Frederick S. Paxton, *Christianizing Death: The Creation of a Ritual Process in Early Medieval Europe* (Ithaca, NY: Cornell University Press, 1996).

[33] Duncan Sayer, "Death and the Family: Developing Generational Chronologies," *Journal of Social Archaeology* 10, no. 1 (2010): 63.

[34] See Jonathan Wyn Schofar, *Confronting Vulnerability: The Body and the Divine in Rabbinic Ethics* (Chicago: University of Chicago Press, 2010), 23.

[35] Françoise Dunand, "Between Tradition and Innovation: Egyptian Funerary Practices in Late Antiquity," in *Egypt in the Byzantine World 300–700*, ed. Roger Bagnall (Cambridge: Cambridge University Press, 2007), 177.

[36] Sofia Torallas Tovar, "Egyptian Burial Practices in Late Antiquity: The Case of Christian Mummy Labels," in *Cultures in Contact: Transfer of Knowledge in the Mediterranean Context. Selected Papers*, ed. Sofia Torallas Tovar and Juan Pedro Monferrer-Sala (Cordoba: Oriens Academic, 2013), 15.

desire for anonymity in death.[37] Given that Mary is known through the vita of her brother, that her identity is tied to her role as his sister and as a monastic guide alone, and that nothing more is said about her following her death, such anonymity marks, in an ideal way, Mary's social humility.

When Mary visits her brother, Pachomius, his immediate instruction facilitates a relationship that will be built on mutual progress in the ascetic life; Mary's expressions of social humilty, performed in words and gestures, are distinctly contextualized in Pachomius's vita by the imminence of their shared fate in death. The emergent stages of this relationship in life, in death, and in afterlife, foreground constructions of social humility, represented as a shared recognition of mortality with accountability for actions taken or avoided in this life, as a central monastic value. Social humility empowers these siblings to interpret the precept to live as a community of individuals "always in the presence of God" as both ethic and end. Social humility informs a relationship between fellow monastics; it grounds a type of Christian friendship that recognizes the place of women and men in the existing social and monastic orders while simultaneously upholding the value of living jointly as "brothers and sisters in Christ."[38] Given this aim, social humility, rooted in a shared commitment to theological humility, follows the example of Christ's servanthood. By placing the needs and the good of the other before the self, Mary and Pachomius serve each other and their respective communities for the benefit of all.

Mary and Eucharistus

In the Roman Empire, the social roles of women were scripted by their female bodies. Jane Rowlandson explains, "The events of birth, marriage, and death punctuated the lives of women in Greek and Roman Egypt, for biology determined their destiny, even as social customs sanctioned and reinforced women's intimate relations with these most important moments

[37] For discussion of the relationship of kinship and death, see David Petts, "Burial and Gender in Late- and Sub-Roman Britain," in *TRAC 97: Proceedings of the 7th Annual Theoretical Roman Archaeology Conference*, University of Nottingham, April 1997, 112–24 (Oxford: Oxbow Books, 1998).

[38] See Augustine, *Confessions* IV.4, trans. R. S. Pine-Coffin (London: Penguin Books, 1961), 75.

in a family's life from one generation to the next."[39] In the period of late antiquity, marriage and childbearing remained defining features of a woman's identity from an early age. Eve D'Ambra aptly asserts that "for women, marriage was a vocation, for men a duty."[40] It marked a life stage for women because "marriage was the socially significant ritual that denoted the end of childhood and transition to adulthood for women."[41] Childbearing was a societal expectation, as attested by the evidence for periods of imperial legislation that imposed regulations on fertility.[42] Remedies for limited fecundity were common.[43] So were methods of contraception. Evidence for the use of contraception, on the part of women and of men, reflects the intent to redirect the purpose of sexual relations and to limit the number of children in the household.

Some early Christian women undertook even more aggressive and more visible means to restrict the societal expectation of childbearing by introducing a counternarrative of chastity in marriage. As Gillian Clark explains, "For women as for men, renouncing sexual activity implied (except in some cases of postmarital chastity) renouncing the life of a parent and householder, and thereby renouncing a clear social identity determined by status and gender."[44] At times, the practice of marital celibacy was adopted when conception was no longer possible. However, marital celibacy was also practiced by younger and potentially fertile couples. Assuming marital celibacy might enable a woman to enter into a type of communion akin to the *virgines subintroductae*, for whom virginity could be a liberatory religious experience.[45] The designation

[39] Jane Rowlandson, *Women and Society in Greek and Roman Egypt* (Cambridge: Cambridge University Press, 1998), 280.

[40] Eve D'Ambra, *Roman Women* (Cambridge: Cambridge University Press, 2007), 47.

[41] Lisa A. Alberici and Mary Harlow, "Age and Innocence: Female Transitions to Adulthood in Late Antiquity," *Hesperia Supplements* 41, *Constructions of Childhood in Ancient Greece and Italy* (2007): 193.

[42] Keith Hopkins, "Contraception in the Roman Empire," *Comparative Studies in Society and History* 8, no. 1 (Oct. 1965): 124–51; see especially 126.

[43] See Rowlandson, *Women and Society in Greek and Roman Egypt*, 287.

[44] Gillian Clark, "Women and Asceticism in Late Antiquity: The Refusal of Status and Gender," in *Asceticism*, ed. Vincent L. Wimbush and Richard Valantasis (Oxford: Oxford University Press, 2002), 39. See also Cloke, *This Female Man of God*, 33–56.

[45] Castelli, "Virginity and Its Meaning," 80–81. See also Burrus, "Word and Flesh," 27–51.

referred to "women who enjoyed a relationship of permanent companionship with a man who was neither father, brother, nor husband to them."[46] For the *virgines subintroductae*, celibacy in cohabitation "offered to men and women a unique opportunity for friendships which involved a high degree of emotional and spiritual intimacy," according to Elizabeth Clark.[47]

Forms of spiritual marriage, and of marital celibacy in particular, are attested in a number of early Christian sources.[48] Among the married couples included in the *Sayings of the Desert Fathers* are the shepherd Eucharistus and his wife, Mary. Their "virginal marriage" attests to a type of ascetic relationship in which a married couple do not consummate their marriage, living chastely, as siblings, mutually recognizing and supporting one another. In their account, Eucharistus emphasizes that he and Mary had lived chastely since their marriage started; he interprets her virginal state in both biological and religious terms.[49] We learn about the couple through the eyes of two monks concerned with spiritual progress. Seeking recognition for their own virtuous status, the monks pray for validation. In response to their prayer, the monks are informed that their virtue does not match that of Eucharistus and Mary, who live nearby. When the monks visit the couple, they find only Mary at home. She responds to their inquiries with a simple declarative statement that her husband is a shepherd who is caring for the sheep. As the monks receive hospitality from Mary, they await Eucharistus's return. When Eucharistus arrives home, he sees the monks and prepares to exercise hospitality by arranging to wash their feet and assisting with their meal. The monks' persistent curiosity prevails as they press Eucharistus for information about his life. Replying "with humility,"[50] Eucharistus provides them with no new information. When the monks then inform Eucharistus that

[46] Brown, *The Body and Society*, 267.

[47] Elizabeth A. Clark, "John Chrysostom and the 'Subintroductae,'" *Church History* 46, no. 2 (June 1977): 171–85.

[48] See the discussion in Dyan Elliott, *Spiritual Marriage: Sexual Abstinence in Medieval Wedlock* (Princeton, NJ: Princeton University Press, 1993), 55–93.

[49] For a positive position on the practice of "virginal marriage," see the example of Paulinus of Nola as discussed in Dyan Elliott, *Spiritual Marriage*, 51–63.

[50] This saying attributed to Eucharistus is included in Ward, *The Sayings of the Desert Fathers*, Eucharistus, *Sayings* 1, p. 60. Variants of this story, like that of the unnamed nun to follow, are found in many monastic sources.

they have been sent by God, he "was afraid" and tells them of their way of life. He explains: "We each live alone. At night we wear hair-shirts and our ordinary clothes by day. No one has known of this till now."[51] Instructed in this manner, the monks depart "giving glory to God."[52]

What does it mean for Eucharistus to reply "with humility"? In the context of ancient hospitality depicted in this saying, the phrase qualifies both why and how Eucharistus responds. As host, Eucharistus treats the visiting monks with deference to their needs; this includes not only their physical well-being but their request for information about his life. And so, it is telling that Eucharistus's response to the monks' request is a negative one. His refusal to supply additional information beyond what the monks have already been told by Mary introduces a tension that he, as host, must also resolve. His decision to provide information about his life deepens the physical vulnerability he bears as host and mirrors that previously borne by Mary during his absence from the home. Eucharistus exercises caution by complying with the monks' request only after he is aware of the reason for their travel. Seemingly unsure of the monks' motive, Eucharistus initially refuses to direct attention to himself and to disclose the details of his monastic life. Such a response is a common trope in similar accounts. In her study of spiritual marriage, Dyan Elliott writes, "Secrecy was an essential element in most narratives treating spiritual marriage, and practical considerations reinforce natural discretion."[53] It is only when Eucharistus learns of the reason for their request that he provides additional information; for Eucharistus, the monks' articulation of a divine source guiding their travel indicates a divine purpose for their visit. As a result, when Eucharistus finally offers a more complete statement about his life, he does so as a witness to this source. Aware of his place before this divine power, Eucharistus is thereby attentive to his role in satisfying the purpose for the monks' visit. By responding to the monks "with humility," Eucharistus acknowledges his human and divine guests as a submissive host, placing all of their needs as primary. By asserting that the monks are the sole bearers of this information, Eucharistus discloses a reality unknown and invisible to others. Such disclosure elevates his, and Mary's, desire for anonymity that, in turn, adds to the depth of his humility.

[51] Ibid.

[52] Ibid.

[53] Dyan Elliott, *Spiritual Marriage*, 62.

When Eucharistus explains, "We each live alone," he names a type of commitment that seeks individual union with a divine power. This commitment is evident in their names, Eucharistus and Mary, which signify a Christian focus for their ascetic practices.[54] In the story, their holiness is recognized, affirmed, and contained in their status, juxtaposed with that of their visitors, as they are identified by the divine for the purpose of educating the visitors in the approved manners of social humility. Their marriage is depicted as a Christian partnership that has at its center neither individual but rather the worship of the divine; living as brother and sister in Christ, each supports, encourages, and works with the other for their jointly ordered purpose and goal. As ecclesiastical authorities debated the Christian orthopraxy of such unions, sources such as the *Sayings of the Desert Fathers* suggest that this and similar expressions of spiritual union enabled some Christians to place theological and social humility at the center of the marriage relationship.[55] Living as a monastic unit, the household of Eucharistus and Mary is structured around this focus.

Since the theological and social humility of Mary and Eucharistus originates and persists in the monastic context of their virginal marriage, to respond "with humility" also signals the content of Eucharistus's reply. The monks approach Mary and Eucharistus as a married couple; when the monks learn about the couple's monastic practices, they realize that they are encountering fellow ascetic practitioners. Mary and Eucharistus are, in fact, peers. As fellow monks, the principles espoused by Mary and Eucharistus are familiar to the visitors; like their hosts, the visitors cultivate chastity, simplicity, ascesis, and prayer. Wearing hair shirts when they are removed from sight indicates the quest for a state of theological humility that continues uninterrupted. However, as the story demonstrates, their theological humility informs a social humility that sets them apart from the visitors. Their social humility is pervasive as it overwhelms the visitors' pride. Moreover, their social humility is formative. Renouncing possessions for the betterment of others indicates their radical dependence on a divine power. Their use of material resources for the larger community expands their social humility to the poor and others in need. Finally, once Eucharistus does speak, his words facilitate change; he

[54] The names explicitly mark a Christian orientation and identity.

[55] See the assessment of Dyan Elliott, *Spiritual Marriage*: "Despite official trepidation, spiritual marriage was simply too adaptable to be suppressed and too useful to be ignored" (63).

responds only because he believes that he has been instructed to do so by the divine who guided the visitors to his home. When the visitors receive his words, they give glory, thereby overturning their initial focus on their own status, evident in their divine query, and redirecting their focus in worship.

In the account of Eucharistus and Mary, an expression of social humility supplies a reminder about an operating theological principle, namely the ongoing, unstated presence of a divine power before which they are radically dependent. Like the exchange between Pachomius and Mary, the exchange between Eucharistus, Mary, and their monastic visitors emphasizes how theological humility produces a way of being in relationship with others. Theological humility serves as the foundation for these expressions of social humility; it permeates the operation of social humility as a Christian value.

The Humility of Seeing

Palladius and the Unnamed Nun

A similar pattern wherein social humility tempers false thinking is found in the story of the unnamed nun included in Palladius's early fifth-century *Lausiac History*. Palladius's work supplies numerous accounts about male and female monks. Palladius had experienced monastic life firsthand, leaving his homeland of Galatia to spend several years under the guidance of many different teachers. He traveled extensively to visit monks and monasteries in Egypt and in Palestine during periods of security and exile. Palladius recalled his experiences and exchanges in the *Lausiac History*, a compendium dedicated to Lausus, who served in the imperial court of Emperor Theodosius II. As Maribel Dietz explains, "Palladius wanted Lausus to learn from and imitate the *Lausiac History*, but he also urged him to seek out actual meetings with holy men and women."[56] Palladius's pedagogical intent, as many scholars have noted, informs not only what and, more specifically, who he recalls but also how he records his monastic encounters. Palladius's stories are intended to instruct; to this end, his stories incorporate description and ethical

[56] Maribel Dietz, *Wandering Monks, Virgins, and Pilgrims: Ascetic Travel in the Mediterranean World, A.D. 300–800* (University Park: Pennsylvania State University Press, 2005), 135.

evaluation.[57] In some cases, like the story of the unnamed nun considered here, Palladius provides evidence of his own education in monastic principles including social humility.

The story of the unnamed nun is embedded in another story about the holy hermit, Piteroum.[58] Palladius explains that an angel appeared to Piteroum, challenging the hermit's prideful thoughts and sense of religious accomplishment. The angel instructs Piteroum to go and meet an unnamed, unidentified nun who "is better than you are" in the monastery of the Tabennisiote community.[59] Obedient to the angel, Piteroum is given entry to the monastery and meets all of the nuns but the one told him by the angel. Feigning mental affliction, this unnamed nun had long been classified as a *sale* by the other nuns.[60] Marginalized and mistreated by the other nuns, the unnamed nun knowingly accepted her self-imposed state of intellectual vulnerability and strove to remain faithful to her religious commitment under the conditions set by the members of her community. Palladius explains that, "taking herself to the kitchen she used to perform every menial service and she was, as the saying goes, 'the sponge of the monastery,' really fulfilling the Scriptures, 'If any man among you seems to be wise in this world, let him become a fool that he may be wise.'"[61] Palladius recounts how the unnamed nun literally embodied this precept by performing, in silence and in isolation, those duties least desired among the members of the community. When Piteroum's request to see the unnamed nun is granted and she appears, he is immediately struck by her blessed state of being. His recognition of her holiness prompts him to rebuke the other nuns, saying, "*You* are the ones who are touched! This woman is spiritual mother to both you and me . . . and I pray that I may be deemed as worthy as she on the day of judgment."[62] When the other nuns then confess their faults against her,

[57] See Matthew W. Dickie, "Narrative-patterns in Christian Hagiography," *Greek, Roman, and Byzantine Studies* 40, no. 1 (Spring 1999): 83–98.

[58] For discussion of its contemporary relevance see Mary Forman, *Praying with the Desert Mothers* (Collegeville, MN: Liturgical Press, 2005), 84–89.

[59] Palladius, *Lausiac History* 34, in Miller, *Women in Early Christianity*, 237.

[60] *Sale* refers to a mental deficiency or dysfunction in this context; Miller's translation refers to this condition as "touched" (238).

[61] Palladius, *Lausiac History* 34.1, in Miller, *Women in Early Christianity*, 237.

[62] Palladius, *Lausiac History* 34.6, in Miller, *Women in Early Christianity*, 238. Italics added.

Piteroum prays with them. Palladius's account concludes with the anonymity of the unnamed nun reclaimed: "And after a few days she was unable to bear the praise and honor of the sisters, and all their apologizing was so burdensome to her that she left the monastery. Where she went and where she disappeared to, and how she died, nobody knows."[63]

The story of the unnamed nun offers a definition of social humility founded on the agency of deception. The intentional deception of the unnamed nun attempts to create an identity marked by madness and produces a type of intellectual vulnerability that defines her tenuous relationship with others. It is telling that Palladius does not judge her intent to deceive or the deception itself; neither is interpreted by Palladius as malicious but, rather, as tied to her virtue, since both allow her to experience and express social humility. Whereas her deception marginalizes her in the community—her actions and tasks are assigned by her chosen isolation—her intent to deceive does not. Furthermore, as Palladius suggests, others' treatment of her is based on these terms. For Palladius she becomes an example: he doesn't dismiss her because of her deceit but does applaud what it makes possible. He commemorates how her deception opens a way of seeking and being and "otherness" that creates space for an expression of social humility informed by anonymity; this anonymity is the vehicle through which she exercises servanthood before the members of her community.

The unnamed nun's decision to feign madness controls not only her actions but others' reactions as well and so drives her story. Mental dysfunction, as Cam Grey explains, "elicited a complex mixture of emotions and responses."[64] In late antiquity, the classification of a mental illness dictated its treatment. Medical evaluation and classification of mental illness shifted significantly under the Greek physician Hippocrates and then developed under his successor, Galen. For Hippocrates, according to Petteri Pietikainen, "mental illnesses were now seen as bodily illnesses, and they were described together with other somatic afflictions."[65] Galen

[63] Palladius, *Lausiac History* 34.7, in Miller, *Women in Early Christianity*, 238. See also Burrus, *Saving Shame*, 90, on the relationship of humiliation and humility in this text.

[64] Cam Grey, "Demoniacs, Dissent, and Disempowerment in the Late Roman West: Some Case Studies from the Hagiographical Literature," *Journal of Early Christian Studies* 13, no. 1 (Spring 2005): 42.

[65] Petteri Pietikainen, *Madness: A History* (London: Routledge, 2015), 20.

retained and advanced his predecessor's classification system of mental illness into melancholy and mania; those in the former category, as "thoughtful, considerate and cautious," exhibit less aggressive temperaments than the latter.[66] Although Palladius's description inconclusively classifies the mental illness of the unnamed nun, it does highlight the ways in which mental dysfunction could impact others. R. D. Milns explains that in the ancient world mental dysfunction could impose additional constraints on the family unit, constraints especially challenging for those of lower social status because "the family or close friends were expected to look after any insane member at home."[67] Limited access to resources for those needing care prohibited many from meeting this expectation. As Milns continues, "The carefully prepared sick room and numerous nurses could only be found in the house of a wealthy person."[68] By feigning madness, the unnamed nun thereby marked not only her own status but also the community's responsibility for her care and well-being.

When the unnamed nun makes the initial decision to feign mental afflication, she risks the role of the marginalized outcast among her peers. As she sustains the guise of her affliction, she chooses a monastic life centered on anonymity, thereby subverting what is normative; indeed, the unnamed nun is exalted and identifed as an example for others in the monastery. Never is the reader introduced to a known individual; the lack of name throughout the entire account is heightened by her social identification with a label ("a *sale*") that sets her apart by objectifying her. Furthermore, as "a *sale*" she is capable of only certain functions in the monastery and those happen to be the most demeaning; in turn, these functions limit her engagement with others to the satisfaction of those duties and tasks that meet the standards of her assumed status. Even her monastic practice is organized around the construction of anonymity, as her interactions are confined to and constrained by the most undesireable aspects of human life. However, her status as "the monastery sponge" produces an unexpected effect, as she is also faithful "mother" (identified first by Piteroum and later by the nuns). The individual and communal ignorance of the nuns in the community is further exaggerated by what the angel, Piteroum, and Palladius know, namely, that the holiness of the

[66] Ibid., 21.

[67] R. D. Milns, "Attitudes to Mental Illness in Antiquity," *Australian and New Zealand Journal of Psychiatry* 20 (1986): 460.

[68] Ibid.

unnamed nun surpasses all others in the monastery. Whereas the other nuns think that she is a fool and for that reason she is set apart, the angel, Palladius, and Piteroum know that her wisdom resides in her faithfulness to gospel principles and teaching. Her quest to preserve her anonymity in the community is paramount as it directs her decision at the conclusion of the story: her disappearance seeks to set right the disruption that comes following her "appearance" before Piteroum; this disappearance is a means of marking anew her marginal status. Her disappearance preserves her social humility because it prevents her from having to continue to confront apologies and glorification by Piteroum and the other nuns. Through anonymity she thereby maintains an intense, solitary focus on a divine power. Her solitude is a self-designed component of this goal: by choosing to be set apart socially, by choosing to perform the most demeaning of tasks, by choosing to accept the rebuke and mistreatment of the other nuns, by choosing to be "the fool" in the Scripture passage, by choosing to remain "the other" in leaving the monastery for an undisclosed location, the unnamed nun embodies theological humility through radical dependence on a divine power.

Palladius maintains that the humility of the unnamed nun is defined by her awareness of the central place of the divine in all of her endeavors. Indeed, it is this awareness that Piteroum recognizes when he asserts before the community, "*You* are the ones who are touched! This woman is a spiritual mother." In his claim, Piteroum names the misguided assumptions operative among the members of the community and challenges their inability to see her holiness and their complicity in her deception (by permitting others to identify her and "construct" her in negative terms). Piteroum champions her capacity as "mother" to serve as model and guide for himself and the members of this community; through her social humility, his own pride and the mistreatment of the other nuns are confronted and overturned. Again, as in the cases of Pachomius and Mary and Eucharistus and Mary, theological humility is the background of significance for the expression of social humility.

Palladius's unnamed nun assumed an anonymity that, in turn, enabled the cultivation of social humility that marked her spiritual motherhood. A similar pattern appears in the story of Domnina, an early Syriac Christian spiritual mother. Here, too, we see the spiritual mother adopt a form of otherness; in this case, Domnina's constructed hiddenness as physical vulnerability informs the cultivation of social humility.

Theodoret of Cyrrhus and Domnina

Suzanne Dixon writes that in Roman society "the pattern of the relationship between mother and daughter was probably established early, with the mother overseeing the girl's training in specifically female areas, both practical and moral."[69] These duties were retained in a Christian context, where mothers continued to bear responsibility for the religious formation of their daughters. In some cases, this formation extended over the course of a lifetime. Susan Ashbrook Harvey keenly observes that "mothers and daughters could sustain their relationship in an ascetic context, in a manner affirming both devotion to God and a personal loyalty to one another of considerable emotional weight."[70] Motherhood is a socially recognized form of female authority that marks a stability of place within the confines and structures of family life, and indicates lifelong relations of interdependence between caregiver and offspring. A mother's responsibility necessarily extends beyond biological relations to include relationships of management and oversight with those who contributed to the upkeep of the household and family life; her identity is tied intentionally to constructions of domesticity. Thus, motherhood is intimately relational; it rests on an authority defined by a place of servitude and submissiveness to the needs of offspring and home. These needs included the education of offspring, with particular implications for the instruction of daughters.[71] The mutual impact of mothers and daughters is located in the story of Domnina.

Domnina's life is included in Theodoret of Cyrrhus's *Religious History*.[72] Theodoret had lived as a monk for many years before he was called to episcopal service, from which he was removed and reinstated due to his position in the Nestorian controversy.[73] Theodoret wrote this

[69] Suzanne Dixon, *The Roman Mother* (London: Croom Helm, 1988), 227.

[70] Harvey, "Sacred Bonding," 28.

[71] D'Ambra, *Roman Women*, 88.

[72] The version used here is Theodoret of Cyrrhus, *A History of the Monks of Syria*, trans. R. M. Price (Kalamazoo, MI: Cistercian Publications, 1985). For the story of Domnina see 186–89.

[73] Istvan Pasztori-Kupan, *Theodoret of Cyrus* (London: Routledge, 2006), 18. See also the discussion of Theodoret in David Rohrbacher, *The Historians of Late Antiquity* (London: Routledge, 2002), 126–34. For the impact of Theodoret's position in his work, see the discussions in Chadwick, *The Early Church*, especially 192–212, and in Christopher C. Craun, "Matronly Monks: Theodoret of Cyrrhus' Sexual Imagery in the Historia

collection of brief hagiograhic accounts while in episcopal office, in 440 CE, a period Istvan Pasztori-Kupan refers to in his study of the theologian as the "'cold war' years between Ephesus and Chalcedon."[74] As David Rohrbacher observes, the *Religious History* "reveals Theodoret's deep attraction to and knowledge of the ascetic, individualized monasticism of Syria. He knew many of his subjects as a child or as an adult, and was familiar as well with the oral tradition of the monks of the recent past. The monastic history makes use of vivid narrative and classical style."[75] Like Palladius, Theodoret was influenced in a formative way by encounters with both male and female ascetics, including Domnina, who was known for her social humility. For this reason, as Derek Krueger writes, Theodoret "conceive[d] composing saints' lives as spiritual practice" and bore personal investment in his subject.[76]

Domnina is one of three females afforded an individual entry in Theodoret's work although, as Theresa Urbainczyk has observed, women are present widely throughout the other accounts included.[77] With regard to the role of the feminine in Theodoret's work, Christopher C. Craun writes that "female saints were frequently used as models of holy masculinity, demonstrating an understanding that, although their bodies may be different to men, their souls were capable of the same endeavors."[78] Theodoret's account of Domnina appears in the final part of his work. He explains that Domnina is supported and advanced as an ascetic by her mother, who allows Domnina to establish a cell connected to their garden and house.

Religiosa," in *Holiness and Masculinity in the Middle Ages*, ed. Patricia H. Cullum and Katherine J. Lewis, 44–57 (Cardiff: University of Wales Press, 2005).

[74] Rohrbacher, *The Historians of Late Antiquity*, 130. On Theodoret's varying positions in the controversy, see Nikolai N. Seleznyov, "Nestorius of Constantinople: Condemnation, Suppression, Veneration," *Journal of Eastern Christian Studies* 62 (3–4): 165–90.

[75] Rohrbacher, *The Historians of Late Antiquity*, 130.

[76] For the influence on Theodoret, see Derek Krueger, "Writing as Devotion: Hagiographical Composition and the Cult of the Saints in Theodoret of Cyrrhus and Cyril of Scythopolis," *Church History* 66, no. 4 (1997): 708. See also Derek Krueger, "Typological Figuration in Theodore of Cyrrhus's Religious History and the Art of Postbiblical Narrative," *Journal of Early Christian Studies* 5, no. 3 (1997): 393–419.

[77] See Theresa Urbainczyk, *Theodoret of Cyrrhus: The Bishop and the Holy Man* (Ann Arbor: University of Michigan Press, 2002), especially the discussion on 103–11.

[78] Craun, "Matronly Monks," 44–57. See also Ellen Muehlberger, "Simeon and Other Women in Theodoret's *Religious History*: Gender in the Representation of Late Ancient Christian Asceticism," *Journal of Early Christian Studies* 23.4 (2015): 583–606.

Domnina attends daily prayer services at the local Christian shrine and convinces her mother and brothers to use their wealth to support those activities.[79] Over time, Domnina's rigorous ascetic feats and disciplines have a marked impact on her body. Theodoret is struck particularly by Domnina's constructed hiddenness, which he describes in these terms: "Though exposed to all who wish to see her, both men and women, she neither sees a face nor shows her face to another, but is literally covered up by her cloak and bent down onto her knees, while she speaks extremely softly and indistinctly, always making her remarks with tears."[80] Domnina's posture and unceasing tears are complemented by her hospitality, of which Theodoret gratefully recalls being the recipient. Theodoret closes his account by informing his readers that Domnina's example was followed by many others who sought to adopt a similar way of life.

Domnina's ascetic practice is contextualized by domesticity, as it is situated directly in the home and is explicitly tied to her mother. It is Domnina's mother, rather than a father, brothers, or other men, who provides material support for her efforts. Theodoret indicates that Domnina's mother supplies emotional and spiritual support for her daughter as well. As Peter Brown succinctly observes, "Female asceticism grew out of the Christian household."[81] Mutual maternal care between mother and daughter blurs the lines of motherhood as exercised in, and extended to, this community through relationships that rest on these values. Since maternal care includes the satisfaction not only of physical needs and protection but spiritual ones as well, it is necessarily given and received by Domnina and her mother to the members of the household. By distributing the responsibility for such forms of maternal care throughout the household, all members facilitate and contribute to the physical, emotional, and spiritual well-being of one another. The household thereby functions as a site of servanthood as members cultivate service to one another. When Theodoret describes the relationship between Domnina and her mother in terms of mutual support, he indicates that the bonds that tie these women are not only biological but spiritual as well.

[79] See also Elizabeth A. Clark, "Authority and Humility."

[80] Theodoret of Cyrrhus, *History of the Monks of Syria* 2, p. 187.

[81] Brown, *The Body and Society*, 263. For the relationship between biological and spiritual motherhood, see Krawiec, "From the Womb of the Church"; see also Schulenburg, *Forgetful of Their Sex*, 261–69; Talbot, "The Byzantine Family and the Monastery."

Exercising care and concern for each other, mother and daughter exercise social humility as each seeks to uphold the progress of the other in the ascetic life. As members of a Christian household, they express aspects of motherhood that transcend their respective biological roles; as spiritual mother to each other they espouse a form of social humility theocentrically focused and oriented beyond the self.

For Theodoret, the elevation of Domnina and her ability to guide others as spiritual matriarch provides his reader with an ideal type that is accessible not only to the women in the household but to the men in her biological family as well. Domnina's ability to serve as a model Christian human being is thereby identified and explained; it is her holiness that Theodoret tells in his account of her life, it is the development of her piety that he offers to his readers as a template for emulation. Theodoret's telling presents a reciprocity between Domnina and her family. Domnina's family was able to extend its own piety through her life and practice as family members assisted in the practices of hospitality that were extended to others. The story of Domnina provides an exemplum that could be applied by all of the members of their household. For every member of the household, social humility, as expressed and exercised in the renunciation of social status and the sharing of material goods, elevates the value of servanthood.

Theodoret's particular attention to Domnina's posture and unceasing tears highlights two characteristics of holiness that inform the construction of social humility in his account. Domnina's posture is an intentional form of physical distanciation. Her posture performs vulnerability. Restricting her vision, her mobility, and her speech, Domnina assumes a penitential stance before all those she encounters; in this way, she asserts a position of submission. Her cloak veils her entire body, shielding her from all forms of undesireable human interaction and creating a form of anonymity in order to preserve a single-minded focus. As Susanna Drake explains, "Ancient writers portrayed women as simultaneously vulnerable (in need of protection from the world) and dangerous (the world must be protected from them). The veil functioned, for women, as a mark of separation and feminine virtue, a sign of their vulnerable social status, and a barrier that guarded them from invasion and protected society."[82]

[82] Susanna Drake, "Origen's Veils: The *Askēsis* of Interpretation," *Church History* 83, no. 4 (December 2014): 815–42.

Lisa Alberici and Mary Harlow explain that "the veiling of holy virgins replicates the wedding ritual in many respects. This suggests that marriage—to Christ or to an earthly husband—remained an important visual and social transition to adulthood for girls."[83] The vulnerability symbolized by Domnina's veil is expressed in her unceasing tears.

Like her posture and cloak, Domnina's tears are an outward manifestation of an interior state of being understood in conjunction with her other practices.[84] Domnina's tears assume several forms and serve several functions. Theodoret observes that Domnina's tears cover her face and garment;[85] tears shape her reply when she speaks;[86] tears contextualize the content of her words. Moved to recall his own hand "soaked" with her tears, Theodoret asks, "What discourse could give due praise to a woman who with such wealth of philosophy weeps and wails and sighs like those living in extreme poverty? For it is fervent love for God that begets these tears, firing the mind to divine contemplation, stinging it with pricks and urging it on to migrate from here."[87] In these terms, Theodoret interprets Domnina's tears as an expression of unceasing prayer. They are also by extension an expression of social humility: it is through her tears that Domnina instructs others in humility. While there is no clear indication about whether her tears are sorrowful or joyful, Theodoret does emphasize that they are "begot" by "fervent love for God," thereby reinforcing that they are a response.[88] Kallistos Ware writes, "Spiritual weeping, when manifested in this outward and bodily fashion, has an immediate relevance for the Christian understanding of the human person. Tears . . . emphasize the integral unity of the human person and show how the body is redeemed and sanctified along with the soul."[89]

[83] Alberici and Harlow, "Age and Innocence," 200.

[84] See Urbainczyk, *Theodoret of Cyrrhus*, 110.

[85] Theodoret of Cyrrhus, *History of the Monks of Syria* 1, p. 186.

[86] Theodoret of Cyrrhus, *History of the Monks of Syria* 2, p. 187.

[87] Ibid.

[88] Ibid. Tears often indicated development and growth in the spiritual life; see *The Syriac Fathers on Prayer and the Spiritual Life*, trans. Sebastian Brock (Kalamazoo, MI: Cistercian Publications, 1987), 44.

[89] Kallistos Ware, "'An Obscure Matter': The Mystery of Tears in Orthodox Spirituality," in *Holy Tears: Weeping in the Religious Imagination*, ed. Kimberley Christine Patton and John Stratton Hawley (Princeton, NJ: Princeton University Press, 2005), 242–53.

Combined with posture and covering, Domnina's tears are illustrative of the central place of a divine power around which she has ordered her life. This rendering accords with what Kimberley Christine Patton observes about the "gift of tears," whereby tears "are a human link to the celestial realm rather than a connection to the earthly realm of travail and embodied emotion."[90] In his account, Theodoret's descriptions of Domnina's posture, covering, and tears juxtapose these private, intimate, and personal efforts with their public and relational outcomes. Domnina compels a response from Theodoret and from others, including her mother and family, by imitating Christ's example in order that 'the immortal bodily experience . . . will redeem the mortal one.' "[91] Such self-reflexivity elicits theological humility, which in turn informs Domnina's capacity to serve as a model of servanthood for others. Theodoret fits the emerging pattern: he reinforces theological humility as the essential context from which social humility is defined and cultivated between Christians. This pattern persists in the later eastern Syriac account of the ascetic woman Shirin, as recorded by Sahdona.

Sahdona and Shirin

Like Palladius and Theodoret before him, the East Syriac Christian Sahdona wrote about Shirin, a holy woman who had a formative impact on his own monastic life.[92] As Sahdona recounts in his *Book of Perfection*, he first learned about Shirin as a child; as an adult, he would come to adopt a monastic life, assume episcopal service, accept exile for theologically divergent views, and "spen[d] the rest of his life, probably as a solitary attached to a monastery, in the vicinty of Edessa."[93] Sahdona readily admits Shirin's influence on his religious formation when he contends, "I myself went to visit her many times in order to pluck bless-

[90] Kimberley Christine Patton, "'Howl, Weep and Moan, and Bring It Back to God': Holy Tears in Eastern Christianity," in *Holy Tears: Weeping in the Religious Imagination*, ed. Kimberley Christine Patton and John Stratton Hawley (Princeton, NJ: Princeton University Press, 2005), 260.

[91] Ibid.

[92] See David Bundy, "Martyrios (Sahdona) (seventh century)," in *Encyclopedia of Early Christianity*, ed. Everett Ferguson, Michael P. McHugh, Frederick W. Norris, and David Scholar (New York: Garland, 1990), 732.

[93] Brock, *The Syriac Fathers on Prayer and the Spiritual Life*, 198.

ings from her, and I would gaze upon her in great astonishment at the ease with which she performed the hardest tasks."[94]

Shirin's impact on Sahdona was cause for her inclusion in the *Book of Perfection*, which Brian Colless describes as "his most important work."[95] As Sebastian Brock explains, "Deeply rooted in the Bible, it is remarkable for the sense of fervour which it conveys. The *Book of Perfection* is a work of edification rather than a theoretical exposition, and in the course of it much information about monastic life in the Syriac Church at the time of the Arab invasions can be gleaned."[96] In his account, Sahdona recollects those characteristics and attributes that mark Shirin's ascetic practice; through analogy with several female biblical figures, he demonstrates that Shirin's spiritual vulnerability, her willingness to be consciously attuned to a divine power, empowered her social humility. Sahdona selected Shirin for inclusion as a representative in his own day of a lineage of biblical predecessors. As exemplar, Shirin embodies theological humility; through hospitality, her example is extended to others who attest to her ability to identify weakness and to overcome demonic forces through radical dependence on a divine power.

In the *Book of Perfection*, Sahdona opens his account of Shirin with the expressed desire to make her spiritual beauty known to others for the benefit of recognition and imitation.[97] His encounter with Shirin as an elderly woman becomes an opportunity for him to applaud the longevity, depth, and rigors of her ascetic practice; as a "blessed spiritual mother, worthy of heavenly bliss,"[98] Shirin prayed intensely with, and for, visitors seeking her blessing. Singing the Psalms, reading Scriptures, and disciplining her body, Shirin also exercised hospitality, especially to women. Shirin's status bears attention; as Susan Ashbrook Harvey has shown, Shirin is among a very small group "in Syriac literature of late antique holy women who were prominent in their public works but do not fit the standard picture we would expect of women whose representation had

[94] Brock and Harvey, *Holy Women of the Syrian Orient*, 180, sec. 74. The story of Shirin is found on 177–81.

[95] Brian E. Colless, *The Wisdom of the Pearlers: An Anthology of Syriac Christian Mysticism* (Kalamazoo, MI: Cistercian Publications, 2008), 84.

[96] Brock, *The Syriac Fathers on Prayer and the Spiritual Life*, 198.

[97] Brock and Harvey, *Holy Women of the Syrian Orient*, 178, sec. 64.

[98] Ibid., 179, sec. 71.

been literarily molded to fit normative social roles."[99] Dwelling in the same village, Sahdona characterizes Shirin as a local spiritual guide extending the influence of her spiritual motherhood beyond the confines of their geographical location.

It is not surprising that in his recollection Sahdona draws on an extended body of categories and terms to describe his subject's ascetic discipline.[100] He also refers to several biblical figures with the effect of heightening the servanthood of his subject. In order to qualify Shirin's comportment before a divine power, Sahdona directly appeals to the example of Daniel. Sahdona draws analogies regarding ascetic discipline and food consumption.[101] Like Daniel, Shirin is "fortified by the grace of the Spirit" in submission and prayer before a divine power.[102] According to the biblical book that bears his name, Daniel's reception of dreams and visions was a mark of his theological humility.[103] Shirin's theological humility is demonstrated in her ascetic hospitality toward others.

Whereas Shirin rightly modeled herself on the examples of male practitioners, an expected practice in this context, Sahdona seeks to situate her influence in the context of her gender. Early in his account, he incorporates key analogies between Shirin and two biblical figures, Jael and the Virgin Mary, in order to locate roles for strength and spiritual vulnerability in Shirin's ascetic life. These analogies identify Shirin's embodiment of male and female virtue and so supply a reason for her accessibility to both male and female visitors. Like Jael, Shirin readily embodies similar soldier- and warrior-like qualities in her battles against "the Evil One" with the weapons of her "visible hardships and hidden prayer;"[104] Shirin, like Jael, is capable and triumphant. Furthermore, Sahdona explains that Shirin is made strong through Christ: "For the

[99] Susan Ashbrook Harvey, "2000 NAPS Presidential Address Spoken Words, Voiced Silence: Biblical Women in Syriac Tradition," *Journal of Early Christian Studies* 9, no. 1 (Spring 2001): 130.

[100] Brock and Harvey observe, "Perhaps the most interesting aspect of Martyrios' [i.e., Sahdona's] short description lies in his portrayal of Shirin as a spiritual advisor to monks as well as to laywomen; this is a feature of feminine sanctity one only rarely finds mentioned in the hagiographical literature" (*Holy Women of the Syrian Orient*, 177).

[101] Brock and Harvey, *Holy Women of the Syrian Orient*, 178, sec. 73.

[102] Ibid.

[103] See Daniel 10:12.

[104] Brock and Harvey, *Holy Women of the Syrian Orient*, 178, sec. 69.

Evil One is greatly shamed: having first of all vanquished a woman and managed to sow his error, he is now himself vanquished by women, thanks to Him who was born of a Virgin and who gave strength to women's nature."[105] Overturning sinfulness, Sahdona contends then that the prayer of holy women like Shirin, coming from pure and humble hearts, attests to a divine power.

Furthermore, Sahdona refers to Shirin in specific terms as equivalent to those males included in "the beauty of the virtuous life."[106] As "equivalent," Shirin's status as a "virtuous one" is measured against the standards of those recognized as holy men. By comparing Shirin to male ascetic forefathers whose examples she followed and emulated, and to female biblical figures whose nature she assumed or overcame, Sahdona demonstrates that Shirin embodies virtuous *human* traits: her fortitude, strength, gentleness, and compassion identify her as a warrior fighting against evil through the self-imposed training and discipline of her body and mind. The comparative element in Sahdona's description is her authority. It is in her capacity as a spiritual mother in these terms that Sahdona presents Shirin as an archetype of social humility accessible to all persons. When Sahdona writes that she is treated as "a holy spiritual mother"[107] by those of like authority, namely, "monks and other strangers to the world"[108] as well as "monastic abbots,"[109] he confirms that Shirin has had a strong influence on others, including himself. Sahdona's account elevates those qualities that define Shirin: her serenity and gentleness, compassionate love, simplicity and purity, joy, hospitality. His purpose is to showcase the influence of these qualities on visitors, including himself. In this case, his perspective is personal, as he recalls how Shirin served as the consummate example to his mother, who, in turn, encouraged extension as the consummate example for her son. Sahdona recalls: "And ever since I was a child she would exhort me to choose to live a life that conformed with Shirin's."[110] Here, Sahdona presents biological motherhood and spiritual motherhood alongside one another not to privilege one over the other, but

[105] Ibid., 178, sec. 69.
[106] Ibid., 178, sec. 64.
[107] Ibid., 180, sec. 77.
[108] Ibid., 180, sec. 77.
[109] Ibid., 179, sec. 71.
[110] Ibid., 181, sec. 78.

to indicate complementarity, as it is the religious zeal shared by both mothers that ignites Sahdona's memory. He upholds the influence of both mothers, biological and spiritual, on his religious development. It is the *example* of Shirin that is given pride of place.

Consider, more closely, how Sahdona offers Jael as an explicitly female role model for Shirin. The story of Jael is contextualized by the military actions recounted in Judges 4–5. While Deborah and Barak arrange their attack against Jabin's army, Deborah announces that "the Lord will sell Sisera into the hand of a woman" (Judg 4:9). As the battle unfolds and Barak's army defeats the army of Jabin, Sisera flees. He arrives at the tent of Jael, the wife of one of his Kenite allies. Sisera seeks protection inside the tent, which Jael provides, and he instructs Jael to lie about his whereabouts if she is asked. While he sleeps, she kills him, splitting his head with a mallet and tent peg. When Barak approaches her tent, she shows him the body of Sisera. Attending to the ambiguity in Jael's actions, scholars debate whether she is a heroine or a victim. Sahdona's analogy of Shirin to Jael bears no such ambiguity. For Sahdona, Jael's actions embolden her to defeat the Israelites' enemy. In kind, Shirin's asceticism empowers her to overcome bodily desire. Sahdona writes, "Like Jael, whom God answered, she [Shirin] pulled out desire like a tent-peg from the tent of her body, brandished it, and laid low at her knees the hidden enemy who fights against the saints: by means of visible hardships and hidden prayer she brought down his entire valor, knocking his head into the ground."[111] It is telling, as Brock and Harvey note, that the epithet "whom God answered" connotes Jael's name in the Syriac Bible. This literary device emphasizes that Jael's actions fulfill Deborah's prophecy. In the context of the analogy with Shirin, the epithet then underscores her satisfaction of a divine purpose. Shirin's actions are just because they are in response to and in accordance with a divine power. Moreover, in each case, conquest represents mental and physical prowess from the least-powerful female figure, Jael and Shirin; defeat provides an unanticipated religious reckoning.

Shirin's social humility is identified in terms similar to those found in the stories of the unnamed nun and Domnina, that is, in a single-minded focus that puts a divine power at the center of the Christian life;

[111] Ibid., 178, sec. 69.

from this focus, social humility orients all other decisions and activities. Moreover, social humility is recognized in these terms by others who seek to emulate it. For the spiritual mother, social humility emerges from vulnerability; it is a product of prayer, as Sahdona contends that "humility of heart is extremely advantageous in our lives, above all at the time of prayer. For prayer requires great attention and needs a proper awareness, otherwise it will turn out to be unacceptable and rejected, and *it will be turned back empty* to our bosom."[112] In the *Book of Perfection*, as Brian Colless explains, Sahdona "tells us that prayer should be an interior offering of the heart, after the heart has been purified of passions; it must be an oblation pleasing to God, without blemish, accompanied by attentiveness and tears; in return God will send 'the fire of his Spirit' to consume our sacrifice, and raise our minds to heaven in the flames."[113] Anonymity as a lack of attention to self-concern in service to others informs the context of Shirin's social humility and of her prayer as "interior offering of the heart."

Anonymous Humility

How does the social humility of these holy women inform the broader construction of Christian humility in this period? Our sources attest to the role of anonymity in social humility. This is telling, given that our authors write precisely to draw attention to the influence of these holy women. In each case, the foundation of theological humility creates a context for expressions of social humility as a form of servanthood. The social humility of these women retains a Christocentric focus that enables a capacity for service as a spiritual good. Desiring to retain their anonymity, these holy women express the servanthood of Christ; in their authoritative status as holy women, they assume a position of service.[114] Although

[112] Brock, *The Syriac Fathers on Prayer and the Spiritual Life*, 208; italics in text identify biblical passage referred to as Isa 55:11.

[113] Brian E. Colless, "Syrian Mysticism," in *The Wiley-Blackwell Companion to Christian Mysticism*, ed. Julia A. Lamm (New York: John Wiley and Sons, 2012), 179; see related texts in Brock, *The Syriac Fathers on Prayer and the Spiritual Life*, 208–9. See also Colless, *The Wisdom of the Pearlers*, 83–86.

[114] See Jan van der Watt, "The Meaning of Jesus Washing the Feet of His Disciples (John 13)," *Neotestamentica* 51, no. 1 (2017): 25–39.

their service may appear in the guise of humilitation, as in the case of the unnamed woman, its intent is not self-concern but concern for the other. These holy women clearly exercise agency in the ways that they perform this feature of the humility of Christ. These holy women thereby offer a way of considering what is qualitatively Christian about social humility by identifying an awareness of existential anonymity.

By highlighting a single-minded focus on theological humility, though not to the exclusion of engagement with others, these sources provide models for social humility that are grounded in prayer. James R. Mensch writes that Christian prayer, with Christ as the "paradigm," entails "both self-emptying and receptivity."[115] As fellow Christians, the male authors who remember these women present their performance of Scripture as social humility. Their prayer, interpreted in terms of "self-emptying and receptivity," requires, as we have seen, an orientation of theological humility as a rightful sense of place with a single-minded focus on a divine power, in the motion of "self-emptying and receptivity," at the center of thought and action; this orientation of prayer, in turn, dictates the holy woman's place before others, as each author stressed her capacity for social humility lived in and through right relations with other persons.

Furthermore, as persons seeking to be holy, the male authors who remember these women ascetics interpret their holiness in terms of the Scripture as lived; Mary, Pachomius's sister, and Mary, Eucharistus's wife, are recalled for demonstrating teachings about service, while the unnamed woman, Domnina, and Shirin are remembered for following notable exemplars. Because of this connection to the interpretation and application of Scripture, their stories become interpretations of the power of the Word as lived in the Christian life: Mary's obedience to Pachomius's request initiates a series of events whereby "they will be saved because of you"; Mary's submission to her husband and her guests makes space for the fruition of insight; Piteroum's declaration, "*You* are *sale*," attests to the unnamed woman as the one who "became foolish that she may be wise"; Theodoret's observation that Domnina's tears originate from a "fervent love for God" upholds contemporary teachings about encountering the divine in contemplation; Sahdona's explanation situates Shirin's quiet fortitude and gentle strength in a lineage of female biblical predecessors.

[115] James R. Mensch, "Prayer as Kenosis," in *The Phenomenology of Prayer*, ed. Bruce Ellis Benson and Norman Wirzba (New York: Fordham University Press, 2005), 68.

As disciples, then, the male authors who remember these women ascetics assert that their humble prayer and constructed holiness serve as a model of Christian behavior. Collectively, these women ascetics are upheld because they represent an effective model of ascetic education in their rightful orientations of theological and social humility. For this reason, it is significant that our authors cast the social humility of their subjects in the context of their surrounding communities; such contextualization situates the choices of these women ascetics against those of their fellow Christians, thereby supplying an evaluative perspective for the audience. Our authors define the social humility of these women ascetics in relation to others. From these comparisons each author extends what is learned about theological and social humility in the immediate context of the woman ascetic to his receiving audience. Our authors demonstrate that the instruction of these ascetic women is an education by example; these stories maintain that spiritual motherhood was a powerful context for social humility as birthing, nurturing, and sustaining a Christian ascetic life. In their anonymity and servanthood, these ascetic women exercised oversight and provided instruction. They functioned as significant interpreters of Scripture and as models of humble prayer.

It is in these contexts of Scripture and prayer that we turn next to consider intellectual humility. As we have seen, theological humility and social humility supply a specifically Christian orientation before a divine power and in relation to other persons. This orientation is possible for those who learn to follow the example of the humility of Christ as presented in Scripture. Intellectual humility, defined here as a capacity for learning through the ongoing interpretation of Scripture, is evident in the patterns of ritual performance described in the travels of the late fourth-century pilgrim Egeria. Here, we will see how Egeria's interpretation of Scripture, in the words and gestures of prayer, creates a decentering of the self that reinforces theological humility and social humility. Such decentering consistently creates bonds of solidarity and informs the construction of community between Egeria and her fellow Christians.

Chapter Four

Patterns of Intellectual Humility

"Stand here."[1]

The women ascetics considered in the previous chapters provide examples for theological and social humility centered in a Christocentric interpretation and application of Scripture. The present chapter builds on this foundation to consider intellectual humilty. Specifically, we will examine women ascetics who pray in community with other Christians from the perspective of a female guest, the fourth-century traveler Egeria. Egeria sought to witness to a divine power in her encounters with fellow Christians; because her account interprets these encounters in the context of Scripture, we can examine how her travels demonstrate a type of intellectual humility connected to theological and social humility.

Egeria's example is but one of many from women travelers in late antiquity. According to an early Egyptian desert abba, the instruction with which this chapter opens was issued by a young woman to her servant before leaving from a visit to the Church of the Holy Sepulchre. The young woman had journeyed to Jerusalem from Constantinople for the purpose of discernment. Trying to determine how to inform her family of her desire to live as an ascetic, she sought time in prayer. Her father, an aristocrat, supported her request, supplying her "with horses, servants,

[1] Samaan El-Souriany, *The Hermit Fathers*, trans. Lisa Agaiby and Mary Girgis (Putty, NSW, Australia: St. Shenouda Coptic Orthodox Monastery, 1993), 35; the story of the unnamed female hermit is on 33–36.

maids and 3000 denarii with which to distribute amongst the holy churches and monasteries."[2] In her travels, the young woman met holy persons and prayed at holy sites. Over time she determined that she would not return to her homeland and to the marriage that awaited her. Following her final words to her servant outside the church, the young woman returned to one of the abbas she had met previously and asked for his assistance. The abba complied. Renouncing all of her remaining possessions and seeking repentance, the young woman prepared for anonymity as a hermit. With shaved head and monastic garment, the young woman submitted willingly to go "wherever God leads me," accompanied by the abba's prayers.[3] Divinely guided to a cave, the young woman lived there as a hermit, uninterrupted for nearly ten years, before she met the narrator of her story.

This story reveals Christian participation in an early type of pilgrimage best characterized, in the words of Mary Campbell, as "significant journeying" whereby "the motion of travel becomes the action of quest."[4] Containing formal and informal elements, according to Brouria Bitton-Ashkelony, "the term *xeniteia* (*ξενιτεία*, usually translated into Latin as *peregrinatio* and borrowed into Syriac as *aksaniutha*) implies wandering, leaving one's birthplace, as well as pilgrimage to holy places, holy men, and the shrines of martyrs."[5] In the case of the young woman, access to formal travel from her homeland to what would come to be referred to as the Holy Land indicates status and means; it recalls a sizable network of relations and of human labor that made her journey possible and safe.[6] This network required an uncommon form of collaboration between men and women, as Peter Brown observes, and provided members

[2] Ibid., 34.

[3] Ibid., 35.

[4] Mary B. Campbell, *The Witness and the Other World: Exotic European Travel Writing, 400–1600* (Ithaca, NY: Cornell University Press, 1988), 15.

[5] Brouria Bitton-Ashkelony, *Encountering the Sacred: The Debate on Christian Pilgrimage in Late Antiquity* (Berkeley: University of California Press, 2005), 148.

[6] For late antique travel, see Maribel Dietz, *Wandering Monks*. See also Gregory I. Halfond, "Transportation, Communication, and the Movement of Peoples in the Frankish Kingdom, ca. 500–900 C.E.," *History Compass* 7/6 (2009): 1554–69. See also E. D. Hunt, *Holy Land Pilgrimage in the Later Roman Empire, AD 312–460* (Oxford: Clarendon Press, 1984), including discussion of the way pilgrimage brought together persons from across social and economic classes.

of both sexes with "moments of unstructured meeting [that] carried with them a warm breath of hope for a lost solidarity and for the lowering of social boundaries that haunted the urban Christian communities of the Mediterranean world."[7] For this young woman, and for others, such formal travel provided a novel opportunity for an uncommon type of encounter and experience. Her specific purpose suggests a willingness to embrace travel as a type of wandering. This aligns well with Georgia Frank's assessment that "ancient Christians spoke of voyaging *orationis causa* ('for the sake of prayer'), to pray (*euchesthai, proseuchesthai*), to venerate (*proskunein*) the holy places."[8] John Wilkinson reminds us that this purpose is neither exceptional nor distinctive of pilgrimage in the ancient world, given that "apart from the fact that his particular places and their interpretations were within a Christian framework, he [i.e., the Christian pilgrim] was undertaking a journey for prayer hardly at all different from the pilgrimages of his pagan contemporaries. Pilgrimage as such was neither the invention nor the monopoly of Christianity."[9] As the work of these and other scholars has shown, such a fluid exchange of ideas and practices affected the development of asceticism for women across the empire.

In general terms, before the fourth century, Western asceticism in and around Rome consisted primarily of individuals or loosely ordered groups dedicated to lives of chastity and prayer, but they remained in the city and often in their family homes. By the end of the fourth century, knowledge of Eastern asceticism was gained through commercial exchange and travel. Travelers carried ascetic literature and their own stories of pilgrimage and visits back to their homes and shared these with others.[10] Exchange of ideas and practices continued to move in both directions. Athanasius of Alexandria encouraged the adoption of Eastern ascetic

[7] Peter Brown, *The Cult of the Saints: Its Rise and Function in Latin Christianity* (Chicago: University of Chicago Press, 1981), 43.

[8] Georgia Frank, "Pilgrimage," in *Oxford Handbook of Early Christian Studies*, ed. Susan Ashbrook Harvey and David G. Hunter, 826 (Oxford: Oxford University Press, 2011). Frank appeals to the scholarship of Pierre Maraval.

[9] John Wilkinson, *Jerusalem Pilgrims Before the Crusades* (Warminster, UK: Aris & Phillips, 1977), 33.

[10] See Philip Rousseau, *Ascetics, Authority and the Church in the Age of Jerome and Cassian* (Oxford: Oxford University Press, 1978).

practices while in exile and traveling in Rome and Milan.[11] Rufinus of Aquileia brought the influence of Basil's monasticism from Bethlehem to Italy through his translation of Basil's Long Rules as well as other ascetic writings.[12]

With regard to women in particular, Athanasius's and Rufinus's contemporary Theodoret of Cyrrhus offers numerous instances of pilgrimage travel in his works that, as Bitton-Askelony maintains, demonstrate the range of "foci of pilgrimage" at the time.[13] Theodoret's *Religious History* includes his visits to two female ascetics, Marana and Cyra. Both, like the young woman at the opening of this chapter and the pilgrim Egeria, were women of means. Marana and Cyra reflect another type of Christian pilgrim alongside these other women. Long engaged in the self-discipline and prayer associated with communal ascetic practice, Marana and Cyra visited the city of Jerusalem and the shrine of Thecla in order "to kindle the firebrand of their love for God."[14] Theodoret interprets their ascetic wandering as an affective component of their Christian identity undertaken for the sake of humble prayer, thereby depicting a distinctive relationship between "asceticism and pilgrimage."[15]

By the late fourth century, the time of Egeria, several women are clearly identified for their role in constructing support networks for Christian pilgrims. Many of these women had undertaken the experience of pilgrimage for themselves and chose to remain in the Holy Land. Upper-class aristocratic women such as Paula traveled from the West to Egypt, toured the monastic sites, and founded religious communities to support pilgrims to Jerusalem. Others, including Poemenia, Silvia, and Melania the Elder, accepted a similar path by remaining in the region and adopting an ascetic lifestyle of service to local monks and pilgrims.[16] Although Egeria's travel account ends with her intent to return to her community,

[11] Marilyn Dunn, "Asceticism and monasticism, II: Western," in *The Cambridge History of Christianity*, vol. 2, ed. Augustine Casiday and Frederick Norris, 669–90 (Cambridge: Cambridge University Press, 2015).

[12] Ibid., 674.

[13] Bitton-Ashkelony, *Encountering the Sacred*, 175.

[14] Theodoret of Cyrrhus, *Hsitory of the Monks of Syria* 7, p. 185.

[15] Bitton-Ashkelony, *Encountering the Sacred*, 179.

[16] See Bernadette McNary-Zak, "Problematizing Women and Pilgrimage in Late Antiquity," *Magistra* 8, no. 2 (Winter 2002): 3–24. See also the discussion of Egeria's *Itinerarium* in Cohick and Hughes, *Christian Women in the Patristic World*, 127–55.

it is possible that she joined those nuns whom she encountered on her travels. Regardless, for those who returned to their homelands and for those who chose to remain "exiled," travel to the Holy Land served as an expression of Christian devotion and Christian orthodoxy.

This chapter considers the role of intellectual humility in the travelogue of Egeria, a Christian woman who spent several years far from her homeland tracing events recorded in Scripture, which she refers to primarily as the "books of Moses."[17] These "books"—the five books of the Torah (Genesis, Exodus, Leviticus, Numbers, and Deuteronomy)—contain the foundational narratives of the Israelites as the chosen people of Yahweh. Egeria's biblical references extended beyond these books to include, among others, appeals to 1 and 2 Kings, Joshua, Job, Judges, and 2 Corinthians. The extant portions of her text indicate that the story of the exodus, in particular, provided the text and the guidebook for her journey.

Scholars continue to debate the details of Egeria's identity and itinerary, as well as the precise dates of her travels. Her extant account is partial and largely contains information about her experiences rather than biographical matter. It suggests that her travels occurred over an extended period of several years, with a dating in the late fourth century, circa 381–384 CE.[18] Egeria was likely, as Maribel Dietz has argued, an "ascetic wanderer(s) practicing a form of monasticism based on itineracy."[19] Hadith Sivan writes that Egeria's travel "demonstrates how pilgrimage created a channel that enabled pious believers of different social classes to enjoy a singular freedom of movement while uniting them in a common enterprise."[20] Like the young woman whose story opens this chapter, Egeria undertook her travels as a form of prayer. Despite certain solitary aspects, Egeria's "itineracy" was a public and communal endeavor. From the start, Egeria was connected to a religious community;

[17] See Hadith Sivan, "Who Was Egeria? Piety and Pilgrimage in the Age of Gratian," *Harvard Theological Review* 81, no. 1 (1988): 71.

[18] See the discussion in Anne McGowan and Paul F. Bradshaw, *The Pilgrimage of Egeria: A New Translation of the* Itinerarium Egeriae *with Introduction and Commentary* (Collegeville, MN: Liturgical Press, 2018), 24–27.

[19] Dietz, *Wandering Monks*, 64. See also the discussion of Egeria on 43–68. For a thorough presentation of the debates regarding Egeria's economic and religious status, see McGowan and Bradshaw, *The Pilgrimage of Egeria*, 3–33.

[20] Sivan, "Who was Egeria?," 72.

she recorded her travels as letters for the members of her Christian community who were unable to join her. Sivan argues that the members of this religious community helped plan Egeria's itinerary through prayer and Scripture reading.[21] Furthermore, Egeria accepted assistance and hospitality from a sizable network of persons, and she prayed regularly with fellow Christians. Mary B. Campbell explains, "Traveling along a route sanctified by Scripture, she reads aloud from the Bible and participates in sacramental rites at every site, working continually to elevate her raw sense experience into a form of communion with that sacred world which *in illo tempore* merged for a while with this one."[22] As Averil Cameron writes, "This pattern was repeated as the journey continued, and Egeria's own account is full of her knowledge of the Hebrew Bible and her enthusiasm to fit what she saw into the biblical text."[23]

Egeria's prayer is indicative of theological humility; her experiences of ascetic hospitality are expressions of social humility. Egeria's experiences of receiving hospitality inform our reading of the ways vulnerability and anonymity factored into her pilgrimage. By attending to the decentering orientation of prayer and of ascetic hospitality provided at each of the sites she visits, Egeria illustrates an ongoing willingness to suspend judgment. The decentering perspective she adopts through the repetition of patterns of prayer with others before a divine presence over the course of her travels indicates a type of intellectual humility, a capacity for learning through the ongoing interpretation of Scripture.[24] Intellectual humility features prominently in her verbal exchanges with those who explain how the sites she visits are connected to their scriptural sources; intellectual humility also factors into how she sees these sites as evidence for the persistent presence of a divine power. Egeria's intel-

[21] Hadith Sivan, "Holy Land Pilgrimage and Western Audiences: Some Reflections on Egeria and Her Circle," *Classical Quarterly* 38, no. 2 (1988): 528–35.

[22] Campbell, *The Witness and the Other World*, 32.

[23] Averil Cameron, "Remaking the Past," in *Interpreting Late Antiquity: Essays on the Postclassical World*, ed. G. W. Bowersock, Peter Brown, and Oleg Grabar (Cambridge, MA: Harvard University Press, 2001), 9.

[24] For related discussion see Pardue, *The Mind of Christ*; see also Grant Macaskill, "Christian Scriptures and the Formation of Intellectual Humility," *Journal of Psychology and Theology* 46, no. 4 (2018): 243–52, especially 246–47. Unfortunately, timing prohibited me from making use of Macaskill's larger monograph (2019).

lectual humility enables her to participate in the ritual practices and in the christianization of the spaces she traverses, with members of the communities she encounters.

Egeria encounters a wide range of holy people on her journey; she greets bishops and visits monks, she befriends female Christian leaders and walks with other pilgrims, she speaks with nuns and recalls the witnessing acts of early martyrs. Egeria's purpose for her "holy wandering" and encounters with "holy persons" inform a type of intellectual humility rooted in prayer and in ascetic hospitality that seeks communion with the divine and with others; through prayer and ascetic hospitality, Egeria becomes a member of a larger "wandering," praying Christian community that acknowledges its radical dependence on a divine power. By focusing on the communal dimension of her journey, we can examine how Egeria's prayer and ascetic hospitality, undertaken in solidarity with others espousing a similar orientation, inform intellectual humility. Here, being led and being guided become humble acts that mirror the examples of biblical predecessors whose faithfulness required movement and relocation as well as commitment and resignation. Regardless of whether Egeria presents "an idealized account of an ideal pilgrimage,"[25] Egeria's account reinforces relationships of theological, social, and intellectual humility as the centerpiece of Christian community.

The Humility of Covenant

In a compelling assessment of Egeria's work, Campbell explains that "it is not just Egeria's self-effacement and purely devotional orientation that separate her from the tradition she helped to engender. It is finally her ecstatic *contemptus mundi*."[26] Building on the earlier work of Leo Spitzer, Campbell attends to Egeria's use of repetition, imagery, and restricted formulaic vocabulary to demonstrate that "her literary task is somehow to depress the reader's interest in herself and the course of her journeying, while at the same time maintaining the presence of that inviting and intercessory first person which makes her meditative tool

[25] Leo Spitzer, "The Epic Style of the Pilgrim Aetheria," *Comparative Literature* 1, no. 3 (Summer 1949): 249.

[26] Campbell, *The Witness and the Other World*, 30.

effective."[27] Egeria's expressions of theological humility are evident in those "moments of awe, reverence, wonder, or gratitude" that further orient the reader beyond the author.[28] Egeria repeatedly names both her "unworthiness" for her travels and her certainty that "God wills" her travels; both are markers of a type of theological humility signifying her awareness of a divine power before whom she is submissive.

Spatial and ideological considerations mark the distinctiveness of Christian pilgrimage in this period. Prayer was a signifying marker in Egeria's travels, as she joins others at sites recollecting biblical events pertaining to Israelite predecessors as well as sites commemorating the more contemporary witness of Christian martyrs. Prayer provides the context for theological humility depicted in her work. In particular, she recalls the theological humility of several exemplars, including Abraham and Moses. These role models reinforce the orientation of theological humility as the product of submission and obedience before a divine power. Their recollection joined a panoply of others who were heralded anew in this period; as E. D. Hunt explains, "The range of Holy Land relics was considerably extended with the sudden awakening, towards the end of the fourth century, of the impetus to discover hitherto unsuspected remains: thus revelations unearthed a succession of Old Testament prophets, Habakkuk, Micah, Zechariah."[29] This was due, in part, to a politically and religiously changed context. Emperor Constantine set a precedent for imperial involvement in the affairs of the developing Christian churches that would culminate in the relocation of the empire in Constantinople. Under Constantine's Theodosian successors, Christianity would continue to assert a dominant position in the religious and political viability of the empire. Under Constantine, John Wilkinson writes, "Christians seem to have been encouraged, by the political favour they had enjoyed . . . to make a take-over bid for everything connected with the Old Testament."[30] Co-optation and colonization of these sites for Christian repurposing was more than cosmetic; Egeria's account, like those of other Christian travelers, served an implicit ideological end by

[27] Ibid., 25.

[28] Ibid., 26. I have added "theological" to these expressions of humility identified by Campbell in order to qualify them further.

[29] Hunt, *Holy Land Pilgrimage*, 131.

[30] John Wilkinson, *Egeria's Travels* (London: SPCK, 1971), 296.

recasting events in the Hebrew Bible to foreshadow and foreground Christian narratives around the persistent presence of a divine power through the incarnation, death, and resurrection of Christ. Such alignment with the political program of Constantine following the Council of Nicea would not only "give Christianity the same public and political visibility enjoyed by other cults of the Empire"[31] but also create tensions between Christians and Jews in the Holy Land. It would also produce the context in which Christian travelers, including Egeria, encountered a type of intellectual humility.

In her travels, Egeria journeys to sites notable for their connection to her Hebrew predecessors Abraham and Moses, and signifies both by appeal to covenant, "the main biblical image for the distinctive relationship of the people of Israel with God."[32] In each case, she recalls a site of education in theological humility. Egeria visits the house of Abraham (20.3), a site of turmoil and trust according to the accounts in Genesis. Events at the site would build on Abraham's faithfulness to God's promise and covenant promise of an heir (Gen 15). The covenant is fulfilled through the actions of Sarah, Hagar, and Abraham with the birth of Ishmael and then of Isaac.[33] Yahweh's protection and ongoing commitment to both male offspring (Gen 17, 21) is evidence for the sustained covenant relationship of trust with the line of Abraham.

This extends to the covenant with Moses. Here, it is telling that Egeria ascends Mount Nebo (10:1–2) recalling the ascent of Moses, who was led there by God. This ascent is a culminating event in the context of the biblical account of Moses; his leadership and authority, depicted as chosen by Yahweh, were consistently questioned and resisted by the Israelites. He had served as a mediator between the Israelites and Yahweh by adjudicating the terms of the covenant. Following periods of oppression and liberation, the covenant reinforced the conditions of Israelite service

[31] F. E. Peters, *Jerusalem: The Holy City in the Eyes of Chroniclers, Visitors, Pilgrims, and Prophets from the Days of Abraham to the Beginnings of Modern Times* (Princeton, NJ: Princeton University Press, 1985), 131. Also see Wilkinson, *Jerusalem Pilgrims*, 35–36.

[32] Steven L. McKenzie, *Covenant* (St. Louis, MO: Chalice Press, 2000), 9.

[33] Leonard Shlain observes the anomaly that this covenant is oral rather than written in *The Alphabet Versus the Goddess: The Conflict between Word and Image* (London: Penguin, 1998), 92.

before Yahweh. Lawrence Boadt explains that "the covenant created the unity of the nation Israel, based not on blood relationship but on submission to the divine will and the confession that he alone is God. In turn, God pledges himself to be Israel's personal protector and helper."[34] It is telling that not only the site but the actions are replicated; Egeria is shown—as was Moses—all of the surrounding places from the mountaintop.[35] This serves as a means of "scriptural illustration" as her guides identify sites recorded in the biblical text for her.[36]

As Wilkinson observes, with regard to the Christian use of sites connected with the Hebrew Scriptures, "the Christians relied on late Jewish tradition for the identification of these sites, and were therefore drawn to make use of the same holy places."[37] In some cases, as with the site of Abraham's house, this entailed intentional co-optation to support a supplemental Christian function. When Egeria reaches the site of the monk-martyr Helpidius in Carrae (Haran), she explains that his martyrium is with a church that now sits on the site of Abraham's house.[38] And so Egeria commemorates both Abraham and Helpidius. Identifying the site for her sisters, she recalls the relevant Scripture passage prompting Abraham to wander under divine protection.[39] The passage signals theological humility, as Abraham's radical dependence on a divine power continued to evolve over the course of his lifetime. And yet, the passage also bears distinct signification in the context of Egeria's present endeavor. It is especially noteworthy that Egeria hearkens to this passage as it serves, in a Christian context, as part of the scriptural basis for the ascetic life and, by association, for the ascetic wandering undertaken by Egeria and other early Christian travelers. Here Abraham is recalled as the consummate model for wandering, trusting completely that he would

[34] Lawrence Boadt, *Reading the Old Testament: An Introduction* (Mahwah, NJ: Paulist Press, 1984), 175.

[35] Egeria, *Travel Journal* 12, p. 340 in *Christianity in Late Antiquity, 300–450 CE: A Reader*, ed. Bart D. Ehrman and Andrew S. Jacobs, 333–47 (Oxford: Oxford University Press, 2003); from Égérie: *Journal de voyage (Itinéraire) et Lettre sur la Béatissime Égérie*, ed. Pierre Maraval, trans. Andrew S. Jacobs (Paris: Cerf, 1982).

[36] Wilkinson, *Jerusalem Pilgrims*, 36. See also Cohick and Hughes, *Christian Women in the Patristic World*, 137.

[37] Wilkinson, *Egeria's Travels*, 296. See also Cohick and Hughes, *Christian Women in the Patristic World*, 155.

[38] Egeria, *Travel Journal* 20.3, in Ehrman and Jacobs, *Christianity in Late Antiquity*, 345.

[39] Ibid. 20.1, p. 345.

be guided and directed. This aligns closely with the ascetic practice of those hermits and monks, as Bitton-Ashkelony explains: "Genesis 12:1—'Get you out of your country and from you kindred and from your father's house to the land that I will show you'—became the maxim of the monks who left their homeland for foreign countries in which they initiated their new life as well as that of the monks who undertook pilgrimage to the Holy Land in the Byzantine period."[40] Fraught with symbolic meaning, then, Abraham serves as a model for Egeria's ascetic wandering as well.

Both Abraham and Moses represent theological humility expressed as "a submissive ('humble') attitude toward the sovereign God of Israel."[41] What Egeria takes from her predecessors appears to be a trust that her purpose was divinely intended and therefore that her pilgrimage is an opportunity for her to be guided by divine will. For our purposes, it is significant that theological humility, in these "moments of awe, reverence, wonder, or gratitude,"[42] is contextualized and supplemented not only by Egeria's appeals to Scripture but by her expressed purpose and by her experience of ascetic hospitality; for this reason they represent a type of social humility informed simultaneously by a divine power and by other persons.[43] Theological humility and social humility orient Egeria to the task of interpretation she assumes in her travels. Theological humility creates a foundation from which she expresses and experiences social humility; both, in turn, influence Egeria's cognitive willingness to learn. By building a community of Christians around prayer and ascetic hospitality, Egeria's travels attest to the Christocentric focus of biblical interpretation as a type of intellectual humility.

The Humility of Dislocation

Egeria's wandering is neither aimless nor unintentional. Egeria writes that she undertook travel "for the sake of prayer,"[44] "for the sake of

[40] Bitton-Ashkelony, *Encountering the Sacred*, 148.

[41] John P. Dickson and Brian S. Rosner, "Humility as a Social Virtue in the Hebrew Bible," *Vetus Testamentum* 54, no. 4 (2004): 459–79.

[42] Campbell, *The Witness and the Other World*, 26.

[43] See Campbell, *The Witness and the Other World*. This chapter intends to complement the studies by Campbell, Spitzer, and others by focusing more directly on how Egeria's experience of decentering, a result of the collective expression of communal prayer and ascetic hospitality, correlates with intellectual humility.

[44] Egeria, *Travel Journal* 17.1, in Ehrman and Jacobs, *Christianity in Late Antiquity*, 343.

religion,"[45] or "for the sake of piety."[46] According to Anne McGowan and Paul F. Bradshaw, "Egeria used the expression 'for the sake of prayer' to indicate the purpose of her own journeys as well as those of other pilgrims, especially to the graves of saints. It seems that by this phrase she had in mind not merely private devotion at the shrine but participation in a corporate liturgical rite that included an appropriate reading and psalm as well as prayer or sometimes the celebration of the Eucharist."[47] The "corporate" dimension of Egeria's wandering signals a relationship: "for the sake of prayer" Egeria's ascetic wandering enables participation in a continuous praying Christian community.

If we turn first to elements of self-disclosure in Egeria's travels, we see how she envisions herself foremost as a Christian disciple. Egeria's wandering, as a means of praying, is situated in a distinctly fourth-century Christian worldview. A certain awareness of a divine power appears to accompany her travels. Indeed, her recurring use of some version of the phrase "God willed" reflects her orientation as well as self-understanding of her stature and place as a traveler. The phrase is often used alongside self-assertions that further contextualize purpose. When Egeria describes her ascent of the Mountain of God, for example, she writes, "So it was *as Christ our God willed*, and *assisted by the prayers* of the holy men who accompanied us and with great toil, since it was necessary for me to climb on foot, since no litter could be carried up—but still I never felt the toil itself. Indeed, I felt no toil, but had only *a desire* to fulfill what *I saw as God's commandment.*"[48] In this passage, Egeria signals that her journey is a result of a divine power, that her desire responds to a divine purpose.[49] Hardly isolated, however, such conjoining of divine will and human desire are acknowledged publicly in the prayers of others. Prayer, individual and communal, serves as the foundation for a Christian interpretation of Egeria's wandering. Working in concert with

[45] Ibid. 19.5, p. 343.

[46] Ibid.

[47] McGowan and Bradshaw, *The Pilgrimage of Egeria*, 50. McGowan and Bradshaw observe that this appears in *Itinerarium Egeriae* 13.1–2, 17.1–2, and 23.3, 10.

[48] Egeria, *Travel Journal* 3.2, p. 334. Italics added. The phrase "Christ our God" is repeated throughout Egeria's work and positions her in line with the teachings of the Council of Nicea (325 CE).

[49] This appears as well later in the text, when Egeria arrives in Constantinople (*Travel Journal* 23.8–9), p. 347.

the divine, then, Egeria and her human guides envision themselves being led in accordance to a mandate beyond her own will. That her "desire" is also divinely imputed appears in a later reference where Egeria expresses a similar sentiment following her visit to Jerusalem.[50] Here, again, the coupling of divine promise and divine fulfillment reveals requisite longing and trust by Egeria. Protection and chosenness are reflected later in Egeria's correspondence when she describes "returning in God's name"[51] to Jerusalem. Gratitude and solace are supplied through "continual thanks"[52] given, Egeria maintains consistently, "as was our custom,"[53] thereby affirming a prayerful response.

Egeria's response, as a recognition of her chosenness, is particularly evident following her visit to the Mountain of God. Returning to Pharan, Egeria writes, "Surely, *I should always give thanks to God in all things* . . . and I could never thank enough all those holy men who saw fit to receive me, in my insignificance, in their monasteries with generous hearts and to guide us with certainty through all the places that I requested, always according to the holy Scriptures."[54] That professions of self-effacement such as Egeria's reflect a common rhetorical strategy in early Christian writings affirms rather than diminishes their capacity to disclose a certain type of self-awareness.[55] What Derek Krueger maintains about the writing of hagiography in this period applies to Egeria's writing as well. Arguing against such claims as "empty tropes," Krueger explains that "recent scholarship on early Christian asceticism has been particularly attentive to the function of self-consciousness as a tool through which the ascetic imagined and formed himself anew. Rather than a rhetoric of false modesty, it might be more accurate to speak of a rhetoric of longed-for humility."[56] Perhaps, then, Egeria's statement attests to a developing self-understanding; her travels, begun for "the sake of prayer," instruct her in itinerancy as a form of continuous prayer. As Egeria

[50] Egeria, *Travel Journal* 10.1–2, in Ehrman and Jacobs, *Christianity in Late Antiquity*, 339.

[51] Ibid. 12.11, p. 341.

[52] Ibid. 15.6, p. 342.

[53] Ibid. 16.2, p. 342.

[54] Ibid. 5.12, p. 337. Italics added. See also *Travel Journal* 23.8–9; 17.3; 18.1, 3, 6.

[55] For the use of these strategies, refer to Campbell, *The Witness and the Other World*.

[56] Krueger, *Writing and Holiness*, 98. See also Sivan, "Who was Egeria?"

progresses in her travels, such informal expressions of gratitude accompany formal expressions of prayer.

Over the course of her travels, Egeria meets other Christians at the holy sites. In these instances we see how Egeria envisions herself as a member of a community of prayer and fellowship. Resembling the daily practice of prayer in local Christian communities, Egeria's descriptions of formal prayer include a Scripture reading and the recitation of the psalms.[57] As Jungmann observes, both practices were common and connected among early Christians.[58] Following her time at Livias, Egeria describes the "custom, whenever we wished to make our way to a place we desired to see: first we said a prayer there, then the appropriate reading was read from the codex, a psalm was recited that was relevant to the matter, and once again a prayer was said. We kept to this custom *because God willed it*, whenever we had managed to arrive at a place we wished to see."[59] Egeria's reference to divine purpose may echo her familiarity with the custom in her local Christian community. On the occasion of her visit to St. John's Garden, Egeria suggests that she prayed the psalms with a number of other Christians, including a group of monks who had traveled to the site for commemoration.[60] Joining other ascetic wanderers in a praying community, Egeria's participation binds her to fellow Christians and maintains her orientation of gratitude.

In her travels, Egeria meets a wide range of Christians with whom she prays informally.[61] Collectively, these Christians express the social humility possible in ascetic hospitality. Individually, these Christians supply educational encounters informing Egeria's self-understanding and reinforcing her religious affiliation. This is evident in her explanation for

[57] See McGowan and Bradshaw, *The Pilgrimage of Egeria*, 50.

[58] Joseph A. Jungmann, *Christian Prayer through the Centuries* (Mahwah, NJ: Paulist Press, 2008), 14–22.

[59] Egeria, *Travel Journal* 10.7, in Ehrman and Jacobs, *Christianity in Late Antiquity*, 339. Italics added. The significance of Scripture has been widely recognized; this includes the role of Scripture as read, as heard, as a centering focus, and as defining place. Likewise, the connection between Scripture and ritual and the role of the ritual pattern on Egeria's pilgrimage are widely explored. See the discussion in McGowan and Bradshaw, *The Pilgrimage of Egeria*, 53–55.

[60] Egeria, *Travel Journal* 11.2–3, p. 340; 15.3–4, p. 342.

[61] See Dietz, *Wandering Monks*, 51; McGowan and Bradshaw, *The Pilgrimage of Egeria*, 38 and 47, for attention to Egeria's emphasis on visiting holy persons.

continued travel to Edessa where Egeria learns from a local bishop about the correspondence of King Abgar to Jesus Christ.[62] In terms that echo Emperor Constantine's confrontation with Maxentius's troops at the Battle of the Milvian Bridge decades earlier, the story of King Abgar includes his appeal to the Christian god whose intervention is believed to thwart the Persian attack on the city.[63] After learning about these events, Egeria receives a copy of the letter from the bishop as a gesture of hospitality. It is expected that she will share both the story and, eventually, this copy of the letter with her sisters.[64] The bishop's exchange with Egeria is framed by acts of prayer; it is in this context that the bishop instructs and guides Egeria, and that Egeria listens and responds.[65] A similar pattern frames Egeria's record of a subsequent visit to Carrae (Haran) as the local bishop assumes responsibility for instructing her about the site. Egeria describes the bishop as "truly holy and a man of God, as well as a monk and confessor,"[66] and she emphasizes his generosity in providing her with additional teaching about Scripture and the local monks.[67] In particular, he supplies information about local practices, answers her questions, and clarifies reports of miracles.[68] In this capacity, the bishop functions distinct from the monks who provide Egeria hospitality at various stops along her travels since, according to Brown, a monk bore "no legal status. . . . He was not a *vir venerabilis*, as was the Christian bishop."[69] Hunt contends, "the demands of hospitality were a matter to which the bishop must give his attention."[70] This is indicated by the development of the regions in and around Jerusalem, in particular,

[62] Egeria, *Travel Journal* 17.1, in Ehrman and Jacobs, *Christianity in Late Antiquity*, 343.

[63] Ibid. 19.13, p. 344.

[64] Ibid. 19.19, pp. 344–45.

[65] See Krueger, *Writing and Holiness*, 153–54.

[66] Egeria, *Travel Journal* 20.2, in Ehrman and Jacobs, *Christianity in Late Antiquity*, 345.

[67] Ibid. 20.13, p. 346.

[68] Ibid.

[69] Peter Brown, *Authority and the Sacred: Aspects of the Christianization of the Roman World* (Cambridge: Cambridge University Press, 1995), 51. See also Peter Brown, *Power and Persuasion in Late Antiquity: Towards a Christian Empire* (Madison: University of Wisconsin Press, 1988), 77.

[70] Hunt, *Holy Land Pilgrimage*, 22.

as holy sites under Emperor Constantine. Egeria's remarks suggest how this layer of episcopal status informs her interpretation.

Relations between the local bishop and monks are featured again when Egeria then goes to visit the water well connected to the biblical figure Jacob.[71] In the company of other Christians, she and the bishop repeat the ritual pattern of prayer and thanksgiving; the bishop then brings Egeria to the monasteries so that she can visit with the monks. Here, too, piety and gratitude are prominent as Egeria is struck by the ascetic hospitality and "generous spirit"[72] of the monks. These are noteworthy experiences for Egeria to share with her sisters; as fellow ascetic wanderers, the monks model a type of lay Christian behavior. Egeria indicates her perceptions of the elevated status of their holiness when she writes "that they saw fit . . . to engage in the kind of speech that is fitting to come forth from their mouths."[73] At the site of the monk-martyr Helpidius, Egeria expresses delight that she is able to worship with a particular group of monks, explaining that "they don't come down from their own places, since these are the sort of men who perform many miracles."[74] That the monks invite her to pray with them attests to the public role of their praying community in solidarity with the local, and larger, church. Their prayer frames Egeria's experience of ascetic hospitality; whereas the monks' hospitality betrays long-standing customs and cultural expectations associated with travel in the ancient world, in the context of a Christian worldview their role as hosts bears particular relevance. Hosts for "the other" travelers, the monks initiate their Christian guests into fellowship. Exercising theological and social humility through prayerful presence, these monks assist not only with their guests' material needs but also their interpretations of their travels. What Bitton-Ashkelony observes of monastic sources also applies to Egeria's account. Bitton-Askelony writes, "The monk is represented in these sources as a stranger, one who can never settle but must wander from his birthplace, leaving his family and becoming estranged from all worldly ties."[75] Egeria's

[71] Egeria, *Travel Journal* 21.5, in Ehrman and Jacobs, *Christianity in Late Antiquity*, 346.

[72] Ibid. 21.3, p. 346.

[73] Ibid.

[74] Ibid. 20.6, p. 345.

[75] Bitton-Ashkelony, *Encountering the Sacred*, 148.

encounters with the monks extend and expand her orientation as a fellow "stranger." Her descriptions of prayer and solidarity with the monks suggest that she envisions them as the consummate "strangers" whose identity is connected directly to their function at each location. Indeed, Dietz observes, for Egeria the role of Scripture is central as "the *sancti monachoi* she meets become personal embodiments of the Scriptures. They are the *dramatis personae* who bring Scripture to life in the very places sacred events occurred years before."[76] According to Wilkinson, many pilgrims were attracted to the monks "to learn about the religious life from the acknowledged originators and experts."[77] Regardless of whether the monks are responsible for the hospitality she receives, the information she obtains, or the prayer she offers, their presence is a consistent reminder of ascetic wandering as a Christian way of life.

This interpretation applies, in particular, to Egeria's description of the deaconess Marthana, who was responsible for the oversight of a community of monks and apotactites (virgins) near the shrine of St. Thecla in Seleucia. Egeria attests to Marthana's holiness and explains, "I got to know her in Jerusalem, where she had gone for the sake of prayer."[78] Like Egeria, Marthana undertakes a form of ascetic itinerancy in communion with other praying Christians. Like the local bishops, so, too, does Marthana instruct and guide Egeria in her capacity as a female Christian leader. Here, again, prayer frames Egeria's interpretation at the site of the martyrium and included a reading of the *Acts of Thecla*.[79] Marthana's oversight of the shrine and the community connected to it contributes to Egeria's interpretation of the shrine.[80] As Stephen Davis explains, at the shrine, as in other places Egeria visits, "the duration of Egeria's pilgrimage visit is ritualized; that is, she conceives all of her activity within the parameters of this liturgical structure."[81] Moreover, "her memory of events in the story would have marked her viewing of

[76] Dietz, *Wandering Monks*, 53.

[77] Wilkinson, *Egeria's Travels*, 23.

[78] Egeria, *Travel Journal* 23.3, in Ehrman and Jacobs, *Christianity in Late Antiquity*, 347. See Daniel F. Stramara, "Double Monasticism in the Greek East, Fourth through Eighth Centuries," *Journal of Early Christian Studies* 6, no. 2 (Summer 1998): 269–312, especially 277–78.

[79] Egeria, *Travel Journal* 23.5, p. 347.

[80] See Stramara, "Double Monasticism."

[81] Stephen J. Davis, *The Cult of Saint Thecla*, 68.

the landscape around Seleucia, brought it into specific relation to the final events of Thecla's life."[82] Occurring with, and in, a community of prayer, Egeria's interpretation of the martyrium as a holy site would have been tied directly to recognition of a divine power.

If it is the case that Egeria met Marthana in Jerusalem, then Marthana may have been present at the liturgical celebrations over the Easter period that Egeria participated in; these liturgical customs were formal opportunities for sacramental prayer. Commemorating the period leading up to and including the death and resurrection of Jesus Christ, their narrative context attests to the theological humility and servanthood of Christ. As "the primary liturgical season in Jerusalem was of course Easter week, when the events of the Gospels could be commemorated on the actual spot where they had taken place,"[83] recollection of humble obedience to a divine power was the central feature of this most solemn Christian ritual. This narrative context would have informed Egeria's visits to the various martyria, including the martyrium of St. Thecla. Marthana assured the commemoration of the theological humility of the martyr through the liturgical and ritual contexts of the cult of the martyr and the reading of the *Acts of Thecla*. Marthana's role as ascetic leader bears added import.[84] Daniel Caner explains, "The chapels and shrines that Christians built in commemoration of martyrs exerted a particularly strong attraction upon monks, who often identified with the martyrs' voluntary sufferings and religious ardor. The Christian conviction in the continuing presence of the martyr's spirit with his buried physical remains gave these shrines a numinous power."[85] Opportunities for prayer, for solidarity, and for fellowship contributed to constructing this "continuing presence."[86]

Martyria containing relics associated with a particular marytr, such as the shrine commemorating St. Thecla, function as significant sites for prayer in Egeria's travels. Like sites connected to biblical figures and

[82] Ibid.

[83] Peters, *Jerusalem*, 149.

[84] See Davis, *The Cult of Saint Thecla*, 69. Daniel Caner, *Wandering, Begging Monks: Spiritual Authority and the Promotion of Monasticism in Late Antiquity* (Berkeley: University of California Press, 2002), 57.

[85] Caner, *Wandering, Begging Monks*, 229.

[86] See William S. Sax, Johannes Quack, and Jan Weinhold, *The Problem of Ritual Efficacy* (Oxford: Oxford University Press, 2010).

events, martyria were sites of intellectual interest and religious devotion for early Christian travelers, attesting to the power and dynamism of the divine through those willing and able to bear witness in death. Interest and devotion are evident in Egeria's accounts of her visits to those martyria she included in her travels; her visits mark local customs connected to specific saints as well as common practices tied to the broader development of a cult of the martyrs in the region. Both features are present in Egeria's description of her visit to the martyrium of Helpidius.[87] Egeria explains that she arrived in time for the annual festival held at the martyrium; as Johan Leemans has demonstrated, such festivals were important periods for a local community to commemorate the martyr and to invoke divine assistance. He writes that the festival often "started around midnight with a vigil. This liturgical service could go on until dawn and was celebrated in the martyrium. . . . The service mainly consisted of the signing of psalms and hymns, both alternately and responsorially to a cantor. There was also room for intercessory prayers, silent prayer and Scriptural readings."[88] These actions could facilitate encounter with what Brown refers to as "the humility of human death" accessible symbolically for the visitor at the martyrium site.[89] Christians of all types and of all social strata, ordained and lay, gathered to remember not only the individual but, through their prayer, the ongoing power of the divine available in intercession.

Prayer situates Egeria's later visit to the martyrium of Euphemia in Chalcedon; whereas Egeria offers scant descriptions, she does indicate that she stayed there.[90] As in her visit to the martyrium of Helpidius, then, we gain that Egeria's prayer at the site would have been joined with that of a mass of worshiping Christians. Visits to Euphemia's martyrium

[87] On debate over the identity of Helpidius, see George Gingras, trans., *Egeria: Diary of a Pilgrimage* (New York: Newman Press, 1970), 208.

[88] Johan Leemans, *"Let Us Die That We May Live": Greek Homilies on Christian Martyrs from Asia Minor, Palestine and Syria C.350–C.450 AD* (New York: Routledge, 2003), 15.

[89] Brown, *The Cult of the Saints*, 61. On the important roles of women in maintaining Roman religious cults, see Sarolta A. Takács, *Vestal Virgins, Sibyls, and Matrons: Women in Roman Religion* (Austin: University of Texas Press, 2008).

[90] Egeria, *Travel Journal* 23.7, in Ehrman and Jacobs, *Christianity in Late Antiquity*, 347.

are attested in other earlier and contemporary sources,[91] and Artemius of Amasea's ekphrasis—which, as Elizabeth Castelli observes, "belongs in a tradition where the graphic narration of martyrs' deaths are used for the spiritual elevation of an audience"—indicates sustained interest in the martyr and her cult.[92] Recollection of Euphemia's persecution, torture, and death was conjoined with a narrative of Christian redemption; the praying martyr models Christian witness for praying visitors, and the martyrium, as a constructed Christian site, informs a collective memory imparting a message of ultimate purpose to participants.

To Egeria, the physical site and the human ascetic both represent the visible and tangible presence of a divine power; she traveled the paths once taken by those predecessors of the faith, recorded in Scripture, because she believed that these holy sites and ascetics are living proof of the credibility of the spiritual path provided by Jesus Christ. Through prayer and ascetic hospitality, Egeria recounts experiences of radical dependence on a divine power in solidarity with her fellow Christians; such demonstrations of theological and social humility are thoroughly informed by Scripture. Her knowledge of Scripture is paramount as it presents an active deity, the same deity that Abraham, Moses, and the people of Israel interacted with as they wandered in the desert. Egeria's intellectual humility is shaped by the encounters of these and other predecessors covenanted and dislocated for the purpose of discipleship.

Decentering Humility

How does the intellectual humility of Egeria and her fellow Christians inform the broader construction of Christian humility in this period? The record of Egeria's travels attests to the role of decentering in intellectual humility. Egeria's ability to suspend judgment, her willingness to learn from and with others, and her capacity to see the sites through the texts of Scripture characterize her intellectual humility. By framing the ex-

[91] Peter Gemeinhardt and Johan Leemans, *Christian Martyrdom in Late Antiquity (300–450 AD): History and Discourse, Tradition and Religious Identity* (Berlin: De-Gruyter, 2012), especially 1–5.

[92] Elizabeth A. Castelli, "Asterius of Amasea *Ekphrasis on the Holy Martyr Euphemia*," in *Religions of Late Antiquity in Practice*, ed. Richard Valantasis (Princeton, NJ: Princeton University Press, 2000), 466.

perience of her travels in terms of prayer and ascetic hospitality, Egeria expands her orientation, situating encounter with a divine power—rather than herself—at the center. Her specifically Christian focus on the ways in which Scripture guides, maps, and interprets her experiences orients and informs her intellectual humility.

Intellectual humility plays a prominent role in the Christian worldview represented in Egeria's *Travels.* We see this in the roles of ritual and of reinterpretation. First, at the center of her account is the recollection of her experiences of encounter with a divine power, her prayer, expressed individually and in communion with others with whom she travels and worships. Catherine Bell's emphasis on "acting ritually"[93] reclaims the synthesis of sensory and cognitive elements in the bodily performances nominally categorized as Christian ritual. Drawing on Bell's work, Davis attends to the liturgical context of Egeria's travel as evidence for the "*ritualization* of pilgrimage travel—the process through which it became more routinized, and privileged, as it was organized in special patterns that made it distinct from conventional travel."[94] Egeria's travel account is a testament to the role of ritualization in imprinting memory. It is a form of biblical reception: Egeria's pilgrimage interprets the texts. By extending past events formative to the identity of the Israelites into the present context of her fellow Christians, Egeria's pilgrimage defines a Christian narrative of salvation history. Churches, martyria, and monastic dwellings are located alongside, and in some cases atop, the dwellings of Hebrew forefathers. The Christian present reiterates and extends the Jewish past.

Ritual performance reinforces intellectual, embodied consent to this Christian narrative. In "A Performative Approach to Ritual," Stanley Tambiah defines ritual as "a culturally constructed system of symbolic communication. It is constituted of patterned and ordered sequences of words and actions."[95] Present during Christian rites of passage while in Jerusalem for the Easter liturgy, and participating frequently in rituals of sacrifice, including the Eucharistic celebration, during her travels, Egeria was in a state of regular communication with a divine power through her

[93] Catherine Bell, *Ritual Theory, Ritual Practice* (Oxford: Oxford University Press, 1992), 7.

[94] Davis, *The Cult of Saint Thecla*, 65. Italics in original.

[95] Stanley Tambiah, *A Performative Approach to Ritual* (Oxford: Oxford University Press, 1979), 119.

prayer. Egeria's formalized prayer at the sites orients her toward a divine power; her pilgrimage confirms the omnipresence of this divine power. As Wilkinson observes, Egeria's travel is contextualized by a "Christian framework." In this context, ritual activity is infused by a type of "receptiv[ity] to the Holy Spirit," according to James R. Mensch.[96] Egeria's travels indicate that this receptivity, as a capacity for *imitatio Christi*, was accessible to all persons.[97] If we recall Brown's observation that operating hierarchical social relations between men and women were often blurred in the context of pilgrimage, the evidence of ritual in Egeria's travels attests to a distinct context for an experience—and expression—of collective intellectual humility. The social context of pilgrimage centered on the guest–host relationship shared those earlier features we witnessed in chapter 3, but on a larger scale. The dislocation of pilgrimage produced a vulnerability and anonymity addressed in the experiences of ascetic hospitality as servanthood; in this context, expressions of social humility constructed explicit bonds of Christian charity. The monastic guides who indicate that "it is customary to pray" at the site control the terms of the exchange in order to orient the entire encounter in an awareness or recognition of a divine power. For this reason, ascetic hospitality was capable of providing a mechanism for the ongoing prayer of the pilgrim, of the type so clearly demonstrated in Egeria's travels. Through prayer born of ascetic hospitality, the pilgrimage space provided a form of communal orientation beyond the self and toward solidarity with other Christians before a divine power. Pilgrimage, as participation in a praying community, reinforced operative theological, anthropological, and eschatological principles for the individual Christian.

As well, the monks Egeria encounters serve as models for a type of intellectual humility. Their interpretation of the sites constructs a Christian framework for biblical reception that performs a type of intellectual humility in the sense that it seeks to recast the covenant relationship depicted in the Hebrew Scriptures in light of the Christian narrative of salvation history. They are the storytellers who control the narrative, and in their retelling they frame the decentering experience of their traveling guests. In addition to economic and material exchange, travelers contributed to the role of Christian storytelling; accounts of their encounters,

[96] Mensch, "Prayer as Kenosis," 68.

[97] Ibid.

their travels, and their experiences were shared with others. Oral and written transmission of their travel stories afforded storyteller and audience an opportunity to continually shape, and reshape, the experience of pilgrimage for which recollection affirmed the biblical narrative as a vehicle for relationship and prayer. Adaptation is a familiar element of storytelling, as storytellers bear responsibility for translating a story written for one purpose into a different context for a different audience; their cultural role rests on their malleability, on their capacity to retain their relevance. Sociologist Gary Alan Fine writes, "Collective memory is about the past—a past filtered and shaped through the needs of the present."[98] Stories often reflect this purpose. Stories bear hermeneutic purchase because they supply a narrative framework for collective memory, fraught with challenge and possibility that invites storyteller and audience to imagine themselves as historical beings. Stories provide contexts for negotiating ambiguity, resilience, and vulnerability; they enable play with situations and ideas. If, as Fine contends, "collective memory is linked to history and historians as a form of *solidified* remembrance,"[99] then Egeria's account of her travels displaces the presumed solidity of her biblical source by situating its values into the particular living worldview of her local audience and by inviting her audience to reflect on how these values from the past will serve their needs in the present. Audience memory through the repetition and retelling of her and others' travel accounts would have continued to affirm the satisfaction of these needs.

As a pilgrim, Egeria's exposure to others' intellectual humility informs her own by supplying added signification as evidence of divine revelation. As Catherine Sider Hamilton contends, "Egeria's journey through the biblical story taken as literal history becomes a journey of spiritual transformation, the soul's journey into the presence of God. In the intersection between Scripture and the land, the biblical story comes alive."[100] Egeria's monastic guides, as storytellers, play no small part in this

[98] Gary Alan Fine, "Rumor, Trust and Civil Society: Collective Memory and Cultures of Judgment," *Diogenes* 54, no. 1 (2007): 7.

[99] Ibid. Italics added.

[100] Catherine Sider Hamilton, "Egeria," 182, in *Handbook of Women Biblical Interpreters: A Historical and Biographical Guide*, ed. Marion Ann Taylor and Agnes Choi (Grand Rapids, MI: Baker Books, 2012).

transformation. Wilkinson argues that the stories Jerusalem pilgrims were told offered "scriptural illustration," that is, "the association of peculiarities in the landscape, real or imaginary with words found in the Scripture (usually the psalms) by identifications, fufillments, or confirmations."[101] These features are clearly at play in Egeria's account of her ascent of Mount Nebo and her queries about the site of Moses' tomb.[102] How do the monks know that this is the site of Moses' burial? There is no indication that this question is of concern to Egeria or her guides. Rather, Egeria's inquiry is met with a response that identifies Moses' burial site as fulfillment and confirmation of Scripture; the monks' explanation fulfills, as the grave remains invisible to human sight, and it confirms, as the invisibility of the grave is evidence for his burial by angels as indicated by a literal rendering of the words of Scripture. Egeria and her guides are concerned that the physical site is rendered religiously significant; because the site can be explained as fulfillment and confirmation of Scripture, its identification is credible. As proof text, Scripture thereby serves as the foundational narrative from which Egeria's monastic hosts frame the stories they told pilgrims. The construction of a church on the site of the burial marks the trajectory of the biblical narrative into Egeria's present context; as a new Moses, Jesus Christ's life, death, and resurrection both fulfill and confirm the prophetic longing for a savior attested in Hebrew Scripture.

The narratives of expressing and encountering theological, social, and intellectual humility examined here and in the previous chapters attest to ongoing efforts on the part of Christian ascetics to routinize humility in the context of ascetic hospitality. As we have seen, such efforts to define humility within an established social structure offered authors and audiences space for considering its benefits and challenges. When we turn to monastic rules in the next chapter, we will see an emphasis on the construction of humble individuals in a humble community through a type of mutual humility that imprints theological, social, and intellectual humility. Monastic communities of women are constructed sites for cultivating mutual humility through ritual performance as a community; the legislation of humility in the monastic rules employs theological

[101] Wilkinson, *Jerusalem Pilgrims*, 36. See also the discussion in Davis, *The Cult of Saint Thecla*, 67–69.

[102] Egeria, *Travel Journal* 12, in Ehrman and Jacobs, *Christianity in Late Antiquity*, 340.

humility as the foundation for expressions of social humility between members; these ties are interpreted by appeal to the interpretation of Scripture accessible through the cultivation of intellectual humility. Routinized and clearly defined, the construction of mutual humility in monastic rules thereby emerges as a core principle for the operation of a specifically monastic Christian community. As part of a community of individuals, each member is servant to other members; as an individual communal body, the community is a servant to its nonmonastic fellow Christians through prayer and hospitality. By legislating a type of mutual humility in monastic rules, male authors provided a means by which women ascetics served as an example of Jesus Christ for the larger Christian community of people like Egeria.

Chapter Five

Rules of Mutual Humility

After becoming bishop, Donatus of Besançon responded to a request from a community of women. The women, who were seeking "to excel yet more"[1] in their monastic life, asked the bishop to design a monastic rule that suited the particular circumstances of their place and practice. Donatus complied. In the prefatory letter attached to the monastic rule Donatus gave them, he admits a "brotherly affection"[2] for the community and acknowledges the intellectual labor required in his response. His response required time, he contends, because he was asked to study the more prominent monastic rules in circulation and to weigh carefully the local conditions of the women's practice. In addition to time, Donatus's response also required a certain level of care. Donatus organized his rule for these women knowing personally those who would strive to adhere to its guidelines. This monastic community of women had included his widowed mother, the noblewoman Flavia, and his sister, Siruda. Donatus extols his mother in the prefatory letter, referring to her as "God's handmaid," and directs his work to the abbess, Gauthstruda, and the members of the community.[3] As it stands, Donatus offers to the community a collation of rules. He writes, "I have chosen a few among the many rules to the right road to Christ which are suitable for you and right for this place and physically

[1] *Rule of Donatus*, prologue, in Jo Ann McNamara, *The Ordeal of Community*, 32.

[2] Ibid., 33.

[3] Ibid., 32. See also Alice-Mary Talbot, "An Introduction to Byzantine Monasticism," *Illinois Classical Studies* 12, no. 2 (Fall 1987): 229–41.

bearable and in agreement with the right teachings of the rule, to which you and those who come after you should hold yourselves bound, with the help of Christ."[4]

Donatus's effort demonstrates how a monastic rule (*regulae*) was composed for a particular community in a specific context. The preservation and transmission of the monastic values of what Autumn Dolan refers to as "a communal spirituality" is a hallmark of a rule.[5] This depository function is present in the earliest iterations of a rule as monastic values were codified into guidelines foundational to a monastic life in the late antique period. Marilyn Dunn explains that, "rather than set down minutely detailed regulations, the earliest monastic rules frequently attempted to capture the essence of the spirit inspiring the groups from which they originated."[6] Extant monastic rules from the fourth century indicate attempts to define core visible "monastic" practices of renunciation and *anachoresis*, or physical withdrawal in periods of isolation. Monastic rules attest to the prominence of Scripture as spoken, read, and prayed in monastic life. These earliest rules operated alongside other emergent writings, including hagiography, sayings, and travelogues like those considered in previous chapters, to facilitate the transmission of monastic teachings and tested practices from representative figures to contemporary practitioners. Like these other early monastic sources, rules were composed while doctrinal orthodoxy emerged in conciliar decrees and ecclesiastical regulations.

Mutual humility, "a giving of the self to the other,"[7] as succinctly identified by Jane Foulcher, was a centerpiece of many monastic rules

[4] *Rule of Donatus*, prologue, in McNamara, *The Ordeal of Community*, 33. For discussion of the relationship between this rule and others, see McNamara's useful opening chapter, "The Ordeal of Community: Hagiography and Discipline in Merovingian Communities," 5–30, as well as Marilyn Dunn, *The Emergence of Monasticism: From the Desert Fathers to the Early Middle Ages* (Oxford: Blackwell, 2000). See also Julie Ann Smith, *Ordering Women's Lives: Penitentials and Nunnery Rules in the Early Medieval West* (Aldershot: Ashgate, 2001), especially 111–53.

[5] Autumn Dolan, "A Revival of Female Spirituality: Adaptations of Nuns' Rules during the Hiberno-Frankish Monastic Movement," *Medieval Feminist Forum: A Journal of Gender and Sexuality* 46, no. 1 (2010): 51. Dolan uses the phrase to refer to several rules in this period.

[6] Dunn, "Asceticism and monasticism, II," 678.

[7] Foulcher, *Reclaiming Humility*, 23. Foulcher's work, especially the overview provided in the first chapter, is a foundational source for understanding this distinct context.

for women, including the rule composed by Donatus. Mutual humility is informed by theological, social, and intellectual humility; in the context of a monastic rule, mutual humility intends to create a monastic community radically dependent on a divine power by empowering individuals who are rightly disposed and oriented in relation to one another. This chapter considers mutual humility in the institutionalized context of monastic life and practice for women. Specifically, it examines how mutual humility is presented in the rules of Donatus and two of his predecessors for monastic communities of women. Donatus's explicit use of the Rule of Caesarius, composed by Caesarius of Arles (470–542 CE), was preceded by Caesarius's direct borrowing from the Rule of Augustine, composed by the infamous bishop of Hippo (354–430 CE). Like Donatus, Caesarius and Augustine were well versed in the monastic life, served their Christian communities as bishop, composed monastic rules for women to whom they were related, and communicated their guidance further with the female monastic communities governed by these rules in letters and in sermons while serving in episcopal office. Given this context, an intertextual approach enables us to consider how specific monastic rules employ biblical interpretation in teachings about mutual humility. Because all three men bind mutual humility to a monastic interpretation of Acts 4:32, comparative assessment highlights the distinct needs and shared concerns across these communities of women. Attending to the relationship of text to context, this chapter examines how Augustine, Caesarius, and Donatus interpret Acts 4:32 as a framework for their constructions of mutual humility for their respective and distinct audiences of women. We will consider closely how they interpret Acts 4:32 as a foundational text in their teachings about mutual humility for their female monastic communities.

Interpretations of Acts 4:32 for this end are neither distinct nor infrequent, as Conrad Leyser observes that "the image of the apostolic community, its members materially and spiritually transparent to each other, dominated the ascetic imagination in the fourth and fifth centuries. From the outset, commentators on the monastic movement were keen to propose a direct historical continuity between the Jerusalem Christians and the desert fathers."[8] Such continuity was possible when the biblical book

[8] Conrad Leyser, *Authority and Asceticism from Augustine to Gregory the Great* (Oxford: Clarendon Press, 2000), 10.

of Acts of the Apostles was read as a continuation of teachings issued directly by Jesus in the Gospel of Luke. William Kurz explains that "the prologue of Acts, with its unambiguous references to the previous account, its explicit parallelism with the Gospel prologue, and its reference to the events of the Gospel as all that Jesus *began* to do and teach (implying more activity by Jesus in the narrative to follow), presents itself self-evidently as a transition from the Gospel into Acts."[9] Kurz further contends that intertextual parallels between the gospel and Acts "provide continuity in plotting disparate episodes through God's overarching plan of salvation from the prophets through Jesus to the disciples in Acts. This biblical principle of continuity then flows easily into further canonical actualisation of similar patterns for lives of later canonical readers of Luke and Acts, as in the motif of imitation of Christ."[10] The implications of such continuity are thereby realized in a distinct type of community formation, as the Pentecost commissioning in the opening of Acts centrally positions the life, death, and resurrection of Christ. A series of passages follows that demonstrates how early followers attempt to retain this focus at the core of their distinctively Christian community by highlighting several recurring features. Acts 1:14 emphasizes that Christian community consists of a fellowship of men and women centered in a life of prayer. This emphasis appears again in Acts 2:43-47, where the sharing of goods effects a certain type of fellowship rooted in solidarity and a redistribution of goods to those in need.[11] These are retained and qualified further in Acts 4:32, which reads: "Now the whole group of those who believed were of one heart and soul, and no one claimed private ownership of any possessions, but everything they owned was held in common." As this early Christian community grew in numbers, "signs and wonders" continued to attest to its credibility in Jerusalem and in the surrounding regions (Acts 5:12-16).

Acts 4:32 signals another significant characteristic of this early Christian community according to Matthew Sleeman, who maintains that Acts

[9] William S. Kurz, "The Open-Ended Nature of Luke and Acts as Inviting Canonical Actualization," *Neotestamenica* 31, no. 2 (1997): 290.

[10] Ibid., 297.

[11] Margaret Aymer, "Acts of the Apostles," in *Women's Bible Commentary*, rev. ed, ed. Carol A. Newsom, Sharon H. Ringe, and Jacqueline E. Lapsey (Louisville, KY: Westminster John Knox Press, 2012): 536–46.

4:31 ("When they had prayed, the place in which they were gathered together was shaken; and they were all filled with the Holy Spirit and spoke the word of God with boldness") marks a notable shift as the site of speaking the word of God now includes Jesus' followers.[12] This shift is then concretized in the description of early Christian community in Acts 4:32. Sleeman explains that Acts "4:32-35 fleshes out the Spirit—filling in 4:31. It narrates Jesus' continuing thirdspace influence among 'the whole group' of 4:32, who constitute the repentant gathered from within Israel, yet still within Israel. The emphatic placement of 'one' (μία) at the end of 4:32a re-emphasises their unity. Contextually 4:32 chimes with the spatiality of a Hellenistic friendship topos, but contextually it heralds Christocentric fulfillment of OT spatialities."[13] Such fulfillment held radical overtones in the context of operating norms and social conventions. Early applications of Acts 4:32 that stressed a care for the poor and needy to a universalizing love toward all persons represented "a political religious act that issued a strong challenge to the status quo" in the context of an empire defined by "extreme class differentiation, patriarchy, and slavery," according to Margaret Aymer.[14] Furthermore, those seeking to uphold Acts 4:32 as an ideal were challenged by the simple fact that, in Boniface Ramsey's terms, early Christianity "had to deal with problems and tensions that inevitably arise when a single body of persons with common goals exists on several different social levels."[15] Early Christian responses to the relationship between the rich and the poor and the use of wealth attest to the various ways distribution and need were regularly defined in the context of community.

Such applications were complemented by emergent monastic interpretations that emphasized various aspects of communal sharing and distribution of goods within a monastic community. Eben Scheffler observes the relationship between "radical sharing and traditional worship," a feature that would carry over into constructions of monastic

[12] Matthew Sleeman, *Geography and the Ascension Narrative in Acts* (Cambridge: Cambridge University Press, 2009), 119.

[13] Ibid., 120.

[14] Aymer, "Acts of the Apostles," 537.

[15] Boniface Ramsey, *Beginning to Read the Fathers* (Mahwah, NJ: Paulist Press, 1985), 183.

community.[16] Glenn W. Olsen indicates that with the rise of monasticism, "a very elaborate ideology had grown up in which the first Christians were seen as having been the first monks . . . [as thinkers came] to see in the apostolic life at Jerusalem the abandoning of private property, as now only the monks did; the possession of unanimity of heart and soul, not likely outside the monastic walls; and the practice of celibacy, which logic suggested must have been the accompaniment of the abandonment of property."[17]

If we take seriously the so-called continuity between the Gospel of Luke and Acts, and the commissioning of a Spirit-filled, Christocentric community with the power to speak the word of God in Acts 4:32, then our examination of monastic rules that refer to this biblical passage as the foundation for mutual humility has added purchase: they signify that the mutual humility to be exercised in a monastic community is overseen by Christ. Here, it is Christ who ultimately guides the monastery of women who are called to follow his example of mutual humility, through a type of dispossession informed by theological, social, and intellectual features, in order to become like him.

Theologically Centered

Deborah Wallace Ruddy observes, "Among the Church Fathers, Augustine is noted for insisting most strongly upon humility's centrality for Christian discipleship."[18] Augustine's insistence extends clearly to the role of humility in the monastic life.[19] Monastic life held special appeal for Augustine following the conversion experience, recounted in book 8 of *Confessions*. In this highly stylized account, Augustine artfully records

[16] Eben Scheffler, "Caring for the Needy in the Acts of the Apostles," *Neotestamentica* 50, no. 3 (2016): 136.

[17] Glenn W. Olsen, "One Heart and One Soul (Acts 4:32 and 34) in Dhouda's 'Manual,'" *Church History* 61, no. 1 (March 1992): 33.

[18] Deborah Wallace Ruddy, "Christian Humility and Democratic Citizenship: St. Augustine and Jacques Maritain," in *Reassessing the Liberal State: Reading Maritain's Man and the State*, ed. Timothy Fuller and John Hittinger (Washington, DC: Catholic University of America Press, 2001): 213.

[19] See Bernadette McNary-Zak, "A Call to Asceticism: Receiving the *Life of Antony*," *Coptica* 13 (2014): 51–64. See also the discussions of humility in Augustine's *Confessions* and in the *Life of Antony* in Foulcher, *Reclaiming Humility*, 26–30 and 59–63.

his conversion experience as a series of frame stories. The thread of humility ties two of the conversion narratives that precede the resolution of Augustine's conflicted soul. In the first narrative, Augustine is told the story of a Christian convert, Victorinus. The story is told by Augustine's colleague Simplicianus. Augustine contends that Simplicianus tells him the story of Victorinus "to encourage me to follow Christ's example of humility."[20] Although the story of Victorinus prompts Augustine to reflection, Augustine remains tormented. It is only when Augustine subsequently hears a story about the impact of the example of Abba Antony of Egypt that this state of affairs changes. This later story about monastic converts is told to Augustine by Ponticianus, a fellow Christian.[21] As a young Alexandrian, Antony believed that he was called by a divine power to renounce material possessions, seek the wisdom of monks dwelling on the outskirts of his village, and then move permanently to practice monasticism in the confines of a desert tomb. Over the course of these movements, Antony grows in theological humility as he is led to increasing states of dependence on a divine power. Antony's initial and ongoing dispossession of material goods and attachments remains a hallmark of this construction of theological humility.

In a frame story, doublets render surplus meaning.[22] Like Antony, whose hagiography indicates that he accepted a call to monastic life only after hearing the Scripture preached a second time, so, too, Augustine. As Ponticianus recalls the dramatic impact of the life of Antony on his fellow Christians, Augustine remains silent. Augustine is drawn to the story of Antony and its impact; the power of Antony's monastic life produces a similar effect on Augustine's own calling as, over the course of listening, he realizes that "while he [i.e., Ponticianus] was speaking, O Lord, you were turning me around to look at myself."[23] Listening and reflection are prominent features of Augustine's descriptions of the

[20] Augustine of Hippo, *Confessions* 8.2, p. 159.

[21] Ibid., 8.6, p. 168.

[22] There is a considerable body of scholarship on Augustine's conversion and on the use of frame narratives. See F. B. A. Asiedu, "Following the Example of a Woman: Augustine's Conversion to Christianity in 386," *Vigilae Christianae* 57, no. 3 (August 2003): 276–306; and Michael Stuart Williams, *Authorised Lives in Early Christian Biography: Between Eusebius and Augustine* (Cambridge: Cambridge University Press, 1986).

[23] Augustine of Hippo, *Confessions* 8.7, p. 169.

tormented state of his soul and release from the bonds of "habit" that bound it to material attachment.[24]

Release requires action. According to *Confessions*, the impact of this sequence of conversion narratives to the monastic life bears intensively on Augustine in another way. Opening an alternative way of thinking about the Christian life, Augustine seeks a similar change of status in monastic life. And yet, as many scholars have demonstrated, Augustine was hardly an uncritical listener to the story of Antony.[25] Augustine would not follow the eremitic path of his monastic predecessor. In his *Life of Augustine*, Possidius (431–439 CE) appeals to those seminal biblical passages relevant to the story of Antony (Matt 19:21 and Luke 12:32-33) as he recounts the bishop's renunciation of worldly ambitions for prayerful service with a small group of like-minded friends. Indeed, the stress on the communal orientation of Augustine's monastic intention is foundational, according to Adolar Zumkeller, who writes, "The chief thought behind his [i.e., Augustine's] ideal of life was to form a community of Christian love and in that community to do everything possible to represent in its perfection the Christian ethic of living. This, above all, is the uniqueness of his monasticism."[26] Later priestly and episcopal appointments position Augustine to realize this vision. When Augustine oversaw the diocese of Hippo Regius, he continued to encourage and support monastic efforts.[27] As George Lawless observes, "Augustine was an innovator; he was feeling his way along the paths of Christian asceticism. He was adapting first-hand observations of monastic life at Milan and Rome to fit his own personal needs as well as the requirements of the north African Church."[28] In his capacities as fellow Christian and ecclesiastical administrator, Augustine endorses and advances the monastic practices of men and women.

[24] Ibid., 8.5, p. 164.

[25] See, for example, Terrence G. Kardong, *Pillars of Community: Four Rules of Pre-Benedictine Monastic Life* (Collegeville, MN: Liturgical Press, 2010); Leyser, *Authority and Asceticism from Augustine to Gregory the Great*, and Adolar Zumkeller, *Augustine's Ideal of the Religious Life*, trans. Edmund Colledge (New York: Fordham University Press, 1986).

[26] Zumkeller, *Augustine's Ideal of the Religious Life*, 430; see also the discussion on 431.

[27] Augustine of Hippo, *The Monastic Rules*, commentary by Gerald Bonner (Hyde Park, NY: New City Press, 2004), 53.

[28] George Lawless, *Augustine of Hippo and His Monastic Rule* (Oxford: Oxford University Press, 1987), 58.

Early hagiographic renderings of the bishop applaud Augustine's efforts. Possidius explains that the bishop issued guidelines for interactions between male and female monks, with specific attention to Augustine's sister and female relatives. According to Possidius, Augustine refused to allow these relatives to live or stay with him in the house he shared with his fellow clerics.[29] In Possidius's recollection, Augustine's apparent concerns with disruption of stability recognize challenges posed to the bishop and to others to uphold and maintain ascetic purity and rigor. Augustine's decision to avoid any form of individual encounter or communication with women by proposing that a requisite number of persons be present is cast by Possidius in terms that emphasize practical consequences. This emphasis is in keeping with the monastic teachings about similar matters in Augustine's *Praeceptum*, the Rule for Men. In a series of teachings situated at the center of this rule, Augustine addresses modesty in clothing, in movement, in speech, and in sight.[30] Augustine differentiates between the mere notice of a woman, which is not problematic as it will likely occur for monks outside the monastery, and staring at a woman, which will raise desire. The latter gives recourse to sin. Akin to the description in Possidius's hagiography, Augustine connects outward signs and inward states, writing, "You cannot claim to have pure minds if you have impure eyes, for an impure eye is the messenger of an impure heart."[31]

Claims about Augustine's behavior regarding monastic life in his *Confessions* and in Possidius's *Life of Augustine* may be positioned alongside two other works for further understanding of the bishop's efforts to support and stabilize the monastic practice. Possidius contends that Augustine, in his capacity as bishop, wrote several letters to a community of nuns who were living a form of urban monasticism in the city of Hippo.[32] These letters are an important historical source for the life and practice of this community; moreover, as scholars readily

[29] Zumkeller, *Augustine's Ideal of the Religious Life*, 426. Such efforts are reflected in earlier models, including those in the *Life of Antony* as well as in the Rule (and *Precepts*) of Pachomius.

[30] See *Praeceptum* 4.1–4.11, in Augustine of Hippo, *The Monastic Rules*.

[31] Augustine of Hippo, *The Monastic Rules*, 114 (Rule 4.4).

[32] See Augustine of Hippo, *Letters 211–270, 1*–29* (Epistulae)*, trans. Roland Teske, ed. Boniface Ramsey (Hyde Park, NY: New City Press, 2005). On the relationship between the rule for men and the rule for women, see Bonner, Augustine of Hippo, *The Monastic Rules*, 11.

acknowledge, they are relevant to discussion of Augustine's views on the monastic life. The composition of these letters betrays interests that were both personal and ecclesiastical. Attention to both the personal and the public was a common feature of epistolary correspondence in late antiquity. Everett Ferguson explains that in the ancient world "the ideals for letter writing were brevity, clarity, suitability to the circumstances and mood of their addressees, and style appropriate to the subject matter,"[33] ideals that would have been tailored to the particular audience, given that "types of letters were influenced by social relationships."[34] In her study of the letters of Paulinus of Nola, a contemporary of Augustine with whom the bishop corresponded, Catherine Conybeare observes the dual influence of classical and early Christian models, referring to the latter as "letters marked by their tension between the personal and the preaching voice, their studied simplicity and directness, and their combination of Christian instruction, admonishment, and reflective exposition."[35] Augustine readily betrays features highlighted by Ferguson and by Conybeare in his letters about monastic life.

Whereas Augustine had envisioned adopting a form of monastic withdrawal with a small group of friends for some time following his conversion, it appears likely that his sister may have preceded him in accomplishing a similar goal. Augustine identifies his sister as the former superior of a community of nuns.[36] Possidius refers to Augustine's sister as a widow "who had lived for a long time in the service of God, right up to the day of her death, as a superior of His handmaidens."[37] Augustine's tone in two letters addressed to her community of women, identified in the corpus as Letter 210 and Letter 211, is firm as he emphasizes his own concerns with a growing source of tension and dissension in the community over its leadership, reminds its members of their shared commitment, and exhorts them to work toward resolution. As John R.

[33] Ferguson, *Backgrounds of Early Christianity*, 114.

[34] Ibid., 115.

[35] Catherine Conybeare, *Paulinus of Nola: Self and Symbols in the Letters of Paulinus of Nola* (Oxford: Oxford University Press, 2000), 20.

[36] See Brent D. Shaw, "The Family in Late Antiquity: The Experience of Augustine," *Past & Present* 115, no. 1 (May 1987): 3–51.

[37] Zumkeller, *Augustine's Ideal of the Religious Life*, 426. Here, Zumkeller provides selections from Possidius's *Life of Augustine*, including the information referenced here, which is found in chapter 26.

Fortin explains, "The principal purpose of *Letter* 210 was to address the concerns of the community that arose over the appointment of a new superior. It summons the sisters to reconciliation and to a revival of the communal life to which they were called. Augustine appends to this letter a copy of the Rule he adapted for them, that is, *Letter* 211."[38] In these letters, Augustine displays a sense of fraternal reponsibility for his sister as well as a resolute exhortation for the continued solidarity of her community. In addition to these personal ends, Augustine was also clearly invested in the workings of this community in his capacity as bishop of Hippo, wanting to ensure that the community was stable and secure in serving the members of the local church to which this community of women was most immediately connected.

The *Regularis Informatio* is the rule Augustine provided for this community of nuns.[39] Acts 4:32-35 opens and permeates the rule. Thomas Kardong attends to one notable alteration to the biblical text made by the archbishop, as Augustine amends Acts 4:32 to close with the phrase "to have one heart and soul, *seeking God*."[40] Kardong explains that Augustine's alteration emphasizes "a dynamic process" whereby "the goal of community is reunion with God."[41] On this foundation, Augustine insists on the distribution of material goods among members of the community "not equally to all because you are not all equally strong, but to each one according to need."[42] Kardong explains, "The point is not dispossession but the elimination of want in the community."[43] Dispossession thereby serves as a means of curbing desire. By exposing an awareness of the individual needs of each of its members, dispossession assures that all contribute to the common life in a sure and secure manner. Building on this exhortation emphasizing a unity of spirit and a oneness of purpose, Augustine instructs the community of nuns, "You should all live united in mind and heart (Acts 4:32) and should in one

[38] John R. Fortin, "Saint Augustine's *Letter* 211 in *The Rule of the Master* and *The Rule of Saint Benedict*," *Journal of Early Christian Studies* 14, no. 2 (Summer 2006): 227.

[39] Augustine of Hippo, *The Monastic Rules*. Bonner writes that this is the "feminine version of the *Praeceptum*" (22).

[40] Kardong, *Pillars of Community*, 171. Italics added.

[41] Ibid., 173.

[42] *Regularis Informatio* 1.3, p. 132, in Augustine of Hippo, *The Monastic Rules*.

[43] Kardong, *Pillars of Community*, 178.

another honor God, whose temples you have become."[44] Dispossession is thus tied to divine ownership as the nun is instructed to recognize herself as a site of divine indwelling. With this teaching, Augustine stresses that each member of the community consider her state of life prior to entry and then relinquish identity based on previous social markers. Neither those who enter as formerly wealthy nor those who enter as formerly impoverished are to draw attention to their former state. Nor should those in either category applaud themselves for dwelling with the other. Rather, in the monastery, all are to be identified by their efforts to "live united in mind and heart." According to Leyser, "Augustine elaborated a theory of needs, and insisted upon its acceptance within the community. There was to be no resentment from any quarter at concessions to the weakness of particular brethren. This would have been a parodic subversion of the whole basis of the community."[45]

Augustine situates mutual humility in the context of the dispossession he reads in Acts 4:32-35. Dispossession of material goods is an act to be undertaken by all members for the benefit of the entire community; it is a defining feature that marks entrance into the community and serves as a consistent measure of equanimity. Kardong reminds us that "Augustine's purpose is not to reduce everyone to a single common denominator of consumption, nor is it even to produce ascetic saints who need almost nothing. Rather, it is to create peace in the community."[46] Dispossession applies equally to all members, although it operates distinctly given the individual circumstances of the new member. Those women of means who dispossess "should not boast if they have contributed anything to the common life from their own means, nor should they take more pride in their riches because they are sharing them in the monastery than they would if they were enjoying them in the world" (1.7). Likewise, those women of poverty who enter the monastery "should not seek to have in the monastery things which they could not have had outside" (1.5). Such expressions of boasting and greed are antithetical to mutual humility. Augustine's construction of dispossession thereby has the capacity to redirect desire; regardless of prior social or economic circumstances, all

[44] *Regularis Informatio* 1.8, p. 134, in Augustine of Hippo, *The Monastic Rules*.

[45] Leyser, *Authority and Asceticism from Augustine to Gregory the Great*, 17. See also the discussion on 11–18.

[46] Kardong, *Pillars of Community*, 180; support is given in 1.8. See also 3.4 and 3.5.

members of the community lack private ownership of material goods. Communal sharing, in itself, should be conducted in a spirit of mutual humility. Meeting the particular situation of the individual thereby assures that each member is able to contribute to the common life. By emphasizing further that mutual humility functions as a communal good when each individual nun accepts her new identity as a member of the community and assumes—equally—responsibility to the common life of the community, Augustine upholds the shared commitment to the shared purpose of the community. Placing individual need in service of communal vision, Augustine's teachings about mutual humility would thus shape a theological anthropology based on the principle of living "united in mind and heart."

Given that the communal focus of a monastic rule intends to have an immediate impact on the shaping of an individual monastic life, precepts about mutual humility aquire meaning in the specific relationships within the community. Manifest as a common or collective good advancing the community to realize its shared mission and purpose, mutual humility defines a particularly Christian context. Grounded squarely in a reorientation of the self in relation to others and before a divine power, Augustine's teachings about mutual humility in the rule resemble those found in his *Confessions*, composed after Letter 210 and Letter 211. In "Augustine's Hermeneutic of Humility: An Alternative to Moral Imperialism and Moral Relativism," Gerald W. Schlabach analyzes the rendering of humility in the *Confessions* and argues convincingly that it rests firmly on Augustine's understanding of the Incarnation. Schlabach observes, "Augustine could hardly imagine any true self-knowledge, much less saving knowledge, without knowledge of God's own humility in Jesus Christ. To admit the knowledge that one not only needs some mediator, but that the scandalously humble Jesus Christ could be that mediator, is to reorient reason and emotion ever after, unless assent itself ceases."[47] Augustine's approach to mutual humility in the *Regularis Informatio* as expressed through attentiveness to the needs of the individual and of the community reinforces his Christocentric construction of humility at the center of monastic life. It is telling that in the rule these teachings are followed by those addressing

[47] Gerald W. Schlabach, "Augustine's Hermeneutic of Humility: An Alternative to Moral Imperialism and Moral Relativism," *Journal of Religious Ethics* 22, no. 2 (Fall 1994): 317. See also Stephen Pardue, *The Mind of Christ*, 74.

prayer. Heightening "awareness of its own weakness," the individual and communal expressions of dependence on and obedience to a divine power, prayer defines the members of this community in the sustained offering of their collective need and purpose.

Augustine's interpretation of mutual humility reflects his insight and experience as a member of his own Christian community.[48] By locating a construction of mutual humility that rests on the "scandalously humble Jesus Christ" at the center of monastic life and practice, Augustine thereby affirms this orientation as a source of Christian charity. Such aims would come to inform those who later adopted and adapted Augustine's Rule for their own particular communities, as in the case of Bishop Caesarius of Arles.[49] Despite their particular contexts, the Rule for Virgins, the "first rule specifically for nuns,"[50] shares select features of the Christocentric construction of mutual humility espoused by Augustine to provide ongoing counsel for the female recipients of this monastic rule.

Socially Oriented

Early in the sixth century, Bishop Caesarius of Arles received a request for a female monastery in the territory of his jurisdiction. Caesarius agreed. Although the request fell under the domain of Caesarius's episcopal duties as defined by official conciliar statements,[51] his consent exceeded mere adherence to ecclesiastical mandate. Prior to his episcopal appointment, Caesarius had joined the monastic community at Lérins, serving for some time as the abbot. Furthermore, the request was issued by a group of women that included Caesarius's own sister. And so, like Augustine, Caesarius had personal interests in the construction of this particular monastic establishment, an establishment that would become, in Leyser's words, both "Caesarius' especial pride—and the focus of opposition towards him."[52]

[48] See Lawless, *Augustine of Hippo and His Monastic Rule*, 160.

[49] Albrecht Diem, "New Ideas Expressed in Old Words: The *Regula Donati* on Female Monastic Life and Monastic Spirituality," *Viator* 43, no. 1 (2012): 11.

[50] Emilie Amt, *Women's Lives in Medieval Europe: A Sourcebook* (New York: Routledge, 1993), 221.

[51] See Dunn, "Asceticism and monasticism, II," 676.

[52] Leyser, *Authority and Asceticism from Augustine to Gregory the Great*, 88.

Despite strong parallels with the foundational monastic texts of several predecessors,[53] Caesarius's Rule for Virgins foregrounds the author's awareness of distinct practical and theological considerations regarding his audience, "the Christianity of the rich laity of Arles."[54] Caesarius's Rule weds monastic custom to monastic innovation. However, as William E. Klingshirn explains, "In addition to providing his sister and her companions with living quarters and a rule, Caesarius also sought to make them self-sufficient and independent of outside control."[55] As a departure and a development from previous teachings and practice, Caesarius's specific emphasis on claustration and autonomy were determined neither lightly nor quickly. He composed the rule in stages; the first version of the rule was issued with the monastery founding in 512 CE, and a recapitulation and final version of the rule was issued in 534 CE.[56]

Caesarius drew heavily from the Rule of Augustine (for virgins) in his monastic rule. As Dunn explains, "The 'Augustinian' sections of the *Rule* (*for Virgins*) lay down the spiritual basis for a community's life—the Gospel precept that all was to be held in common and no one should possess any private property."[57] Dispossession appears early in the Rule for Virgins. Caesarius appeals to Matthew 19:21 and Luke 14:26, insisting that "nuns who have possessions cannot have perfection."[58] He includes specific precautions for those members who may be in a position

[53] See the discussion in Caesarius of Arles, *Sermons*, vol. 3 *(187–238)*, trans. Mary Magdeleine Mueller (Washington, DC: Catholic University of America Press, 1981), 63–65. See also Conrad Leyser, "Augustine in the Latin West, 430–ca. 900," in *A Companion to Augustine*, ed. Mark Vessey, 451–64 (Malden, MA: Wiley-Blackwell, 2012).

[54] Leyser, *Authority and Asceticism from Augustine to Gregory the Great*, 91.

[55] William Klingshirn, *Caesarius of Arles: The Making of a Christian Community in Late Antique Gaul* (Cambridge: Cambridge University Press, 1994), 122. See also Dunn, "Asceticism and monasticism, II," 677–80. See also Jane Tibbetts Schulenberg, "Women's Monastic Communities, 500–1100: Patterns of Expansion and Decline," *Signs: Journal of Women in Culture and Society* 14, no. 2 (1989): 261–92.

[56] See the discussions in Caesarius of Arles, *Sermons*, 9, and in Dunn, *The Emergence of Monasticism*, 99.

[57] Dunn, *The Emergence of Monasticism*, 100.

[58] Maria Carita McCarthy, *The Rule for Nuns of St. Caesarius of Arles: A Translation with a Critical Introduction* (Washington, DC: Catholic University of America Press, 1960), Rule 5, p. 172. See also Rule 52, p. 188, for repeated appeal to these biblical passages. McCarthy draws attention to Caesarius's belief that the nuns should deed their property to the poor; she links this belief to the teaching in Rule 21.

of property ownership upon the death of their parents. These nuns should learn, in fear, from the negative example of Ananias and Sapphira, "who, though they said they had offered all to the Apostles, gave part and perfidiously kept a part for themselves, which is neither becoming, permissible, nor proper."[59] Dispossession is a firm requirement for monastic life. As with Augustine, dispossession is also a mark of mutual humility. There are two direct teachings about humility in the Rule for Virgins. The first teaching alludes to the biblical passage that grounds Augustinian monastic life.[60] Referencing the same text, Acts 4:32, in the Rule for Virgins, Caesarius interprets its capacity for illuminating mutual humility as a requisite for monastic life, in particular when he instructs that "those who had something in the world shall, when they enter the monastery, humbly offer it to the mother to be of use for the common needs."[61] Caesarius's departure from his predecessor enforces obedience. As Leyser writes, for Caesarius "community of property forms neither the economic nor the spiritual basis of the community along the lines envisaged by Augustine,"[62] given the strictly elite composition of the community and therefore the emphasis on the abbess's authority over distribution.

Coupled with this teaching, Caesarius contends that humility should inform the approach toward and conditions of monastic labor. Here he offers an independent perspective on mutual humility as he writes, "Let them receive with humility their daily task to be done in the wool work, and let them strive to fulfill it with great industry."[63] Ceasarius's qualification, "with humility," extends the communal dimension of manual labor contained in the Rule of Augustine. Regarding work, Augustine writes that "no one should work at anything for herself. . . . All your work should be shared together with greater care and more ready eagerness than if you were doing things for yourself alone" (5.2). Caesarius focuses more on the role of manual labor in the spiritual life of the com-

[59] McCarthy, *The Rule for Nuns*, Rule 6, p. 173.

[60] McCarthy keenly observes about "the persistent exhortation 'to prepare' found in the *Rule*, and its correlative 'to renounce'" (*The Rule for Nuns*, 56) as signaling Caesarius's distinct emphases.

[61] McCarthy, *The Rule for Nuns*, Rule 21, p. 176. See the discussion in Leyser, *Authority and Asceticism from Augustine to Gregory the Great*, 91–92.

[62] Leyser, *Authority and Asceticism from Augustine to Gregory the Great*, 91.

[63] McCarthy, *The Rule for Nuns*, Rule 16, p. 175.

munity. Both of Caesarius's teachings about humility emphasize the obedience of the individual nun; furthermore, the teachings juxtapose concrete actions of offering possessions and receiving materials with humility in the context of specific moments in the monastic life (upon entrance and during periods of manual labor), thereby indicating a place for mutual humility in the daily monastic life of the nuns.

This interpretation of mutual humility is the assumed framework for Caesarius's sermons to this monastic community; in principle, the sermons facilitate the cultivation of teachings and guidelines contained in the rule. For his sermons, Caesarius often turned to the work of others, as William M. Daly explains: "In the midst of his busy life, Caesarius began to edit, shorten, simplify, and make more didactically effective, sermons available to him from the existing patristic tradition."[64] By employing familiar rhetorical features and appeals to local ecological imagery, in Sermon 237 Caesarius built on the interpretation of mutual humility presented in the rule to highlight more specifically *how* mutual humility should operate in the life of this community.

According to Nicholas De Maeyer and Gert Partoens, "Preaching occupied a central place in the activities and writings of the Arlesian bishop," for which he was remembered and celebrated by contemporaries and biographers.[65] Klingshirn elaborates: "Where Caesarius differed from many of his colleagues was not so much in the act of preaching (although he may have preached more often than most bishops), but rather in the art of preaching, which set his authority as a preacher on a different footing."[66] Klingshirn later writes, "Caesarius worked hard to deliver sermons that were clear, convincing, and above all memorable. To this end, he accommodated his rhetorical style to his pastoral intentions."[67] In Sermon 237, delivered to the recipients of his monastic rule, Caesarius focused

[64] William M. Daly, "Caesarius of Arles, A Precursor of Medieval Christendom," *Traditio* 26 (1970): 8. See also Eric Rebillard, "Sermons, Audience, Preacher," 87–102, in *Preaching in the Patristic Era: Sermons, Preachers, and Audiences in the Latin West*, ed. Anthony Dupont, Shari Boodts, Gert Partoens, and Johan Leemans (Leiden: Brill, 2008); and Nicholas De Maeyer and Gert Partoens, "Preaching in Sixth-Century Arles: The Sermons of Bishop Caesarius," 198–223, also in this volume.

[65] De Maeyer and Partoens, "Preaching in Sixth-Century Arles," 198.

[66] Klingshirn, *Caesarius of Arles*, 147.

[67] Ibid., 150.

directly on the topic of humility.[68] A brief analysis of his teachings about humility in his rule and in this sermon illustrates explicitly another relevant site of departure and development in his thought. Building on Leyser's observation that "the determination to establish a regime of strict surveillance in an elite culture of ostentation conditioned Caesarius' assimilation of the writings of Augustine,"[69] we can examine how Caesarius selectively adjusts his predecessor's emphasis on the Christocentric construction of mutual humility for his own audience in his Rule for Virgins. This construction lays the foundation for Caesarius's teachings about humility in Sermon 237. In this sermon, Caesarius couples familiar rhetorical strategies with local ecological imagery to invite his female monastic audience to interpret mutual humility as a private and a public good for the benefit of the entire Christian community.

In brief, Sermon 237 is an exegesis of Romans 14:7, "None of us lives for himself alone, and none of us dies for himself alone."[70] Caesarius situates this biblical teaching in the particular monastic context of his audience when he invites consideration of the responsibility that they each bear, individually, for the states of their own souls as well as the souls of those influenced by their example. In the first of a series of juxtapositions intended to stimulate audience reflection and application, Caesarius observes that the nuns' example may encourage others "to humility, charity and obedience" or to "disobedience and pride."[71] The

[68] The title of Sermon 237 indicates a mixed audience in which the group of nuns under the Rule for Virgins would be included. There is debate about whether this was a double monastery. For information about the preservation and transmission of this text, see Césaire d'Arles, *Oeuvres Monastiques*, vol. 1: *Oeuvres Pour Les Moniales*, introduction, text critique, translation and notes by Adalbert de Vogüé and Joël Courreau (Paris: Editions du Cerf, 1988).

[69] Leyser, *Authority and Asceticism from Augustine to Gregory the Great*, 91. Leyser's statement, relevant to the Rule for Virgins, can be applied to the question of mutual humility and to Sermon 237.

[70] Caesarius of Arles, *Sermons*, 214 (sec. 1). See Lawrence Wills, "The Form of the Sermon in Hellenistic Judaism and Early Christianity," *Harvard Theological Review* 77:3–4 (1984): 277–99. Wills demonstrates the consistent deployment of a basic tripartite structure: exempla, conclusion, and exhortation in early Christian sermons (279). This basic structure and intent are reflected in Caesarius's Sermon 237.

[71] Caesarius of Arles, *Sermons*, 215 (sec. 1). Here, humility cf. Latin *humilitatem*, French *l'humilité* (Césaire d'Arles, *Oeuvres Monastiques*, 121).

former rightly orients the mind toward the divine and is therefore especially susceptible to the devil's attentions. Caesarius encourages his audience to consider that the devil operates insidiously in expressions of anger, sloth, and gossip. The bishop exhorts his audience to remain on guard against temptations and to reflect closely on the grace of God; those nuns needing to reform should work hard to apply "the medicine of humility" as antidote to "this wound of pride."[72]

Attention to the chiastic structure of Sermon 237 indicates that Caesarius contextualizes his exegesis in the familiar Christian narrative of creation, fall, and redemption.[73] At the opening of the sermon, Caesarius upholds the natural stability embedded in a divinely ordered symbiotic relationship between human beings; for him, the monastery and the monastic life have the potential to exemplify this order internally and for those in the local Christian community. Seeking to disrupt this order from within the monastery, the devil preys on those who "are lukewarm and careless."[74] In turn, these nuns infiltrate and perpetuate disorder by the impact of their false thinking on others. Recognizing their fallenness, they should appeal for relief that they may recognize again "the gift of Christ" that enables restoration and the cultivation of humility, charity, and obedience.[75] Caesarius's concern was both internal to the monastery and external to those in the local community. Although claustration restricted access to and accessibility for the nuns, their isolation was not a mark of absence. Indeed, as Leyser observes, "Of all the ascetic groups in the city, the consecrated virgins—whom few would ever see again once they had entered the convent enclosure—were to serve as the most potent emblem of the moral purity evoked so fervently by the bishop in

[72] Ibid., 219 (sec. 5).

[73] The chiastic structure can be seen in the following:

A—Symbiotic relationship established
  B—Relationship tested
    C—Symbiotic relationship disrupted
  B'—Relationship reformed
A'—Symbiotic relationship re-established

This basic structure resembles that found in Genesis 3. See Robert Ouro, "The Garden of Eden Account: The Chiastic Structure of Genesis 2–3," *Andrews University Seminary Studies* 40, no. 2 (2002): 219–43.

[74] Caesarius of Arles, *Sermons*, 216 (sec. 3).

[75] Ibid., 218 (sec. 5).

his homilies to the people."[76] The example of the nuns mattered, then, as it was believed to affect the lives of members of the larger Christian community in congregations beyond the confines of the monastery.

Caesarius reinforces this specifically Christocentric rendering of mutual humility by adopting rhetorical strategies employed by Augustine. A cursory review of the exordium of Sermon 237 demonstrates this well. The exordium bears resemblance to what David Vincent Meconi defines as "recapitulative tropes" in Augustine's sermons, whereby the bishop "invites his listeners to reflect on some past experience and emotion, offers Christ as the lone healer of those pains or satisfier of those desires, and then shows how the Lord fulfills his promises"[77] in order to create a "triadic connection between his words, his hearers' desires, and the Lord's promises."[78] This basic pattern presents in the exordium of Sermon 237 as Caesarius invites his audience into a moment of self-reflection on a feature of their individual and collective experience, on a factor pertaining to their fallen human condition, when he beckons them in conditional language: "*If you notice carefully* beloved brethren or venerable daughters, *you realize clearly. . . .*"[79] Caesarius then suggests that his audience extend reflection beyond their immediate lives to the example and presence of Christ when he shifts to the parallel claim in Romans 14:7. Caesarius's inclusion of this biblical verse draws the attention of an audience well versed in Scripture to consider a broader implicit eschatological purpose. The audience is then called toward the resolution of their fallenness through Christ.[80] Here, Caesarius demonstrates resolution of the condition to which he drew attention in his opening invitation.

Caesarius advances this specifically Christocentric rendering of humility in the exordium of Sermon 237 through content parallels to Augustine's treatise on holy virginity, *De sancta virginitate*, a work with which Caesarius was certainly familiar. In his treatise, Augustine draws attention to pride as the antithesis of humility and to envy as the opposite of charity. As "daughter and handmaid," as "offspring and companion" to pride,

[76] Leyser, *Authority and Asceticism from Augustine to Gregory the Great*, 89.

[77] David Vincent Meconi, "Recapitulative Tropes in Augustine's Sermons," *New Blackfriars* 95, no. 1060 (2014): 689.

[78] Ibid.

[79] Caesarius of Arles, *Sermons*, 214 (sec. 1). Italics added.

[80] Caesarius of Arles, *Sermons*, 215 (sec. 1).

envy is also connected directly to the work of the devil. In respective order, humility begets charity and works against these vices in obedience to the example of Jesus Christ, whom Augustine refers to as the "teacher of humility."[81] Although this ordering may not have been shared by Caesarius, in the exordium of Sermon 237 he does maintain humility as the antithesis of pride; as we would expect, his appeals to the work of the devil and to the christological model are also shared.[82] Finally, Caesarius betrays a similar intent; Augustine's exhortation, "Let those who persevere in your company be an example to you, but let those who fall by the wayside increase your fear" (*De virg*. 52, p. 208), resembles the claim to serve as an example for others in the reference to Romans 14:7 that opens Sermon 237.

Attending to the social location of his audience, Caesarius "uses examples and analogies drawn from everyday life, in order to appeal to his audience's common experience and to present practical remedies for sinful habits" in Sermon 237.[83] If we return to the chiastic structure of Sermon 237, we see the inclusion of ecological imagery in service of these ends. Caesarius's references to ecological imagery clarify and ground his teaching; these appeals prompt the audience to imagine the direct expression of a biblical reference in the familiar, mundane context of daily life. Although ecological imagery is located in sections two (B), three (C), and four (B') of the sermon,[84] the parallel arrangement of sections two and four clearly highlights this intent: in each section, Caesarius offers an observation about the state of the soul that is then supported by appeal to a biblical passage or allusion and followed by a

[81] In the *Retractationes* (ca. 401 CE), Augustine explains that in *De Sancta Virginitate* "he showed how great a gift of God it [i.e., virginity] was and with what humility it needed to be maintained" (Augustine of Hippo, *Revisions*, trans. Boniface Ramsay [Hyde Park, NY: New City Press, 2010], 131).

[82] Leyser has shown divergence from Augustine, as Caesarius maintains that "humility derives from charity, the mother of all virtues, and pride from desire" in Sermon 48 (*Authority and Asceticism from Augustine to Gregory the Great*, 92).

[83] De Maeyer and Partoens, "Preaching in Sixth-Century Arles," 205. See also Igor Filippov, "Legal Frameworks in the Sermons of Caesarius of Arles," *Medieval Sermon Studies* 58, no. 1 (2014), 68. Unfortunately, I was unable to use Antonio Salvatore, *Sermo humilis, sensus mysticus: esegesi e linguaggio da Paolino di Nola a Cesario di Arles* (Napoli: Loffredo, 1995).

[84] See note 73.

statement of application illustrated by reference to ecological imagery. The intended teaching is reinforced in a concluding statement.[85]

Looking more closely at the use of ecological imagery in the case of the slothful soul in section two, Caesarius describes the devil's activity as similar to that of a hunter or bird catcher.[86] Caesarius attends to these two actors in order to demonstrate the actions of the devil to tempt any soul. Just as a hunter or bird catcher locates a single prey, weakens it, and then uses it as a decoy to trap others, so, too, does the devil act insidiously among those in monastic community to create in a member or two decoys to trap the others into laxity, pride, and disobedience. Both the hunter and the bird catcher, like the devil, inflict violence and conquest, employing cunning strategies to lure and contain their prey. Additionally, both the hunter and the bird catcher devote considerable time and care to their respective crafts.[87] In financial terms, such labor was costly; Robert Fossier observes that it "required specialized personnel, time, and space."[88] These variant interpretations of the expense involved in acquiescing to the devil's temptations would not have been lost on Caesarius's audience. Indeed, his analogy is instructive and vividly didactic as it depicts not only the tactics of the devil but how the nun should act to avoid these pitfalls. As a result, the analogy serves the exegetical function for Romans 14:7 by drawing attention to the way in which the nun can serve as an example of an evil life that influences not only herself but others through their imitation.[89]

When Caesarius turns to the sorrowful soul in section four, he describes those who have succumbed to pride as "caus[ing] shipwreck to both themselves and others."[90] In this case, water imagery beckons Caesarius's audience to consider again their local context, dependent for life and livelihood on the Rhone River, in a highly particular and practical way. This analogy of the religious life as nautical maneuvers draws on

[85] This pattern resembles that found in the exordium.

[86] Caesarius of Arles, *Sermons*, 215 (sec. 2).

[87] Ibid., 215–16.

[88] Robert Fossier, *The Axe and the Oath: Ordinary Life in the Middle Ages*, trans. Lydia G. Cochrane (Princeton, NJ: Princeton University Press, 2010), 201.

[89] Caesarius of Arles, *Sermons*, 216 (sec. 2).

[90] Ibid., 218 (sec. 4).

a common Christian trope for the soul in a manner that hearkens to the specificity of Arles as a highly influential commercial port city in late antiquity. This was an unstable context, for, as Eric Shuler writes, "Arles and its neighbors faced a challenging first half of the sixth century. The boundaries of the post-Roman kingdoms were in flux, producing a series of wars in the region."[91] Water gains renewed currency as it would have "dictated the city layout and provided security."[92] Harnessing, channeling, and using water required an incredibly sophisticated infrastructure of manual labor and expense. Mechanisms of sea travel and technologies of navigation prioritized "safety," and "storms were impossible to predict."[93] These allusions to additional forces of uncertainty and change heighten the effects of those nuns whose demise comes at the expense of a privileged self-will. Here, too, Caesarius's closing appeal serves the exegetical function for Romans 14:7 when he advises that "those who protect themselves in the midst of the sea are more praiseworthy than those who sink in port."[94]

Marking a shift from the potential influence of the devil on the slothful soul in section two to the realized repentance of the sorrowful soul in section four, Caesarius shamelessly appeals to biblical ecological imagery in the climax of the sermon in section three. This section centers on an exegesis of Proverbs 26:11 that links the actions of an animal to those of the soul in order to stress the habitual nature of sin under the persuasive influence of the devil. Succinctly pairing the first part of this proverb with the analogy he seeks to draw, Caesarius states, "As the dog that returns to his vomit becomes hateful, so is the sinner that returns to his sin."[95] Here, the dog drawn ineluctably to that which is most vile for its well-being, to that which pollutes and defiles it, is akin to the fallen soul forgoing the grace of God in order to return even more fully to its vices. Describing the souls of those who have lost their zeal and fervor due to carelessness and sloth, Caesarius employs inner-biblical interpretation

[91] Eric Shuler, "Caesarius of Arles and the Development of the Ecclesiastical Tithe: From a Theology of Almsgiving to Practical Obligations," *Traditio* 67 (2012): 55.

[92] Fossier, *The Axe and the Oath*, 157.

[93] Ibid., 161.

[94] Caesarius of Arles, *Sermons*, 218 (sec. 4).

[95] Ibid., 217 (sec. 3).

of this proverb as found in 2 Peter.[96] Building on Petrine interpretation, Caesarius then reinforces the application of the proverb for his audience, admonishing them to consider and evaluate the consequences of this shift on the state of their own souls.[97]

The ecological imagery in Sermon 237 serves explanatory and exhortatory functions related to ongoing monastic concerns about essential commitments to humility, charity, and obedience through conventional means. Caesarius betrays an acute awareness of his particular audience when he enlivens and interprets specific biblical and monastic teachings through ecological imagery. Hearkening to the blinded bird, the wrecked ship, and the bilious dog, Caesarius appeals to the audience of Sermon 237 as a fellow monk and bishop; the credibility of his words rests on the validity of his shared experience. Through this ecological imagery Caesarius thereby addresses his audience as fellow sensory beings capable of engaging empathetically; their own lived experience attests to the truthfulness of the biblical passages and allusions drawn. In this way, Caesarius's consistent connections between text and context build the exegetical argument for an interpretation of Romans 14:7 that is reasonable and relevant. Stressing personal accountability for the consequences of one's example, it is telling that Caesarius finishes his instruction by requesting that his audience satisfy the conditions pregnant in his opening words. In closing, he instructs his audience to pray as intercessors on behalf of those outside the monastery.[98]

When Caesarius assumed responsibility for the foundation of a female monastery in Arles, he attended to the ways in which prior constructions could inform present concerns. Advocating for the application of general monastic principles in a particular monastic context, he advanced a process of thinking about mutual humility that would extend beyond his immediate efforts. As an essential component of the monastic life, as a virtue bound to charity and obedience, as the antithesis of pride, and as a necessary element of Christian community, vestiges of Caesarius's teachings about mutual humility would continue to bear fruit in the efforts of later monastic thinkers.

[96] Ibid.

[97] Ibid.

[98] Ibid., 219 (sec. 5).

Intellectually Grounded

With the seventh-century Rule of Donatus, we turn from the claustration required by the Rule of Caesarius to a different type of relationship between the monastic and the local nonmonastic Christian communities. Although "monastic life appeared to be a positive option, a safe sanctuary for aristocratic women"[99] in this period, as Donald Hochstetler explains, "Donatus wrote his rule to scotch any revolt by the consecrated women of Besançon."[100] Like Caesarius, Donatus emphasizes teachings pertaining to obedience. Such emphasis would prove instrumental to their purpose. Autumn Dolan contends, "In the female community, whose members were closely tied to local families, the most effective way to separate the convent from its secular influences was to enforce the rule and to immerse the nuns in a communal spirituality."[101] Classified as a proprietary nunnery, this community was particularly suited to retaining features of family life that resembled the earlier monastic environments.[102] According to Susanna Wemple, a proprietary nunnery "usually remained quite small, representing no more than an extended household, that is, an aristocratic house turned into a family cult center. As opposed to the prestige of the greater houses, a proprietary convent offered the comfort of familiar faces and surroundings."[103] Serving as a public institution, a nunnery could be a significant site of female leadership, according to Judith Herrin, who explains that "while it required outside intervention and could not function completely autonomously, it was not necessarily dominated by the secular clergy."[104] In his episcopal capacity, Donatus maintained oversight over the monastic community at Jussanum. The

[99] Schulenburg, "Women's Monastic Communities," 273.

[100] Donald Hochstetler, *A Conflict of Traditions: Women in Religion in the Early Middle Ages, 500–840* (Lanham, MD: University Press of America, 1992), 140. Citing the prologue to the Rule of Donatus, Smith observes, "The sisters of the nunnery under the care of Donatus of Besançon declared the rule of Benedict unsuitable because of its masculine expectations" (*Ordering Women's Lives*, 121).

[101] Dolan, "A Revival of Female Spirituality," 51.

[102] These include the monastic forms of Emmelia and her daughter, Macrina.

[103] Suzanne Fonay Wemple, *Women in Frankish Society: Marriage and the Cloister, 500–900* (Philadelphia: University of Pennsylvania Press, 1981), 163.

[104] Judith Herrin, "Public and Private Forms of Religious Commitment among Byzantine Women," in *Women in Ancient Societies: 'An Illusion of the Night,'* ed. Léonie J. Archer, Susan Fischler, and Maria Wyke, 181–203 (New York: Routledge, 1994), 185.

Rule of Donatus is centered on mutual humility tied to obedience between its members. Locating a role for each member, the teachings in Donatus's monastic rule orient the nuns toward a common spirituality for those seeking to "excel yet more" in the monastic life.

When Donatus composed his rule, centered on the creation of a non-cloistered monastic community of women, he drew extensively from three rules in circulation, the Rule of Caesarius, the Rule of Benedict, and the Rule of Columbanus. In Donatus's day, the practice of collation was widespread and "appears to have been the norm rather than the exception in Gaul,"[105] according to Marilyn Dunn. Donatus adopted principal teachings in these rules for his specifically urban and female audience and attended more directly not only to distinguishing characteristics of monastic life but also to principles of governance and structure. As Albrecht Diem has shown, the overlap between monastic rules is an opportunity for scholars. Diem observes, "Reading the text *against* other texts and especially against the monastic rules Donatus uses helps us to access discontinuities in the rise of monasticism and dissent among those who founded and organized monastic communities."[106] Given that a monastic rule serves as a living document, interpreted and applied in context, the differences across these rules attest to the ways in which a particular rule sought to locate monastic practice in a distinct environment. Diem's examination of Donatus's Rule alongside the Rule of Caesarius, the Rule of Benedict, and the Rule of Columbanus demonstrates that Donatus's efforts were no mere borrowing. Donatus "succeeds in producing an entirely new and innovative monastic program through conscious omissions, rearrangement of his material, and subtle shifts in terminology."[107] Diem argues that there are distinct communal spiritualities at play that account for Donatus's alterations and that these reflect different theological emphases. With regard to the teachings in Acts 4:32-35, Diem demonstrates that for Donatus, "though everything belongs to the community, the nuns may receive, keep and store certain objects, gifts and food for themselves under the strict condition that the abbess knows about it and gives her permission."[108] This distinction, namely the explicit per-

[105] Marilyn Dunn, "Mastering Benedict: Monastic Rules and Their Authors in the Early Medieval West," *English Historical Review* 105, no. 416 (July 1990): 569.

[106] Diem, "New Ideas Expressed in Old Words," 5.

[107] Ibid., 1.

[108] Ibid., 23.

mission of the abbess or one of her representatives, signals a shift that contributes, in Diem's comparative assessment, to Donatus's differentiation from a communal spirituality under his monastic predecessors that was marked by "a system of monastic discipline based on prohibition, blind obedience and punishment towards control, knowledge and permission."[109] This shift is evident in the ways Donatus alters Benedict's teachings about humility.[110] Donatus abandons Benedict's view that "true humility is acknowledging one's fundamentally helpless and incurable state and being aware of the constant danger of eternal damnation."[111] In its place, Donatus proposes a monastic worldview that "gives the individual nun, if supported by the prayer of the community and by the guidance of the abbess, a much more active role in her own salvation."[112] This principle is certainly reflected when we look more closely at Donatus's teachings about mutual humility in his rule. Of its seventy-seven chapters, just under a third address humility in some manner.

Mutual humility is explicitly tied to dispossession of material goods in Donatus's Rules 7 and 8. Rule 7 pertains to the form of dispossession required upon entrance into the monastery. Here, dispossession is tied again to Jesus' teachings in Matthew 19:21 and Luke 14:33. As in Caesarius's Rule for Virgins, the pairing of these passages in this order reinforces the idea that perfection is possible in and through discipleship.[113] Together, these passages encapsulate the call and *vocatio* of the Christian nun. That these passages are illustrative of the dispossession required of the monastic life is evident when Donatus juxtaposes them with the example of Ananias and Sapphira (Acts 5:1-11) in order to offer a cautionary tale for those who will need to dispossess at a later time. Like Caesarius, Donatus instructs that those in the monastery avoid the example of Ananias and Sapphira because it does not meet the mandate to "reserve nothing in their power which they are seen to ordain or possess privately" for admittance.[114] The nuns are called to respond to Christ's

[109] Ibid., 27.

[110] Ibid., 32–34.

[111] Ibid., 33.

[112] Ibid., 34; Diem observes that Donatus merges Rule of Benedict 5 and 7 (80). See also Albrecht Diem, "Columbanian Monastic Rules: Dissent and Experiment," in *The Irish in Early Medieval Europe: Identity, Culture and Religion*, ed. Roy Fletcher and Sven Meeder, 68–85 (London: Palgrave, 2016).

[113] See Scheffler, "Caring for the Needy in the Acts of the Apostles," 134–35.

[114] McNamara, *The Ordeal of Community*, 39.

teachings by dispossessing of material goods and resources completely.[115] Donatus reinforces that the requirement of dispossession of private property in Rule 7 contributes to the fulfillment of Acts 4:32 when he turns to Rule 8. Here, he offers a literal rendering of the biblical text: "Everything must be held in common by all, as it is written, 'And they had all in common.' (Acts 4:32)."[116] Such rendering suggests that the Rule of Donatus links explicitly to and parallels an intertextual interpretation by which, as Scheffler explains, the "radical sharing of goods [in Acts] was interpreted by Luke as being a way of obedience (amongst others) to Jesus's instruction or advice in Luke 12:33 to sell one's possessions and give alms."[117] In the context of the Rule of Donatus, this interpretation instills mutual humility, as indicated in Rule 9, "That none may make a private work without orders," which reads, "Anyone who had anything in the world must offer it humbly to the mother on entering the monastery for the future use of the community. Nor let any seek in the monastery for what they did not have in the world."[118] This precept receives more extensive treatment in Rule 10, "That none may despise her sister," where Donatus explains that the goal of these teachings is to "live in all unanimity and concord and mutually honour God, Whose temple you have deserved to be, in yourselves," a virtual paraphrase of Acts 4:34.[119] Dispossession thereby defines a community of mutual humility through a more complete sharing of resources.[120]

Mutual humility is given a concentrated focus in Rules 37 through 48. Donatus's dependence on the sixth-century Rule of Benedict is especially apparent in these chapters, and the bishop adopts and adapts his predecessor's work with regard to the placement and presentation of his teachings about humility. Whereas in the Rule of Benedict humility is given its own chapter early in the text (Rule 7), Donatus places it much later, toward the close of his monastic rule. Furthermore, when Donatus does address

[115] Donatus's appeal to the example of Ananias and Sapphira here is closer to that in Caesarius's Rule for Virgins (Rules 5 and 6) and to the Rule of the Master (Rule 82) on poverty than to the Rule of Benedict.

[116] McNamara, *The Ordeal of Community*, 40. See David R. McCabe, *How to Kill Things with Words: Ananias and Sapphira under the Prophetic Speech-Act of Divine Judgment (Acts 4.32–5.11)* (New York: T & T Clark, 2011).

[117] Scheffler, "Caring for the Needy in the Acts of the Apostles," 135.

[118] McNamara, *The Ordeal of Community*, 41.

[119] Ibid.

[120] See also Rule of Donatus 21 for direct appeal to Acts 4:34.

humility, he distributes his teachings about humility across several chapters, expanding on the more concentrated form of presentation in the Rule of Benedict. Finally, as Diem also observes, Donatus links obedience to humility.[121] Specifically, Donatus likens the obedience of the nun to her superior with that of Christ to the will of the Father.[122] Donatus's direct appeals to the example and teaching of Christ build an explicit connection between his teachings and the cultivation of mutual humility by Christ. As a result, Donatus stresses the relationship between the nun and Christ; it is in service to Christ that the nun espouses mutual humility. As a form of obedience, Donatus reinforces the place of the nun before Christ; her submission to the rule and to this service cultivates a state of mutual humility by rightly reorienting the nun. By choosing consciously to place her relationship with Christ at the center of her life, the nun conforms her self-will to be directed, guided, and shaped in relation to this end. Donatus suggests that from this foundation, a series of other forms of obedience naturally flow, including obedience to the prioress.[123]

When Donatus reframes an emphasis on obedience and humility, he makes extensive use of Scripture and, in particular, of the gospels. Such emphasis and use may be explained if we turn our attention to his employment of teachings from the sixth-century Rule of Columbanus.[124] Donatus may have appealed to the Rule of Columbanus for reasons of certitude; this was a monastic rule with which he was particularly familiar, given that he was trained under its direction. Donatus and his family had long-standing connections to Columbanus; Alexander O'Hara explains that the *Life of Columbanus* recounts an early exchange between the monastic founder and Donatus's parents prior to his birth. According to the vita, Donatus "was conceived after his barren parents had sought the help of Columbanus but only after they had agreed to the conditions of the hard-bargaining holy man. He would only pray on their behalf if they agreed that their first-born would be consecrated to the religious life."[125] And so

[121] Diem, "New Ideas Expressed in Old Words," 33.

[122] McNamara, *The Ordeal of Community*, 53.

[123] Ibid.

[124] Diem, "New Ideas Expressed in Old Words," 33–34, observes intertextual parallels with regard to the role of the abbess and the place of penance; I wish to draw connections between the Rule of Columbanus and the Rule of Donatus regarding mutual humility.

[125] Alexander O'Hara, "The Vita Columbani in Merovingian Gaul," *Early Medieval Europe* 17, no. 2 (2009): 139.

Donatus assumed monastic life under the Rule of Columbanus and later founded a monastery employing this rule during his episcopal tenure.[126] Although the influence of Columbanus and his rule on Donatus manifests specifically, as Caitlin Corning explains, in teachings pertaining to "instructions and punishments,"[127] it is not surprising that influence is found in other rules as well, including the Rule of Donatus 37. Distinct from the Rule of Benedict, Rule of Donatus 37 resembles one of the teachings about humility in the Rule of Columbanus. The Rule of Columbanus is frequently noted for the severity of punishment and the emphasis on penance contained.[128] To these ends, the teachings about mutual humility appear most succinctly in a single statement tied to obedience and mortification, as the Rule of Columbanus instructs that the monk follow "the example of the Lord and Savior, Who says, 'I came down from heaven not to do My will, but the will of Him Who sent Me, the Father.'"[129] Appealing directly to the Gospel of John in this way, the Rule of Donatus and the Rule of Columbanus emphasize mutual humility as grounded in obedience to the example of Christ. Indeed, the Rule of Columbanus contends that "monks must everywhere beware of a proud independence, and learn true lowliness as they obey without murmuring or hesitation, that according to the Lord's word they may feel the yoke of Christ pleasant and His burden light."[130] Connecting obedience and humility thereby emphasizes its redemptive value as accessible to the nun without the burden of dependence but, rather, with the agency of choice.[131]

Dispossessing Humility

How does mutual humility, as defined and instructed by the episcopal family members of these holy women, inform the broader construction

[126] Ibid., 139–40.

[127] Caitlin Corning, *The Celtic and Roman Traditions: Conflict and Consensus in the Early Medieval Church* (New York: Springer, 2006), 60.

[128] See Dunn, "Mastering Benedict," for discussion of the relationship between the Rule of Donatus, the Rule of Benedict, and the Rule of Columbanus.

[129] Rule of Columbanus 9, in *Regular Life: Monastic, Canonical, and Mendicant Rules*, ed. Daniel Marcel La Corte and Douglas J. MacMillan (Kalamazoo, MI: Medieval Institute Publications, 2004), 92.

[130] Ibid.

[131] This supports Diem, "New Ideas Expressed in Old Words," 37.

of Christian humility in this period? The Christocentric focus of Christian humility is stabilized in written rules that create a community spirituality around a type of mutual humility emerging from dispossession. In the Rule of Augustine (for virgins), the Rule of Caesarius, and the Rule of Donatus, the dispossession called for in Acts 4:32-35 becomes the foundation for a monastic Christian community of women. In none of the rules examined here is dispossession an end in itself. Rather, dispossession becomes the hermeneutic framework for interpreting mutual humility. Given the particularity of dispossession, the role and meaning of mutual humility fluctuates. For Augustine, dispossession contributes to harmony in the monastic Christian community. Dispossession orients the nun to mutual humility. Augustine's insistence on the distribution of material goods among members of this community "not equally to all because you are not all equally strong, but to each one according to need"[132] hearkens to the example of the Jerusalem community in the Acts of the Apostles, and of Acts 4:32 in particular, by featuring radical dependence on a divine power. These teachings are adopted and adapted by Caesarius of Arles. Whereas Augustine defines monastic Christian practice in the context of urban life, intentionally and necessarily aware of relations between lay and monastic Christians, Caesarius advances the specific need for claustration. For Caesarius, dispossession demonstrates obedience as a submission of one's will. Dispossession creates relationships of mutual humility. Caesarius's requirements for the dispossession of private ownership emphasize redistribution to meet the needs of all members of the community. Donatus of Besançon appeals to teachings about humility in the Rule of Caesarius. For Donatus, dispossession engenders trust. Dispossession sustains mutual humility, benefits the community by addressing its practical needs, and empowers each nun to exercise agency in the role of material goods under the guidance of her superior.

Our sources also attest to the ways in which theological, social, and intellectual humility inform mutual humility as "a giving of the self to the other."[133] In each case, the mutual humility that emerges from dispossession ties to theological humility by reinforcing the characteristic radical dependence on a divine power; dispossession creates an attitude

[132] *Regularis Informatio* 1.3, p. 132, in Augustine of Hippo, *The Monastic Rules*.

[133] Foulcher, *Reclaiming Humility*, 23.

toward material goods and persons that attempts to retain the encounter with that power at the center. Mutual humility connects with social humility by emphasizing shared dependence among a community of persons espousing this common value of dispossession; all are equally in need, and it is the responsibility of all persons to meet the material needs of all members. Mutual humility connects explicitly to intellectual humility by providing a scriptural context or basis for this shared practice of dispossession. In this context, the practice of dispossession thus unites the members of the community and connects them to a lineage, as followers or imitators of the example of the earliest Christian community, as instituted and commissioned by Christ. Mutual humility is constructed with elements or features of theological humility as the foundation from which social humility and intellectual humility emerge in the institutionalized context of monastic Christian community. Mutual humility permeates these communities as a form of Christian or spiritual friendship between fellow Christians. As "sisters in Christ," the nuns' monastic ties of mutual humility are rooted in a shared commitment of radical dependence on a divine power with others in accordance with the example and teachings of Scripture. They elicit a type of charity (love) that destabilizes operating social norms. This countercultural orientation of Christian humility, upholding forms of vulnerability, anonymity, decentering, and dispossession in concomitant structures of authority, servanthood, solidarity, and charity, is the focus of our final chapter.

Chapter Six

The Challenge of Christian Humility

Now that we have seen some of the ways Christian humility was shown to operate as a relational value in the period of late antiquity, we can return to Leander of Seville's exhortation that his audience, "Picture in your mind His humility,"[1] at the opening of this book. When we consider Leander's work, we must remember that "Leander's rule bears little resemblance to other rules for nuns or monks known at the time and was not concerned with daily practice within the community. Rather he focused on the virtues necessary for the proper fulfilment of the religious life for women. . . . He also emphasised the necessity for the nuns to distance themselves from worldly contacts."[2] Leander's exhortation was complicated by the fact that by the time of his writing the humility of Christ was securely associated with the humility of the Godhead; the humanity of Christ was now positioned more explicitly alongside the growing popularity of Marian devotion. Although Mary had been a role model for ascetic women from earliest times, her prominence positioned her even more centrally as an exemplar of humility; through her submission to divine will and perfect virginity, ascetic women were provided with a model that reflected a confounding ideology of gender.

Interpreting Leander's exhortation requires us to account for his anti-Arian, post-Chalcedonian position. Leander's Christian worldview upholds the humanity and divinity of Jesus Christ and the prominent role of Mary

[1] Barlow, *Iberian Fathers*, 206.

[2] Smith, *Ordering Women's Lives*, 127.

as Theotokos, that is, as Virgin and Mother of God. If we are attendant to the dual identities of both figures, then we can approach Leander's exhortation constructively using the discussion of humility in the preceding chapters. We do so by following cues from Leander himself when he directs Florentina to interpret rightly by advising her, "Do not fear to imitate Him because He is God; but remember that He is more to be imitated because He is man. This He did and this He taught; He judged it possible to be done."[3] By stressing imitation of the embodied Christ who lived, moved, and acted in ways both observable and accessible to human beings, Leander maintains that this example is accessible to all persons because it is based on the human quality of Christ (and not on the maleness of Christ).

Leander's emphasis guides us to consider the ways in which Jesus and Mary offer examples to these ascetic women from which they might participate in a pedagogy of humility and learn how to become humble as fellow human beings. Here, Jesus and Mary present functioning examples for human beings in their own capacity as fellow human beings. If we first parse the ways Jesus and Mary operate separately and independently to instruct these ascetic women in theological, social, intellectual, and mutual humility, we can see that Leander appeals to those external behaviors and internal values embedded in the Christian humility of both figures in order to invite his audience to follow their example.[4]

Leander frames a pedagogy of theological humility intended to encourage Florentina to learn to be a model for others by attaining a certain type of authority obtained through and cultivated in humility. Specifically, Jesus' radical dependence on a divine power heightens the role of vulnerability in the acquisition of his authority. Moreover, it imbues a type of social humility that rests on servanthood, as Leander writes, "He [i.e., Jesus] loved equally all mankind, so that, just as His death is our life and His humility is the curing of our pride, so our integrity was bought with His wounds."[5] Leander's claim about the universal impact of Jesus' sac-

[3] Barlow, *Iberian Fathers*, 206.

[4] See Peter Brown, "The Saint as Exemplar in Late Antiquity," in *Saints and Virtues*, ed. John Stratton Hawley, 2–14 (Berkeley: University of California Press, 1987). Regarding the imitation of Christ, Brown explains, "Though the phrase does not, to my knowledge, occur among Late Antique Christian writers in this context, *repraesentatio Christi*, making Christ present by one's own life in one's own age and region, appears to be the aim and effect of the early Christian *imitatio Christi*" (7).

[5] Barlow, *Iberian Fathers*, 186 (here Barlow quotes Jerome).

rifice rests on a juxtaposition between Jesus' humility and human pride. As the cure of human pride, Jesus' humility (as a type of "true humility") requires, in this context, a doctrine of atonement that maintains the full suffering and death of Jesus.

Leander's appeals to the theological humility of Mary originate in his reflections on Jesus' humility. Leander advocates that in order to follow Jesus' example as Mary did, Florentina and her fellow nuns must assume a form of isolation: "It is believed that she [i.e., Mary] avoided all contacts with men, because she was alone when the angel found her, because she trembled at seeing in the angel the male sex which she was avoiding. See what glory she attained to become the Mother of Christ by avoiding men."[6] Mary's anonymity thereby contributes to her social humility as a form of servanthood by attesting, as Fiona J. Griffiths contends, to Leander's beliefs about his sister as a female monastic. Griffiths explains that "the presumed efficacy of her [Florentina's] prayers was based on Leander's sense of her spiritual potential, rooted in her sex and specifically in her gendered physical purity and status as a bride of Christ. Leander assumed that, as a woman and as a virgin, Florentina was more perfectly positioned to plead with Christ than he (or, frankly, any man, whether virgin or not, ordained or not) could be."[7]

According to Leander, Mary participates in Jesus' salvific act in her capacity as "the Mother and guide of virgins," writing, "blessed that fertility, which in bearing filled the world and won heaven as its reward, yet did not lose the veil of virginity."[8] Through imitation of the theological humility of Mary, "that outstanding example of virginity," and "the model and leader of all virgins,"[9] Florentina and the nuns are invited to participate in the salvific act of Christ as well. Leander exhorts, "Let your heart, my sister, burn with that fire which Christ sent on earth. Be aroused by the flame of that fire; behold in your mind's eye the bands of maidens accompanying Mary; follow those bands, join them with eager heart."[10] This call for Florentina and her fellow nuns to cultivate mutual humility,

[6] Ibid., 200.

[7] Fiona J. Griffiths, *Nuns' Priests' Tales: Men and Salvation in Medieval Women's Monastic Life* (Philadelphia: University of Pennsylvania Press, 2018), 142.

[8] Barlow, *Iberian Fathers*, 200.

[9] Ibid.

[10] Ibid., 188.

as "a giving of the self to the other,"[11] encourages them to create a monastic Christian community radically dependent on a divine power by empowering individuals who are rightly disposed and oriented in relation to one another through a type of dispossession that informs charity.

Analogous to Mary, the virgin undergoes a "conception from above" that, in turn, "gives birth to virtues."[12] Again, in a way similar to Mary, the virgin is neither sterile nor unchaste.[13] The birthing virgin, like Mary, conceives virginally and retains her purity after the birth of the virtues. Leander explains to Florentina, "By one conception with the Holy Spirit, you will produce many births. The first child of a virgin is the virtue of modesty, the second patience, the third sobriety, the fourth humility, the fifth temperance, the sixth charity, the seventh chastity, that it might be fulfilled, as it is said, that: 'The barren hath borne seven.' Lo, by one conception of the sevenfold Spirit, you have borne seven sons."[14] Leander's allusion to the relationship of the Zuphite Elkanah and his barren wife, Hannah, in this passage recalls one of the couple's visits to the temple in Shiloh. In prayer for a male child, Hannah draws the attention of Eli, the priest, who confirms her request (1 Sam 1:9-19). When Hannah later gives birth to Samuel, she honors her promise to dedicate him to the Lord's service in the temple. In her song of thanksgiving, Hannah proclaims that with the Lord, "The barren has borne seven sons" (1 Sam 2:5). Leander's reference thereby illustrates both the barrenness and the fruitfulness of the virgin who remains committed to her divine bridegroom. The implicit connection between Hannah and Mary further emphasizes the place of the virgin in a lineage of chosen women whose service participates in the realization of a christianized eschatology.[15] Here, Leander draws on a type of intellectual humility informed by a Christocentric interpretation and application of Scripture that decenters the individual by emphasizing solidarity with others.

Leander's attention to those practical forms of theological, social, intellectual, and mutual humility exemplified by Jesus and by Mary

[11] Foulcher, *Reclaiming Humility*, 23.

[12] Barlow, *Iberian Fathers*, 193.

[13] Ibid.

[14] Ibid., 194.

[15] See Griffiths, *Nuns' Priests' Tales*, 164–67, for discussion of the challenges posed by Hannah as a biblical model for women's prayerfulness.

demonstrates attainable ends for his audience. Such ends, however, are situated in the broader context of an ideal of divine humility, the humility of Jesus Christ as God incarnate in humanity through Mary. Here, we turn to the fact that, for Leander, humility holds redemptive value because of the incarnation, an act of union between Jesus and Mary, as God becomes man through the God-bearer.[16] The divine humility of Christ required both an emphasis on his divinity and an emphasis on Mary's virginity. Leander maintains that divine humility rests on both, on incarnation and crucifixion. Instructing Florentina and her fellow nuns, "Be humble after the law of your Bridegroom,"[17] Leander explains this "law" of "infinite humility" in the incarnation and crucifixion. He exhorts, "You, certainly, if you love your Bridegroom, must observe his death, must picture in your mind His humility, and must press solidly to your intellect as on a coin the virtues which He bore in the flesh after the manner of man."[18] Referring to humility in the incarnation of Christ and then to humility in the death of Christ, Leander builds on the precondition for such "imprinting" by maintaining that, due to Florentina's state of being, she should be able to access, through love, a type of observation that will, in turn, enable her to be in solidarity with his humility as conducted in the crucifixion. Explicit attention to Christ's divine humility, in birth and in death, thereby depicts the place of humility over the course of the entire human lifespan. By birthing humility these ascetic women participate in the existential dimension of human humility and in the incarnational dimension of divine humility. Given their training, then, they can serve as role models, as representatives, of Christian humility.

Christian Humility and Ascetic Women

In the period of late antiquity, discipleship entailed following Christ in his example of humility; to do so is to acknowledge the self as Christ, that is, *to be* a human person incarnate, suffering, dying, and rising. The appeal to ascetic women, by Leander and by those we have examined in this book, as a symbol for Christ indicates their perceived value in

[16] While Leander was in Constantinople he would have encountered strong endorsements of the emerging cult of the Theotokos.

[17] Barlow, *Iberian Fathers*, 206; this is "Chapter 11: A Nun Shall Be Humble."

[18] Ibid.

defining a particularly Christian type of humility. Such a construction reflected emerging sensibilities; Gillian Clark observes that the ascetic practice of early Christians sought "a sharing of suffering not so much with the poor as with Christ and the martyrs."[19] Operating types of humility (theological, social, intellectual, and mutual), as well as their external behaviors (authority, servanthood, solidarity, and charity) and internal values (vulnerability, anonymity, decentering, and dispossession) were christianized. Such distinction set Christian humility apart from its Greco-Roman and Judaic counterparts.

The rhetorical construction of these types of humility in our sources intentionally locates this Christocentric focus in decisions based in human thought and behavior; as a result, humility affords consistently an awareness of one's place as creature in the presence of creator. Here, humility rests on an intellectual orientation rooted in a reconception of the self, emphasizing a Christocentric focus that moves the subject beyond self-concern. Concern is directed toward a divine power even when it is in service of other human beings. Given that Christ's humility entailed a rightly ordered and directed self-will, our sources uphold the capacity of the human person. To imitate Christ as the epitome of Christian humility required vulnerability, anonymity, decentering, and dispossession in order to espouse orientation of prayerful service toward others. To follow Christ as disciple was to serve others before the self and to do so without attention to self-concern. Those Christians who were set apart by the quality or caliber of their imitation, of their discipleship, could serve as role models. Indeed, as Caesarius and others suggest, such persons are required to do so, as they will be held accountable for those who follow.

Within this Christocentric context, this background of significance, humility demonstrates a course of action that is both real and ideal; our sources point out how an individual chooses to act and how an individual *should* choose to act. Our sources contain and reify moments of interrogation and decision embedded in the element of choice. As a choice, humility accounts for knowingly exercising individual agency in solidarity with (and for the larger benefit of) another. By "textualizing" Christian humility through the example of the ascetic woman, our sources supplied contemporary human examples for their audiences. Whereas early Chris-

[19] Gillian Clark, "Women and Asceticism in Late Antiquity," 43.

tian audiences would recognize well the operative "ideology of gender differences,"[20] they may also have been attuned to the ways humility could "point out moments of slippage, spaces where the self-evidency of gender conventions and the relationships for which they were foundational might have been thought otherwise," in the words of Elizabeth Castelli.[21] And so with the risk of Christian humility. When the ascetic woman functioned as a symbol for Christian humility, audiences were aware of the selective use of an image that espoused its countercultural principles. They understood the boundaries by which it framed interpretation and application. Vestiges of what Caroline Walker Bynum observes of reversal images in the later Middle Ages are evident here as well. Bynum writes, "The male writer who saw his soul as a bride of God or his religious role as womanly submission and humility was conscious of using an image of reversal. He sought reversal because reversal and renunciation were at the heart of a religion whose dominant system is the cross—life achieved through death. . . . Because women were women, they could not embrace the female as a symbol of renunciation. Because society was male-dominated, they could not embrace the male as a symbol of renunciation."[22] At the margins of the normative social system, the ascetic woman undertook a form of renunciation of self that could enable her to function for both females and males as a symbol of Christian humility.

For this reason, the use of ascetic women to demonstrate the choice required by learning, teaching, and cultivating Christian humility demonstrates *how* countercultural such a value could be. The use of ascetic women was simultaneously affirmative of biblical precedent and subversive of societal norms. Constructed as malleable, ascetic women were deployed in service of an author's intent to disorient in order to reorient an audience. The presentation of her assertions and her assertiveness betrayed the scriptural foundation of Christian humility and conveyed a life lived in explicit accordance with an unrealized eschatology. Her

[20] Castelli, "'I Will Make Mary Male': Pieties of the Body and Gender Transformation of Christian Women in Late Antiquity," in *Body Guards: The Cultural Politics of Gender Ambiguity*, ed. Julia Epstein and Kristina Straub (New York: Routledge, 1991), 46.

[21] Ibid., 47. See also Gillian Cloke, *This Female Man of God*, 212–21.

[22] Caroline Walker Bynum, *Fragmentation and Redemption: Essays on Gender and the Human Body in Medieval Religion* (New York: Zone Books, 1992), 171.

expressions of humility, often in the context of ascetic hospitality, symbolized the radical overturning required in a way of being centered on prayer and service to a particular Christian community. Preserving societal, ecclesiastical, and patriarchal norms that bound her access and agency, in these expressions of humility, she stood *for* and *in the place of* Jesus Christ.

Bibliography

Alberici, Lisa A., and Mary Harlow. "Age and Innocence: Female Transitions to Adulthood in Late Antiquity." *Hesperia Supplements* 41, *Constructions of Childhood in Ancient Greece and Italy* (2007): 193–203.

Amt, Emilie. *Women's Lives in Medieval Europe: A Sourcebook.* New York: Routledge, 1993.

Amundson, Darrel, and Gary Ferngren. "Virtue and Medicine from Early Christianity through the Sixteenth Century." In *Virtue and Medicine*, edited by Earl E. Shelp, 23–61. Dordrecht: D. Reidel, 1985.

Aristarkhova, Irina. "Hospitality and the Maternal." *Hypatia* 27, no. 1 (Winter 2012): 163–81.

Asiedu, F. B. A. "Following the Example of a Woman: Augustine's Conversion to Christianity in 386." *Vigilae Christianae* 57, no. 3 (August 2003): 276–306.

Augustine of Hippo. *Confessions.* Translated by R. S. Pine-Coffin. London: Penguin Books, 1961.

———. *Letters 211–270, 1*-29* (Epistulae).* Translated by Roland Teske. Edited by Boniface Ramsey. Hyde Park, NY: New City Press, 2005.

———. *The Monastic Rules.* Commentary by Gerald Bonner. Hyde Park, NY: New City Press, 2004.

———. *Revisions.* Translated by Boniface Ramsay. Hyde Park, NY: New City Press, 2010.

Aymer, Margaret. "Acts of the Apostles." In *Women's Bible Commentary*, revised and updated ed. Edited by Carol A. Newsom, Sharon H. Ringe, and Jacqueline E. Lapsey, 536–46. Louisville, KY: Westminster John Knox Press, 2012.

Barbu, Liviu. "The 'Poor in Spirit' and Our Life in Christ: An Eastern Orthodox Perspective on Christian Discipleship." *Studies in Christian Ethics* 22, no. 3 (2009): 261–74.

Barlow, Claude W., trans. *Iberian Fathers*, vol. 1, *Martin of Braga, Paschasius of Dumium, Leander of Seville.* Washington, DC: Catholic University of America Press, 1969.

Barrett-Lennard, R. J. S. "The Canons of Hippolytus and Christian Concern with Illness, Health, and Healing." *Journal of Early Christian Studies* 13, no. 2 (Summer 2005): 137–64.

Beaucamp, Joelle. "Women." In *Late Antiquity: A Guide to the Postclassical World*, edited by G. W. Bowersock, Peter Brown, and Oleg Grabar, 749. Cambridge, MA: Harvard University Press, 1999.

Beeley, Christopher A. *The Unity of Christ: Continuity and Conflict in Patristic Tradition*. New Haven, CT: Yale University Press, 2012.

Bell, Catherine. *Ritual Theory, Ritual Practice*. Oxford: Oxford University Press, 1992.

Bitton-Ashkelony, Brouria. *Encountering the Sacred: The Debate on Christian Pilgrimage in Late Antiquity*. Berkeley: University of California Press, 2005.

Boadt, Lawrence. *Reading the Old Testament: An Introduction*. Mahwah, NJ: Paulist Press, 1984.

Boodts, Shari, and Anthony Dupont. "Augustine of Hippo." In *Preaching in the Patristic Era: Sermons, Preachers, and Audiences in the Latin West*, edited by Anthony Dupont, Shari Boodts, Gert Partoens, and Johan Leemans, 177–97. Leiden: Brill, 2008.

Booth, Phil. *Crisis of Empire: Doctrine and Dissent at the End of Late Antiquity*. Berkeley: University of California Press, 2014.

Brakke, David. *Demons and the Making of the Monk: Spiritual Combat in Early Christianity*. Cambridge, MA: Harvard University Press, 2006.

———. "The Lady Appears: Materializations of 'Woman' in Early Monastic Literature." *Journal of Medieval and Early Modern Studies* 33, no. 3 (Fall 2003): 387–402.

Braun, Willi. "Body, Character, and the Problem of Femaleness in Early Christian Discourse." *Religion and Theology* 9, nos. 1–2 (2002): 108–17.

Brereton, Virginia Lieson. *From Sin to Salvation: Stories of Women's Conversion, 1800 to the Present*. Bloomington: Indiana University Press, 1991.

Brock, Sebastian, trans. *The Syriac Fathers on Prayer and the Spiritual Life*. Kalamazoo, MI: Cistercian Publications, 1987.

Brock, Sebastian, and Susan Ashbrook Harvey. *Holy Women of the Syrian Orient*. Berkeley: University of California Press, 1987.

Brown, Peter. *Authority and the Sacred: Aspects of the Christianization of the Roman World*. Cambridge: Cambridge University Press, 1995.

———. *The Body and Society: Men, Women, and Sexual Renunciation in Early Christianity*. New York: Columbia University Press, 1988.

———. *The Cult of the Saints: Its Rise and Function in Latin Christianity*. Chicago: University of Chicago Press, 1981.

———. *Late Antiquity*. Cambridge, MA: Harvard University Press, 1998.

———. *Power and Persuasion in Late Antiquity: Towards a Christian Empire*. Madison: University of Wisconsin Press, 1988.

———. "The Saint as Exemplar in Late Antiquity." In *Saints and Virtues*, edited by John Stratton Hawley, 3–14. Berkeley: University of California Press, 1987.

Bundy, David. "Martyrios (Sahdona) (seventh century)." In *Encyclopedia of Early Christianity*, edited by Everett Ferguson, Michael P. McHugh, Frederick W. Norris, and David Scholar, 732. New York: Garland, 1990).

Burrus, Virginia. *Saving Shame: Martyrs, Saints, and Other Abject Subjects*. Philadelphia: University of Pennsylvania Press, 2008.

———.*The Sex Lives of Saints: An Erotics of Ancient Hagiography*. Philadelphia: University of Pennsylvania Press, 2004.

———. "Word and Flesh: The Bodies and Sexuality of Ascetic Women in Christian Antiquity." *Journal of Feminist Studies in Religion* 10, no. 1 (Spring 1994): 27–51.

Burton-Christie, Douglas. *The Word in the Desert: Scripture and the Quest for Holiness in Early Christian Monasticism*. Oxford: Oxford University Press, 1993.

Bynum, Caroline Walker. *Fragmentation and Redemption: Essays on Gender and the Human Body in Medieval Religion*. New York: Zone Books, 1992.

Caesarius of Arles. *Sermons*, vol. 3 *(187–238)*. Translated by Mary Magdeleine Mueller. Washington, DC: Catholic University of America Press, 1981.

Cameron, Averil. "Remaking the Past." In *Interpreting Late Antiquity: Essays on the Postclassical World*, edited by G. W. Bowersock, Peter Brown, and Oleg Grabar. Cambridge, MA: Harvard University Press, 2001.

Campbell, Mary B. *The Witness and the Other World: Exotic European Travel Writing, 400–1600*. Ithaca, NY: Cornell University Press, 1988.

Caner, Daniel. *Wandering, Begging Monks: Spiritual Authority and the Promotion of Monasticism in Late Antiquity*. Berkeley: University of California Press, 2002.

Carden, Michael. "Review of Virginia Burrus, *Saving Shame: Martyrs, Saints and Other Abject Subjects* (Philadelphia: University of Pennsylvania Press 2008)." *The Bible and Critical Theory* 5, no. 2 (2009): 29.1–29.5.

Castelli, Elizabeth A. "Asterius of Amasea *Ekphrasis on the Holy Martyr Euphemia*." In *Religions of Late Antiquity in Practice*, edited by Richard Valantasis, 464–68. Princeton, NJ: Princeton University Press, 2000.

———. "'I Will Make Mary Male': Pieties of the Body and Gender Transformation of Christian Women in Late Antiquity." In *Body Guards: The Cultural Politics of Gender Ambiguity*, edited by Julia Epstein and Kristina Straub, 29–49. New York: Routledge, 1991.

———. "Mortifying the Body, Curing the Soul: Beyond Ascetic Dualism in *The Life of Saint Syncletica*." *differences: A Journal of Feminist Cultural Studies* 4, no. 2 (1992): 134.

———. "Virginity and Its Meaning for Women's Sexuality in Early Christianity." *Journal of Feminist Studies in Religion* 2, no. 1 (1986): 61–88.

Césaire d'Arles. *Oeuvres Monastiques*, vol. 1, *Oeuvres Pour Les Moniales*. Introduction, text critique, translation and notes by Adalbert de Vogüé and Joël Courreau. Paris: Les Editions du Cerf, 1988.

———. *Oeuvres Monastiques*, vol. 2, *Oeuvres Pour Les Moniales*. Introduction, text critique, translation and notes by Joël Courreau and Adalbert de Vogüé. Paris: Les Editions du Cerf, 1994.

Chadwick, Henry. *The Early Church*. London: Penguin Books, 1984.

Clark, Elizabeth A. *Ascetic Piety and Women's Faith: Essays on Late Ancient Christianity*. Lewiston, NY: Edwin Mellen Press, 1986.

———. "Authority and Humility: A Conflict of Values in Fourth-Century Female Monasticism." *Byzantinische Forschungen* 9 (1985): 17–33.

———. "The Celibate Bridegroom and His Virginal Brides: Metaphor and the Marriage of Jesus in Early Christian Ascetic Exegesis." *Church History* 77, no. 1 (March 2008): 1–25.

———. "Ideology, History, and the Construction of 'Woman' in Late Ancient Christianity." *Journal of Early Christian Studies* 2, no. 2 (1994): 155–84.

———. "John Chrysostom and the 'Subintroductae.'" *Church History* 46, no. 2 (June 1977): 171–85.

———. "The Lady Vanishes: Dilemmas of a Feminist Historian after the 'Linguistic Turn.'" *Church History* 67, no. 1 (March 1998): 1–31.

Clark, Gillian. "Women and Asceticism in Late Antiquity: The Refusal of Status and Gender." In *Asceticism*, edited by Vincent L. Wimbush and Richard Valantasis, 33–48. Oxford: Oxford University Press, 2002.

———. *Women in Late Antiquity: Pagan and Christian Lifestyles*. Oxford: Clarendon Press, 1994.

Cloke, Gillian. *This Female Man of God: Women and Spiritual Power in the Patristic Age, AD 350–450*. New York: Routledge, 1995.

Cohick, Lynn H., and Amy Brown Hughes. *Christian Women in the Patristic World*. Grand Rapids, MI: Baker Academic, 2017.

Colless, Brian E. "Syrian Mysticism." In *The Wiley-Blackwell Companion to Christian Mysticism*, edited by Julia A. Lamm, 77–89. New York: John Wiley and Sons, 2012.

———. *The Wisdom of the Pearlers: An Anthology of Syriac Christian Mysticism*. Kalamazoo, MI: Cistercian Publications, 2008.

Conybeare, Catherine. *Paulinus of Nola: Self and Symbols in the Letters of Paulinus of Nola*. Oxford: Oxford University Press, 2000.

Coon, Lynda L. *Sacred Fictions: Holy Women and Hagiography in Late Antiquity*. Philadelphia: University of Pennsylvania Press, 1997.

Cooper, Kate. *Band of Angels: The Forgotten World of Early Christian Women*. New York: Overlook Press, 2013.

———. *The Virgin and the Bride: Idealized Womanhood in Late Antiquity*. Cambridge, MA: Harvard University Press, 1996.

———. "Virginity." In *Late Antiquity: A Guide to the Postclassical World*, edited by G. W. Bowersock, Peter Brown, and Oleg Grabar, 744. Cambridge, MA: Harvard University Press, 1999.

Corning, Caitlin. *The Celtic and Roman Traditions: Conflict and Consensus in the Early Medieval Church*. New York: Springer, 2006.

Corrigan, Kevin. "Syncletica and Macrina: Two Early Lives of Women Saints." *Vox Benedictina* 6, no. 3 (July 1989): 241–57.

Cottingham, John. "What Difference Does It Make? The Nature and Significance of Theistic Belief." *Ratio (new series)* 19, no. 4 (December 2006): 401–20.

Craun, Christopher C. "Matronly Monks: Theodoret of Cyrrhus' Sexual Imagery in the Historia Religiosa." In *Holiness and Masculinity in the Middle Ages*, edited by Patricia H. Cullum and Katherine J. Lewis, 44–57. Cardiff: University of Wales Press, 2005.

Cunneen, Sally. *In Search of Mary: The Woman and the Symbol*. New York: Ballantine Books, 1996.

Daly, William M. "Caesarius of Arles, A Precursor of Medieval Christendom." *Traditio* 26 (1970): 1–28.

D'Ambra, Eve. *Roman Women*. Cambridge: Cambridge University Press, 2007.

Davis, Stephen J. *The Cult of Saint Thecla: A Tradition of Women's Piety in Late Antiquity*. Oxford: Oxford University Press, 2001.

De Maeyer, Nicholas, and Gert Partoens. "Preaching in Sixth-Century Arles: The Sermons of Bishop Caesarius." In *Preaching in the Patristic Era: Sermons, Preachers, and Audiences in the Latin West*, edited by Anthony Dupont, Shari Boodts, Gert Partoens, and Johan Leemans, 198–223. Leiden: Brill, 2008.

Dickie, Matthew W. "Narrative-patterns in Christian Hagiography." *Greek, Roman, and Byzantine Studies* 40, no. 1 (Spring 1999): 83–98.

Dickson, John P., and Brian S. Rosner, "Humility as a Social Virtue in the Hebrew Bible." *Vetus Testamentum* 54, no. 4 (2004): 459–79.

Diem, Albrecht. "Columbanian Monastic Rules: Dissent and Experiment." In *The Irish in Early Medieval Europe: Identity, Culture and Religion*, edited by Roy Fletcher and Sven Meeder, 68–85. London: Palgrave, 2016.

———. "New Ideas Expressed in Old Words: The *Regula Donati* on Female Monastic Life and Monastic Spirituality." *Viator* 43, no. 1 (2012): 1–38.

Dietz, Maribel. *Wandering Monks, Virgins, and Pilgrims: Ascetic Travel in the Mediterranean World, A.D. 300–800*. University Park: Pennsylvania State University Press, 2005.

Dixon, Suzanne. *The Roman Mother*. London: Croom Helm, 1988.

Dolan, Autumn. "A Revival of Female Spirituality: Adaptations of Nuns' Rules during the Hiberno-Frankish Monastic Movement." *Medieval Feminist Forum: A Journal of Gender and Sexuality* 46, no. 1 (2010): 38–62.

Drake, Susanna. "Origen's Veils: The *Askēsis* of Interpretation." *Church History* 83, no. 4 (December 2014): 815–42.

Dreyer, Susan. "Syncletica: Urban Ascetic and Desert Mother." Graduate Papers/Theses, Paper 14, College of Saint Benedict/Saint John's University, School of Theology and Seminary, 2006.

Dunand, Françoise. "Between Tradition and Innovation: Egyptian Funerary Practices in Late Antiquity." In *Egypt in the Byzantine World 300–700*, edited by Roger Bagnall, 163–86. Cambridge: Cambridge University Press, 2007.

Dunn, Marilyn. "Asceticism and monasticism, II: Western." In *The Cambridge History of Christianity*, vol. 2, edited by Augustine Casiday and Frederick Norris, 669–90. Cambridge: Cambridge University Press, 2015.

———. *The Emergence of Monasticism: From the Desert Fathers to the Early Middle Ages*. Oxford: Blackwell, 2000.

———. "Mastering Benedict: Monastic Rules and Their Authors in the Early Medieval West." *English Historical Review* 105, no. 416 (July 1990): 567–94.

Egeria. *Travel Journal*. In *Christianity in Late Antiquity, 300–450 CE: A Reader*, edited by Bart D. Ehrman and Andrew S. Jacobs, 333–47. Oxford: Oxford University Press, 2003. From Égérie: *Journal de voyage (Itinéraire) et Lettre sur la Béatissime Égérie*, edited by Pierre Maraval, translated by Andrew S. Jacobs. Paris: Cerf, 1982.

Ehrman, Bart, and Andrew S. Jacobs, eds. *Christianity in Late Antiquity, 300–450 CE: A Reader*. Oxford: Oxford University Press, 2004.

Elliott, Allison Goddard. *Roads to Paradise: Reading the Lives of the Early Saints*. Hanover, NH: University Press of New England, 1987.

Elliott, Dyan. *Spiritual Marriage: Sexual Abstinence in Medieval Wedlock*. Princeton, NJ: Princeton University Press, 1993.

Elm, Susanna. *"Virgins of God": The Making of Asceticism in Late Antiquity*. Oxford: Oxford University Press, 1994.

El-Souriany, Samaan. *The Hermit Fathers*. Translated by Lisa Agaiby and Mary Girgis. Putty, NSW, Australia: St. Shenouda Coptic Orthodox Monastery, 1993.

Ferguson, Everett. *Backgrounds of Early Christianity*, 2nd ed. Grand Rapids, MI: William B. Eerdmans, 1993.

Filippov, Igor. "Legal Frameworks in the Sermons of Caesarius of Arles." *Medieval Sermon Studies* 58, no. 1 (2014): 65–83.

Fine, Gary Alan. "Rumor, Trust and Civil Society: Collective Memory and Cultures of Judgment." *Diogenes* 54, no. 1 (2007): 5–18.

FitzGerald, Kyriaki Karidoyanes. "Hospitality: Keeping a Place for the 'Other.'" *Greek Orthodox Theological Review* 56, nos. 1–4 (2011): 161–77.

Fontaine, Carole. *Smooth Words: Women, Proverbs and Performance in Biblical Wisdom.* London: Sheffield Academic Press, 2002.

Forman, Mary. "Amma Syncletica: A Spirituality of Experience." *Vox Benedictina* 10, no. 2 (1993): 199–237.

———. *Praying with the Desert Mothers.* Collegeville, MN: Liturgical Press, 2005.

Fortin, John R. "Saint Augustine's *Letter* 211 in *The Rule of the Master* and *The Rule of Saint Benedict*." *Journal of Early Christian Studies* 14, no. 2 (Summer 2006): 225–34.

Fossier, Robert. *The Axe and the Oath: Ordinary Life in the Middle Ages*, translated by Lydia G. Cochrane. Princeton, NJ: Princeton University Press, 2010.

Foulcher, Jane. *Reclaiming Humility: Four Studies in the Monastic Tradition.* Collegeville, MN: Liturgical Press, 2015.

Frank, Georgia. "Macrina's Scar: Homeric Allusion and Heroic Identity in Gregory of Nyssa's Life of Macrina." *Journal of Early Christian Studies* 8, no. 4 (2000): 511–30.

———. "Pilgrimage." In *Oxford Handbook of Early Christian Studies*, edited by Susan Ashbrook Harvey and David G. Hunter, 826–41. Oxford: Oxford University Press, 2011.

Fullam, Lisa. "Humility and Magnanimity in Spiritual Guidance." *Reflective Practice: Formation and Supervision in Ministry* 32 (2012): 36–47.

Geanellos, Rene. "Exploring Ricoeur's Hermeneutic Theory of Interpretation as a Method of Analysing Research Texts." *Nursing Inquiry* 7, no. 2 (2000): 112–19.

Gemeinhardt, Peter, and Johan Leemans. *Christian Martyrdom in Late Antiquity (300–450 AD): History and Discourse, Tradition and Religious Identity.* Berlin: DeGruyter, 2012.

Gerhart, Mary. *Genre Choices, Gender Questions.* Norman: University of Oklahoma Press, 1992.

Gingras, George, trans. *Egeria: Diary of a Pilgrimage.* New York: Newman Press, 1970.

Grey, Cam. "Demoniacs, Dissent, and Disempowerment in the Late Roman West: Some Case Studies from the Hagiographical Literature." *Journal of Early Christian Studies* 13, no. 1 (Spring 2005): 39–69.

Griffiths, Fiona J. *Nuns' Priests' Tales: Men and Salvation in Medieval Women's Monastic Life.* Philadelphia: University of Pennsylvania Press, 2018.

———. "Siblings and the Sexes within the Medieval Religious Life." *Church History* 77, no. 1 (March 2008): 26–53.

Halfond, Gregory I. "Transportation, Communication, and the Movement of Peoples in the Frankish Kingdom, ca. 500–900 C.E." *History Compass* 7/6 (2009): 1554–1569.

Hall, Stuart, ed. *Representation: Cultural Representations and Signifying Practices*. Thousand Oaks, CA: Sage Publications, 1997.

Hamilton, Catherine Sider. "Egeria." In *Handbook of Women Biblical Interpreters: A Historical and Biographical Guide*, edited by Marion Ann Taylor and Agnes Choi. Grand Rapids, MI: Baker Books, 2012.

Harakas, Stanley. "The Eastern Orthodox Tradition." In *Caring and Curing: Health and Medicine in the Western Religious Tradition*, edited by Ronald L. Numbers and Darrel Amundson. Baltimore, MD: Johns Hopkins University Press, 1986.

Harmless, William. *Desert Christians: An Introduction to the Literature of Early Monasticism.* Oxford: Oxford University Press, 2004.

Harvey, Susan Ashbrook. "2000 NAPS Presidential Address Spoken Words, Voiced Silence: Biblical Women in Syriac Tradition." *Journal of Early Christian Studies* 9, no. 1 (Spring 2001): 105–31.

———. "Sacred Bonding: Mothers and Daughters in Early Syriac Hagiography." *Journal of Early Christian Studies* 4, no. 1 (1996): 27–56.

———. "Women and Words: Texts by and about Women." Chap. 35 (pp. 382–90) in *The Cambridge History of Early Christian Literature*. Cambridge: Cambridge University Press, 2008.

Hedstrom, Darlene L. Brooks. "The Geography of the Monastic Cell in Early Egyptian Monastic Literature." *Church History* 78, no. 4 (December 2009): 756–91.

Herrin, Judith. "Public and Private Forms of Religious Commitment among Byzantine Women." In *Women in Ancient Societies: 'An Illusion of the Night,'* edited by Léonie J. Archer, Susan Fischler, and Maria Wyke, 181–203. New York: Routledge, 1994.

Hinson-Hasty, Elizabeth. "Revisiting Feminist Discussions of Sin and Genuine Humility." *Journal of Feminist Studies in Religion* 28, no. 1 (2012): 108–14.

Hochstetler, Donald. *A Conflict of Traditions: Women in Religion in the Early Middle Ages, 500–840*. Lanham, MD: University Press of America, 1992.

Hopkins, Keith. "Contraception in the Roman Empire." *Comparative Studies in Society and History* 8, no. 1 (Oct. 1965): 124–51.

Hunt, E. D. *Holy Land Pilgrimage in the Later Roman Empire, AD 312–460.* Oxford: Clarendon Press, 1984.

Jabbur, Jibrail S. *The Bedouins and the Desert: Aspects of Nomadic Life in the Arab East*. New York: SUNY Press, 1995.

Jacobs, Andrew S. " 'Let Him Guard Pietas': Early Christian Exegesis and the Ascetic Family." *Journal of Early Christian Studies* 11, no. 3 (2003): 265–81.

Jensen, Joseph. *God's Word to Israel*. Wilmington, DE: Michael Glazier, 1988.

Jungmann, Joseph A. *Christian Prayer through the Centuries*. Mahwah, NJ: Paulist Press, 2008.

Kardong, Terrence G. *Pillars of Community: Four Rules of Pre-Benedictine Monastic Life*. Collegeville, MN: Liturgical Press, 2010.

Kazhdan, Alexander. "Byzantine Hagiography and Sex in the Fifth to Twelfth Centuries." *Dumbarton Oaks Papers* 44 (1990): 131–43.

Kellenberger, James. *Dying to Self and Detachment*. New York: Routledge, 2016.

———. "Humility." *American Philosophical Quarterly* 47, no. 4 (2010): 322–36.

———. *Relationship Morality*. University Park: Pennsylvania State University Press, 1995.

King, Margot H. *The Desert Mothers: A Survey of the Feminine Anchoretic Tradition in Western Europe*. Toronto, ON: Peregrina, 1984.

Klingshirn, William. *Caesarius of Arles: The Making of a Christian Community in Late Antique Gaul*. Cambridge: Cambridge University Press, 1994.

Konkola, Kari. "Have We Lost Humility?" *Humanitas* 18, nos. 1–2 (2005): 182–207.

Kraemer, Ross Shephard. *Unreliable Witnesses: Religion, Gender, and History in the Greco-Roman Mediterranean*. Oxford: Oxford University Press, 2011.

Krawiec, Rebecca. "'From the Womb of the Church': Monastic Families." *Journal of Early Christian Studies* 11, no. 3 (2003): 283–307.

Krueger, Derek. "Typological Figuration in Theodore of Cyrrhus's Religious History and the Art of Postbiblical Narrative." *Journal of Early Christian Studies* 5, no. 3 (1997): 393–419.

———. *Writing and Holiness: The Practice of Authorship in the Early Christian East*. Philadelphia: University of Pennsylvania Press, 2004.

———. "Writing and the Liturgy of Memory in Gregory of Nyssa's Life of Macrina." *Journal of Early Christian Studies* 8, no. 4 (2000): 483–510.

———. "Writing as Devotion: Hagiographical Composition and the Cult of the Saints in Theodoret of Cyrrhus and Cyril of Scythopolis." *Church History* 66, no. 4 (1997): 707–19.

Kupfer, Joseph. "The Moral Perspective of Humility." *Pacific Philosophical Quarterly* 84 (2003): 249–69.

Kurz, William S. "The Open-Ended Nature of Luke and Acts as Inviting Canonical Actualization." *Neotestamenica* 31, no. 2 (1997): 289–308.

La Corte, Daniel Marcel, and Douglas J. MacMillan, eds. *Regular Life: Monastic, Canonical, and Mendicant Rules*. Kalamazoo, MI: Medieval Institute Publications, 2004.

Larsen, Lillian I. "The Apophthegmata Patrum and the Classical Rhetorical Tradition." *Studia Patristica* 39 (2006): 409–16.

———. "The Apophthegmata Patrum: Rustic Rumination or Rhetorical Recitation." *Patristica Nordica Annuaria* 23 (2008): 23–31.

———. "Excavating the Excavations." In *Monastic Education in Late Antiquity: The Transformation of Classical Paideia*, edited by Lillian I. Larsen and Samuel Rubenson, 101–24. Cambridge: Cambridge University Press, 2018.

Lawless, George. *Augustine of Hippo and His Monastic Rule*. Oxford: Oxford University Press, 1987.

Leemans, Johan. *"Let Us Die That We May Live": Greek Homilies on Christian Martyrs from Asia Minor, Palestine and Syria C.350–C.450 AD*. New York: Routledge, 2003.

Leyser, Conrad. "Augustine in the Latin West, 430–ca. 900." In *A Companion to Augustine*, edited by Mark Vessey, 451–64. Malden, MA: Wiley-Blackwell, 2012.

———. *Authority and Asceticism from Augustine to Gregory the Great*. Oxford: Clarendon Press, 2000.

Louf, Andre. *The Way of Humility*. Translated and introduced by Lawrence S. Cunningham. Monastic Wisdom Series. Kalamazoo, MI: Cistercian Publications, 2007.

Macaskill, Grant. "Christian Scriptures and the Formation of Intellectual Humility." *Journal of Psychology and Theology* 46, no. 4 (2018): 243–52.

Marinides, Nicholas. "Religious Toleration in the *Apophthegmata Patrum*." *Journal of Early Christian Studies* 20, no. 2 (2012), 235–68.

McCabe, David R. *How to Kill Things with Words: Ananias and Sapphira under the Prophetic Speech-Act of Divine Judgment (Acts 4.32–5.11)*. New York: T & T Clark, 2011.

McCarthy, Maria Carita. *The Rule for Nuns of St. Caesarius of Arles: A Translation with a Critical Introduction*. Washington, DC: Catholic University of America Press, 1960.

McGowan, Anne, and Paul F. Bradshaw. *The Pilgrimage of Egeria: A New Translation of the* Itinerarium Egeriae *with Introduction and Commentary*. Collegeville, MN: Liturgical Press Academic, 2018.

McKenzie, Steven L. *Covenant*. St. Louis, MO: Chalice Press, 2000.

McNamara, Jo Ann. *The Ordeal of Community*, 2nd ed. Toronto, ON: Peregrina, 1993.

———. *Sisters in Arms: Catholic Nuns through Two Millennia.* Cambridge, MA: Harvard University Press, 1996.

McNary-Zak, Bernadette. "A Call to Asceticism: Receiving the *Life of Antony*." *Coptica* 13 (2014): 51–64.

———. "'Like a Motionless Stone in His Hands': Forgiveness in the Stories of the Harlot Saints," *Magistra* 8, no. 2 (Winter 2006): 54–69.

———. "Problematizing Women and Pilgrimage in Late Antiquity." *Magistra* (Winter 2002): 3–24.

———. "The Soul is Like a Ship: Sailing Imagery in Early Egyptian Monastic Literature." *Coptica* 8 (2009): 41–51.

McNulty, Tracy. *The Hostess: Hospitality, Femininity, and the Expropriation of Identity.* Minneapolis: University of Minnesota Press, 2007.

Meconi, David Vincent. "Recapitulative Tropes in Augustine's Sermons." *New Blackfriars* 95, no. 1060 (2014): 689–97.

Mensch, James R. "Prayer as Kenosis." In *The Phenomenology of Prayer*, edited by Bruce Ellis Benson and Norman Wirzba, 63–87. New York: Fordham University Press, 2005.

Merrills, Andrew H. "Monks, Monsters, and Barbarians: Re-defining the African Periphery in Late Antiquity." *Journal of Early Christian Studies* 12, no. 2 (2004): 217–44.

Miller, Patricia Cox. "Is There a Harlot in This Text? Hagiography and the Grotesque." *Journal of Medieval and Early Modern Studies* 33, no. 3 (Fall 2003): 419–35.

———. "Visceral Seeing: The Holy Body in Late Ancient Christianity." *Journal of Early Christian Studies* 12, no. 4 (Winter 2004): 391–411.

———. ed. *Women in Early Christianity: Translations from Greek Texts.* Washington, DC: Catholic University of America Press, 2005.

Milns, R. D. "Attitudes to Mental Illness in Antiquity." *Australian and New Zealand Journal of Psychiatry* 20 (1986): 458–62.

Mitchell, W. J. Thomas. *Picture Theory: Essays on Verbal and Visual Representation.* Chicago: University of Chicago Press, 1995.

Morgan, Vance G. "Humility and the Transcendent." *Faith and Philosophy* 18, no. 3 (July 2001): 307–22.

Muehlberger, Ellen. "Simeon and Other Women in Theodoret's *Religious History*: Gender in the Representation of Late Ancient Christian Asceticism." *Journal of Early Christian Studies* 23.4 (2015): 583–606.

Newman, Jay. "Humility and Self-Realization." *Journal of Value Inquiry* 16 (1982): 275–85.

O'Hara, Alexander. "The Vita Columbani in Merovingian Gaul." *Early Medieval Europe* 17, no. 2 (2009): 126–53.

Olsen, Glenn W. "One Heart and One Soul (Acts 4:32 and 34) in Dhouda's 'Manual.'" *Church History* 61, no. 1 (March 1992): 23–33.

Ouro, Robert. "The Garden of Eden Account: The Chiastic Structure of Genesis 2–3." *Andrews University Seminary Studies* 40, no. 2 (2002): 219–43.

Overmyer, Sheryl. "Exalting the Meek Virtue of Humility in Aquinas." *Heythrop Journal* 56, no. 4 (2015): 650–62.

Pachomian Koinonia, vol. 1, *The Life of Pachomius and His Disciples*. Translated and with an introduction by Armand Veilleux. Kalamazoo, MI: Cistercian Publications, 1980.

Pachomian Koinonia, vol. 2, *Pachomian Chronicles and Rules*. Translated and with an introduction by Armand Veilleux. Kalamazoo, MI: Cistercian Publications 1981.

Pardue, Stephen. "Kenosis and its Discontents: Towards an Augustinian Account of Divine Humility." *Scottish Journal of Theology* 65, no. 3 (2012): 271–88.

———. *The Mind of Christ: Humility and the Intellect in Early Christian Theology*. London: Bloomsbury, 2013.

Parker, Annabelle. "The Vita Syncleticae in the Synagoge: The Citations of Synkletike of Alexandria Used by Paul of Evergetis." In *Work and Worship at the Theotokos Evergetis: 1050–1200*, edited by Margaret Mullett and Anthony Kirby, 143–51. Belfast Byzantine Texts and Translations 6.2. Belfast: Belfast Byzantine Enterprises, 1997.

Pasztori-Kupan, Istvan. *Theodoret of Cyrus*. London: Routledge, 2006.

Patton, Kimberley Christine. "'Howl, Weep and Moan, and Bring It Back to God': Holy Tears in Eastern Christianity." In *Holy Tears: Weeping in the Religious Imagination*, edited by Kimberley Christine Patton and John Stratton Hawley, 255–73. Princeton, NJ: Princeton University Press, 2005.

Patton, Kimberley Christine, and John Stratton Hawley, eds. *Holy Tears: Weeping in the Religious Imagination.* Princeton, NJ: Princeton University Press, 2005.

Paxton, Frederick S. *Christianizing Death: The Creation of a Ritual Process in Early Medieval Europe*. Ithaca, NY: Cornell University Press, 1996.

Pelikan, Jaroslav. *Mary through the Centuries: Her Place in the History of Culture*. New Haven, CT: Yale University Press, 1996.

Perrin, Norman, and Dennis C. Duling. *The New Testament: An Introduction*, 2nd ed. New York: Harcourt Brace Jovanovich, 1982.

Peters, F. E. *Jerusalem: The Holy City in the Eyes of Chroniclers, Visitors, Pilgrims, and Prophets from the Days of Abraham to the Beginnings of Modern Times*. Princeton, NJ: Princeton University Press, 1985.

Petts, David. "Burial and Gender in Late- and Sub-Roman Britain." In *TRAC 97: Proceedings of the 7th Annual Theoretical Roman Archaeology Conference*, 112–24, University of Nottingham, April 1997. Oxford: Oxbow Books, 1998.

Pietikainen, Petteri. *Madness: A History*. London: Routledge, 2015.

Porterfield, Amanda. *Healing in the History of Christianity*. Oxford: Oxford University Press, 2005.

Pseudo-Athanasius. *The Life and Regimen of the Blessed and Holy Syncletica*. Translated with notes by Elizabeth Bryson Bongie. Toronto, ON: Peregrina, 1999.

Ramsey, Boniface. *Beginning to Read the Fathers*. Mahwah, NJ: Paulist Press, 1985.

Ranft, Patricia. *Women and Spiritual Equality in Christian Tradition*. New York: St. Martin's Press, 1998.

Rapp, Claudia. "Figures of Female Sanctity: Byzantine Edifying Manuscripts and Their Audience." *Dumbarton Oaks Papers* 50 (1996): 313–44.

———. "Storytelling as Spiritual Communication in Early Greek Hagiography: The Use of Diegesis." *Journal of Early Christian Studies* 6, no. 3 (1998): 431–48.

Rebillard, Eric. "Sermons, Audience, Preacher." In *Preaching in the Patristic Era: Sermons, Preachers, and Audiences in the Latin West*, edited by Anthony Dupont, Shari Boodts, Gert Partoens, and Johan Leemans, 87–102. Leiden: Brill, 2008.

Reynolds, Thomas E. "Toward a Wider Hospitality: Rethinking Love of Neighbour in Religions of the Book." *Irish Theological Quarterly* 75, no. 2 (2010): 175–87.

Roberts, Michelle Voss. "Retrieving Humility: Rhetoric, Authority, and Divinization in Mechthild of Magdeburg." *Feminist Theology* 18, no. 1 (2009): 50–73.

Rohrbacher, David. *The Historians of Late Antiquity*. London: Routledge, 2002.

Rönnegård, Per. *Threads and Images: The Use of Scripture in* Apophthegmata Patrum. Winona Lake, IN: Eisenbrauns, 2010.

Rousseau, Philip. *Ascetics, Authority and the Church in the Age of Jerome and Cassian*. Oxford: Oxford University Press, 1978.

———. *Pachomius: The Making of a Community in Fourth-Century Egypt*. Berkeley: University of California Press, 1999.

Rowlandson, Jane. *Women and Society in Greek and Roman Egypt*. Cambridge: Cambridge University Press, 1998.

Rubenson, Samuel. *The Letters of Antony: Monasticism and the Making of a Saint*. Minneapolis: Fortress Press, 1995.

Rubin, Miri. *Mother of God: A History of the Virgin Mary*. New Haven, CT: Yale University Press, 2010.

Ruddy, Deborah Wallace. "Christian Humility and Democratic Citizenship: St. Augustine and Jacques Maritain." In *Reassessing the Liberal State: Reading Maritain's Man and the State*, edited by Timothy Fuller and John Hittinger, 209–27. Washington, DC: Catholic University of America Press, 2001.

Sahas, Daniel J. "Hagiography." In *Encyclopedia of Early Christianity*, edited by Everett Ferguson, Michael P. McHugh, Frederick W. Norris, and David M. Scholar, 409. New York: Garland, 1990.

Saiving, Valerie. "The Human Situation: A Feminine View." *Journal of Religion* 40 (1960): 100–112.

Sax, William S., Johannes Quack, and Jan Weinhold. *The Problem of Ritual Efficacy*. Oxford: Oxford University Press, 2010.

Sayer, Duncan. "Death and the Family: Developing Generational Chronologies." *Journal of Social Archaeology* 10, no. 1 (2010): 59–91.

Scheffler, Eben. "Caring for the Needy in the Acts of the Apostles." *Neotestamentica* 50, no. 3 (2016): 131–65.

———. "Reflecting on Jesus' Teaching on Humility from a Positive Psychological Perspective." *Neotestamentica* 51, no. 1 (2017): 95–111.

Schlabach, Gerald W. "Augustine's Hermeneutic of Humility: An Alternative to Moral Imperialism and Moral Relativism." *Journal of Religious Ethics* 22, no. 2 (Fall 1994): 299–330.

Schlesinger, George N. "Truth, Humility, and Philosophies." In *God and the Philosophers: The Reconciliation of Faith and Reason*, edited by Thomas V. Morris, 248–62. Oxford: Oxford University Press, 1994.

Schofar, Jonathan Wyn. *Confronting Vulnerability: The Body and the Divine in Rabbinic Ethics.* Chicago: University of Chicago Press, 2010.

Schroeder, Caroline T. "Women in Anchoritic and Semi-Anchoritic Monasticism in Egypt: Rethinking the Landscape." *Church History* 83, no. 1 (March 2014): 1–17.

Schulenburg, Jane Tibbetts. *Forgetful of Their Sex: Female Sanctity and Society, ca. 500–1100.* Chicago: University of Chicago Press, 1998.

———. "Women's Monastic Communities, 500–1100: Patterns of Expansion and Decline." *Signs: Journal of Women in Culture and Society* 14, no. 2 (1989): 261–92.

Schultz, Jennifer. "Doctors, Philosophers, and Christian Fathers on Menstrual Blood." In *Wholly Woman, Holy Blood: A Feminist Critique of Purity and Impurity*, edited by Kristin De Troyer, Judith A. Herbert, Judith Ann Johnson, and Anne-Marie Korte, 97–116. Harrisburg, PA: Trinity Press, 2003.

Seleznyov, Nikolai N. "Nestorius of Constantinople: Condemnation, Suppression, Veneration." *Journal of Eastern Christian Studies* 62, nos. 3–4: 165–90.

Shaw, Brent D. "The Family in Late Antiquity: The Experience of Augustine." *Past & Present* 115, no. 1 (May 1987): 3–51.

Shlain, Leonard. *The Alphabet Versus the Goddess: The Conflict between Word and Image*. London: Penguin, 1998.

Shuler, Eric. "Caesarius of Arles and the Development of the Ecclesiastical Tithe: From a Theology of Almsgiving to Practical Obligations." *Traditio* 67 (2012): 43–69.

Sivan, Hadith. "Holy Land Pilgrimage and Western Audiences: Some Reflections on Egeria and Her Circle." *Classical Quarterly* 38, no. 2 (1988): 528–35.

———. "Who was Egeria? Piety and Pilgrimage in the Age of Gratian." *Harvard Theological Review* 81, no. 1 (1988): 59–72.

Sleeman, Matthew. *Geography and the Ascension Narrative in Acts*. Cambridge: Cambridge University Press, 2009.

Smith, Julie Ann. *Ordering Women's Lives: Penitentials and Nunnery Rules in the Early Medieval West*. Aldershot: Ashgate, 2001.

Snow, Nancy E. "Humility." *Journal of Value Inquiry* 29, no. 2 (1995): 203–16.

Spiegel, James S. "The Moral Irony of Humility." *Logos: A Journal of Catholic Thought and Culture* 6, no. 1 (2003): 131–50.

Spitzer, Leo. "The Epic Style of the Pilgrim Aetheria." *Comparative Literature* 1, no. 3 (Summer 1949): 225–58.

Stausberg, Michael, and Steven Engler, eds. *The Routledge Handbook of Research Methods in the Study of Religion*. Routledge Handbooks in Religion. London: Routledge, 2013.

Stocking, Rachel L. *Bishops, Councils, and Consensus in the Visigothic Kingdom, 589–633*. Ann Arbor: University of Michigan Press, 2000.

Stramara, Daniel F. "Double Monasticism in the Greek East, Fourth through Eighth Centuries." *Journal of Early Christian Studies* 6, no. 2 (Summer 1998): 269–312.

Swan, Laura. *The Forgotten Desert Mothers: Sayings, Lives, and Stories of Early Christian Women*. Mahwah, NJ: Paulist Press, 2001.

Takács, Sarolta A. *Vestal Virgins, Sibyls, and Matrons: Women in Roman Religion*. Austin: University of Texas Press, 2008.

Talbot, Alice-Mary. "The Byzantine Family and the Monastery." *Dumbarton Oaks Papers* 44 (1990): 119–29.

———. "An Introduction to Byzantine Monasticism." *Illinois Classical Studies* 12, no. 2 (Fall 1987): 229–41.

Tambiah, Stanley. *A Performative Approach to Ritual*. Oxford: Oxford University Press, 1979.

Theodoret of Cyrrhus. *A History of the Monks of Syria*. Translated with an introduction and notes by R. M. Price. Kalamazoo, MI: Cistercian Publications, 1985.

Tovar, Sofia Torallas. "Egyptian Burial Practices in Late Antiquity: The Case of Christian Mummy Labels." In *Cultures in Contact: Transfer of Knowledge in the Mediterranean Context. Selected Papers*, edited by Sofia Torallas Tovar and Juan Pedro Monferrer-Sala, 13–24. Cordoba: Oriens Academic, 2013.

Urbainczyk, Theresa. *Theodoret of Cyrrhus: The Bishop and the Holy Man*. Ann Arbor: University of Michigan Press, 2002.

Valantasis, Richard. *The Making of the Self: Ancient and Modern Asceticism*. Eugene, OR: Cascade Books, 2008.

Van Dam, Raymond. *Saints and Their Miracles in Late Antique Gaul*. Princeton, NJ: Princeton University Press, 1993.

van der Watt, Jan. "The Meaning of Jesus Washing the Feet of His Disciples (John 13)." *Neotestamentica* 51, no. 1 (2017): 25–39.

Vasilescu, Lucretia. "Desert Spirituality: *Amma*, a Spiritual Directress." *Diacronia* (2013). http://www.diacronia.ro/ro/indexing/details/A233/pdf.

Ward, Benedicta. *Harlots of the Desert: A Study of Repentance in Early Monastic Sources*. Kalamazoo, MI: Cistercian Publications, 1987.

———, trans. *The Sayings of the Desert Fathers: The Alphabetical Collection*. Rev. ed. Kalamazoo, MI: Cistercian Publications, 1975; rev. ed., 1984.

Ware, Kallistos. " 'An Obscure Matter': The Mystery of Tears in Orthodox Spirituality." In *Holy Tears: Weeping in the Religious Imagination*, edited by Kimberley Christine Patton and John Stratton Hawley, 242–53. Princeton, NJ: Princeton University Press, 2005.

Wemple, Suzanne Fonay. *Women in Frankish Society: Marriage and the Cloister, 500–900*. Philadelphia: University of Pennsylvania Press, 1981.

Wengst, Klaus. *Humility: Solidarity of the Humiliated: The Transformation of an Attitude and Its Social Relevance in Graeco-Roman, Old Testament-Jewish, and Early Christian Tradition*. Philadelphia: Fortress Press, 1988.

Wheeler, Rachel. "Growing Wings Like Eagles: Women's Bodies and Women's Work in *The Life of Syncletica*." *Magistra* (Summer 2014): 76–96.

Wheeler-Reed, David. *Regulating Sex in the Roman Empire*. New Haven, CT: Yale University Press, 2017.

Whittow, Mark. "Early Medieval Byzantium and the End of the Ancient World." *Journal of Agrarian Change* 9, no. 1 (2009): 134–53.

Wilken, Robert Louis. *The Spirit of Early Christian Thought: Seeking the Face of God*. New Haven, CT: Yale University Press, 2003.

Wilkinson, John. *Egeria's Travels*. London: SPCK, 1971.

———. *Jerusalem Pilgrims before the Crusades*. Warminster, UK: Aris & Phillips, 1977.

Williams, Michael Stuart. *Authorised Lives in Early Christian Biography: Between Eusebius and Augustine*. Cambridge: Cambridge University Press, 1986.

Wills, Lawrence. "The Form of the Sermon in Hellenistic Judaism and Early Christianity." *Harvard Theological Review* 77:3–4 (1984): 277–99.

Winslow, Donald F. "Humility." In *Encyclopedia of Early Christianity*, 2nd ed., edited by Everett Ferguson, 547–48. New York: Garland, 1998.

Young, Frances M., with Andrew Teal. *From Nicaea to Chalcedon: A Guide to the Literature and Its Background*, 2nd ed. Grand Rapids, MI: Baker Academic, 2010.

Zumkeller, Adolar. *Augustine's Ideal of the Religious Life.* Translated by Edmund Colledge. New York: Fordham University Press, 1986.

Index